THINKERTOYS

THINKERTOYS

A HANDBOOK OF CREATIVE-THINKING TECHNIQUES

2ND EDITION

MICHAEL MICHALKO

TEN SPEED PRESS
Berkeley | Toronto

Ten Speed Press
P.O. Box 7123
Berkeley, California 94707
www.tenspeed.com

Distributed in Australia by Simon & Schuster Australia, in Canada by Ten Speed Press Canada, in New Zealand by Southern Publishers Group, in South Africa by Real Books, and in the United Kingdom and Europe by Airlift Book Company.

Cover design by Nancy Austin based on a design by Fifth Street Design
Text design by Sarah Levin
Typesetting by Tasha Hall

Library of Congress Cataloging-in-Publication Data
Michalko, Michael, 1940–
    Thinkertoys : a handbook of creative-thinking techniques / Michael Michalko.—2nd ed.
        p. cm.
    Includes index.
    Original title: Thinkertoys : a handbook of business creativity.
    ISBN-13: 978-1-58008-773-5
    ISBN-10: 1-58008-773-6
    1. Creative ability in business. 2. Creative thinking. I. Title.
HD53.M53 2006
650.01'9—dc22
                                    2005036213

Printed in China

2 3 4 5 6 7 8 9 10 — 10 09 08 07 06

Figure on page 7 from *Drawing on the Artist Within* copyright © 1989 by Betty Edwards. New York: Simon & Schuster. Used by permission of the publisher.

Figure on page 10 from "Pattern recognition and modern computers" by O. G. Selfridge. Published in the proceedings of the Western Joint Computer Conference, New York. Copyright © 1955 by IRE (now IEEE). Used by permission.

Figure on page 12 from Ripley's Believe It or Not, property of Ripley's International, Inc., Toronto, Ontario. Used by permission.

Figure on page 25 from "Subjective Contours" by Gaetano Kanisza, illustration by Jerome Kuhl. Copyright © 1976 by *Scientific American*, New York. Used by permission of the publisher.

Figure on page 35 from *Can You Believe Your Eyes* copyright © 1989 by J. R. Block and H. E. Yuker. New York: Gardner Press, Inc. Used by permission of the publisher.

Figure on page 95 from *Can You Believe Your Eyes* copyright © 1989 by J. R. Block and H. E. Yuker. New York: Gardner Press, Inc. Used by permission of the publisher.

Figure on page 157 from "The Amateur Scientist" by Michael Goodman, illustration by Jearl Walker. Copyright © 1988 by *Scientific American*, New York. Used by permission of the publisher.

Figure on page 175 from "Figural aftereffects: an investigation of visual processes" by W. Kohler and H. Wallach. Published in the proceedings of the American Philosophical Society, 88, 269–357, copyright © 1944. Used by permission.

Figure on page 199 from *The Journal of General Psychology*, 7, 481–482 copyright © 1932. Published by Heldref Publications. Used by permission of the publisher.

Figure on page 227 from "The role of frequency in developing perceptual sets" by B. R. Bugleski and D. A. Alampay, published in the *Canadian Journal of Psychology*, 15, 205–211. Copyright © 1961 by the Canadian Psychological Association. Used by permission of the publisher.

Figure on page 289 from "Subjective Contours" by Gaetano Kanisza, illustration by Ilel Arbel. Copyright © 1976 by *Scientific American*, New York. Used by permission of the publisher.

DEDICATION

This book and my love are dedicated to Anne, my wife and partner, who has free rent in my heart, forever.

ACKNOWLEDGMENT

I thank Charlotte Bruney, Parish Administrator of St. Vincent de Paul in Churchville, New York, for reawakening my faith and for reminding me of the single most important thing in life, which I had forgotten long ago. Charlotte reminded me that the real nature of human feeling is mostly the same from person to person, mostly the same in every person everywhere on earth. Of course there is that part of human feeling where we are all different. Each one of us has our own idiosyncrasies and our own unique human character. That is the part people are talking about when they are talking about feelings and comparing feelings. But that part is about ten percent of the feelings we feel. Ninety percent of all our feelings is stuff in which we are all the same and feel the same things. This shared universal human feeling has been forgotten by most people, hidden in the mess of opinion, conflicts, and personal differences voiced by governments, religions, politicians, academics, celebrities, and, of course, the omnipresent and omnipotent mass media. These voices of disharmony and disunity have disconnected us from each other and have rusted our hearts. We need to ignore these voices of discord and reawaken each other to honor and respect this huge ocean—this ninety percent—in which our feelings are all alike. Maybe, if we do that, we will have "heaven on earth."

CONTENTS

Warning:
This Book Is for Monkeys

Your business attitude determines your potential for innovation, creativity, even genius, and success in your field. There are two basic business attitudes, which I call the "kitten" and the "monkey," because of how each animal deals with stress and change.

If a small kitten is confused or in danger, it will do nothing but mew until its mother comes and carries it to safety. By contrast, a baby monkey will run to its mother and jump on her back at the first sign of trouble. The baby monkey then rides to safety, hanging on for itself.

This book can do little for people with the "kitten" attitude—those who cry for help when faced with a challenge or problem. Thinkertoys is designed for the "monkeys," who are willing to work on themselves, work to develop their business creativity, and work on coming up with innovative ideas . . . and are ready to enjoy the very real benefits of that work.

If you have the "monkey" attitude and want a wealth of original ideas to improve your business or personal life, this book is for you. I invite you to take these Thinkertoys and use them to create the ideas you need to change your life. Thinkertoys are solid, creative techniques that show you how to get ideas. The rest is up to you.

(Hope for those with the "kitten" attitude: If you want to change, you will find the help you need in Chapter One, Original Spin, with exercises and encouragement for developing the "monkey" attitude.)

PREFACE TO THE NEW EDITION

"The general chooses the road to safety or to ruin."

SUN TZU

Think about the trees along a wild and windblown lake. The pattern of these trees is so made that when the wind blows they all bend in concert, and all of the forces in the system stay in balance. The pattern of the bending trees, plants, and roots makes them all self-maintaining and whole.

Now think about a piece of land that is very steep and where erosion takes place. There aren't enough trees to hold the earth together. It rains in torrents, and water carries the earth down streams, which form gullies. Here the pattern of the trees and plants is poor. The earth is not bound together because there are not enough roots or plants. Each time the wind blows or it rains, the erosion deepens. The pattern of this system is such that the forces that it gives birth to in the long run act to destroy the system. The system is self-destroying. It does not have the capacity to contain the forces that arise within it.

Nature doesn't care if patterns are creative or destructive. What matters to nature is the way things self-organize, the way they cooperate to form coherent patterns. When you look at nature's patterns, contents aren't contained anywhere but are revealed only by the dynamics. With the trees, form and content are inextricably connected and can't be separated. The healthy pattern of trees bending in concert creates harmony and beauty, whereas the other pattern is destructive and ugly.

It is the same with people. With the trees, it is the wind, rain, roots and erosion that form the patterns; with people, it is a common body of human behaviors from which patterns blend together to create the person. A positive self-image is like the pattern of the trees and wind and is self-maintaining and creative; a poor self-image is like the pattern of the gullies and rain and is self-destructive.

Take three blank sheets of paper and place them side by side a few inches apart. Leave the center one blank. On the right one draw a small

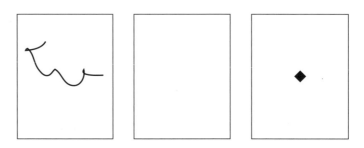

diamond-shaped dot in the middle of the page. On the left one draw an irregular squiggle.

Which sheet of paper is more like your real self? Which of the three sheets seem like a better picture of all of you, with all your hopes, fears, and weaknesses, as you are at this point of time. Which comes closest to representing the way you feel about yourself?

The majority of people choose either the squiggle or the blank sheet. Almost none chose the diamond-shaped dot. Yet, the sheet with the dot is the most centered and solid and has the most feeling and potential. The blank sheet feels empty and meaningless. The one with the squiggle creates an impression of disturbance and incoherence.

You may wonder if the descriptions are accurate. To convince you, let me propose a thought experiment. Suppose you are with the person you love more than any other person on the face of the earth. And suppose you just made the three pieces of paper we have been looking at. Imagine that you are asked to give the sheet of paper that most represents your love to the person. Which of the three do you give? Most likely, you will give the one on the right because it feels valuable, feels worth giving, and feels the most meaningful of the three.

The majority of us feel an emptiness and incoherence in our lives, which is why we think of ourselves as blanks or squiggles instead of diamonds. We know the diamond-shaped dot was what we wanted to select but, in some way, our sense of self made us feel unworthy, and so we rationalized why we selected the squiggle or the blank. It is the same way in life.

We are tacitly taught that we exist and just are the way we are. We have been taught that all people are true to their own genes, environment, and nature. We are conditioned to be objects. We are taught to be "me," instead of "I." When you think of yourself as "me," you are limited. The "me" is always limited because it is a passive *object*, rather than an active *subject*. The "me" doesn't act; it is acted upon by outside forces.

When you see yourself as an object, you believe how others (parents, teachers, peers, colleagues, and so on) describe you. You become that. You might want to be an artist, but others might tell you that you have no talent, training, or temperament to be an artist. The "me" will say, "Who do you think you are? You are just an ordinary person. Get real."

Richard Cohen is the author of *Blindsided: Lifting a Life Above Illness,* and he lives a life defined by illness. He has multiple sclerosis, is legally blind, has almost no voice, and suffers chronic pain that makes sleeping difficult and leaves him constantly exhausted. Two bouts of colon cancer in the past five years have left his intestines in disarray. And though he is currently cancer-free, he still lives with constant discomfort.

Cohen worked as a producer for CBS until he was physically unable. Being precluded from many activities because of his chronic illness and physical disability initially left him feeling worthless. Friends and relatives encouraged him to seek professional help from psychologists, but he refused. He felt psychologists always focus on what's wrong with you, explain why you feel worthless, and why it's not your fault. He saw no value in this kind of treatment.

Cohen realized the inevitable consequences of his illness, but he also realized that he, and he alone, controlled his destiny. Cohen says, "The one thing that's always in my control is what is going on in my head. The first thing I did was to think about who I am and how I could prevail. By choosing my feelings on a conscious level, I am able to control my mood swings and feel good about myself most of the time." He cultivated a positive attitude toward life by interpreting all of his experiences in a positive way.

He said his life is like standing on a rolling ship. You're going to slip. You're going to grab onto things. You're going to fall. And it's a constant challenge to get up and push yourself to keep going. But in the end, he said, the most exhilarating feeling in the world is getting up and moving forward with a smile.

Richard Cohen is the subject of his life and controls his own destiny. People who live as subjects are wonderfully alive and creative. Once, on a rainy Sunday afternoon in a café in Old Montreal, I saw a woman rise from her table and, for no apparent reason, start to sing opera. She had a certain smile, and I knew she was perfectly at home with herself as she sang. She was wearing a great wide hat, her arms were flung out in an expansive gesture, and she was utterly oblivious to everything but what was in her and around her at that second.

As you read this, you may be thinking of people you know who are alive and people who are, in comparison, lifeless. This woman was wonderfully alive and self-creating. When you meet people like Richard Cohen or the woman in Montreal you get a vague feeling that you "ought to be" something more. You already know this feeling. You get this feeling when you recognize the thing in others that you long to be. The feeling that you ought to be like that seems so trivial, so fundamental that you dare not admit it to others. You long to become more alive and creative in your personal and business lives. The feeling for it is the most primitive feeling a person can have. The feeling for it is as primitive as the feeling for your own well-being.

It is not easy to put this feeling into words. The person who believes he is a *subject* is frank, open-minded, sincerely going ahead, facing the situation freely, and looking for ways to make things work and get things done. The person who believes she is an *object* is inhibited, pushed, driven, acting by command or intimidation, has a one-track mind, and is always looking for reasons things can't be done or why things can't work. They cannot deal with life as free and happy people; they are narrowed and enslaved by their attitude.

When you look at the behaviors of creative geniuses such as Leonardo da Vinci, Thomas Edison, Albert Einstein, Pablo Picasso, and so on throughout history, you will find that, like the patterns of the trees, the form and contents of their behaviors are inextricably connected and can't be separated. Creators are joyful and positive. Creators look at "what is" and "what can be" instead of "what is not." Instead of excluding possibilities, creators include all possibilities, both real and imagined. They choose to interpret their own world and do not rely upon the interpretations of others. And most importantly, creators are creative because they believe they are creative.

Can you imagine a Vincent van Gogh bemoaning his failure to sell his paintings as evidence of his lack of talent? A Thomas Edison giving up on his idea for a light bulb when he failed 5,000 times? A Leonardo da Vinci who is too embarrassed to attempt much of anything because of his lack of learning? An Albert Einstein who is fearful of looking stupid for presenting theories about the universe as a patent clerk? A Michelangelo refusing to paint the ceiling of the Sistine Chapel because he had never painted fresco? A weeping and wailing Mozart blaming an unfair world for his poverty? A Walt Disney giving up his fantasies after being fired from his first job as a newspaper editor because he lacked imagination? A Henry Ford giving up his dreams after the experts explained that he didn't have the capital to compete in the automobile industry? Or a depressed Pablo Picasso shuffling down the street with his head down, hoping no one notices him?

It's impossible to be creative if you are negative. Most people presume that our attitudes affect our behavior, and this is true. But it's also true that our behavior determines our attitudes. You can pretend or act your way into a new attitude. We choose to be positive or to be negative.

Every time we pretend to have an attitude and go through the motions, we trigger the emotions we create and strengthen the attitude we wish to cultivate. Think, for a moment, about social occasions—visits, dates, dinners out with friends, gatherings, birthday parties, weddings, and so on. Even when we're unhappy or depressed, these occasions force us to act as if we were happy. Observing other's faces, postures, and voices, we unconsciously mimic their reactions. We synchronize our movements, posture, and tone of voice with theirs. Then, by mimicking happy people, we become happy.

We do not choose to be born. We do not choose our parents. We do not choose our historical epoch, or the country of our birth, or the immediate circumstances of our upbringing. We do not, most of us, choose to die; nor do we choose the time or conditions of our death. But within this realm of choicelessness, we do choose how we shall live: with purpose or adrift, with joy or with joylessness, with hope or with despair, with humor or with sadness, with a positive outlook or a negative outlook, with pride or with shame, with inspiration or with defeat, and with honor or with dishonor. We decide what makes us significant or insignificant. We decide to be creative or to be indifferent. No matter how indifferent the universe may be to our choices and decisions, these choices and decisions are ours to make. We decide. We choose. In the end, our own creativity is decided by what we choose to do or what we refuse to do. And as we decide and choose, so are our destinies formed.

THE BARKING CAT

What would you think of someone who said, "I would like to have a cat, provided it barked"? The common desire to be creative, provided it's something that can be easily willed or wished, is precisely equivalent. The thinking techniques that lead to creativity are no less rigid than the biological principles that determine the characteristics of cats. Creativity is not an accident, not something that is genetically determined. It is not a result of some easily learned magic trick or secret, but a consequence of your intention to be creative and your determination to learn and use creative-thinking strategies.

The illustration below shows the word "FLOP," which we all know and understand. Look at it again. Can you see anything else?

Once we see the word "FLOP," we tend to exclude all other possibilities, despite the strange shapes of the letters. Yet if you look at the "O" in flop, you can see a white "I." Now if you read the white outlines as letters with the "I," you will see the word "FLIP." Flip-flop is the complete message. Once found, it seems so obvious that you wonder why you were, at first, blind to it.

By changing your perspective, you expand your possibilities until you see something that you were unable to see before. This is what you will experience when you use Thinkertoys. You will find yourself looking at the same information everyone else is looking at yet seeing something different. This new and different way of seeing things will lead you to new ideas and unique insights.

Thinkertoys train you how to get ideas. They are specific hands-on techniques that enable you to come up with big or small ideas; ideas that make money, solve problems, beat the competition, and further your career; ideas for new products and new ways of doing things.

The techniques were selected for their practicality and range from the classic to the most modern. They are divided into *linear* techniques, which allow you to manipulate information in ways that will generate new ideas, and *intuitive* techniques, which show you how to find ideas by using your intuition and imagination.

A popular children's puzzle shows six fishermen whose lines are tangled together to form a sort of maze. One of the lines has caught a fish; the problem is to find which fisherman it belongs to. You are supposed to do this by following each line through the maze, which may take up to six tries, depending on your luck. It is obviously easier to start at the other end and trace the line from the fish to the fisherman, as you have only one possible starting place, not six.

This is how I researched and developed Thinkertoys. Instead of presenting a catalog of all known creative techniques and abandoning you to puzzle out which ones actually work, I started with the *ideas* (fish) and worked backwards to each creator (fisherman). Then I identified the technique that caught the idea.

Some readers will feel that they profit more from the linear techniques and will discount the intuitive ones. Others will prefer the intuitive and discount the linear. You can produce ideas using both the linear and intuitive techniques, and should not limit yourself to one or the other—the more ideas you generate the better.

This book will change how you perceive your own creativity, while stripping creativity itself of its mystique. You will, perhaps for the first time, see endless possibilities stretching before you. You will learn how to:

- Generate ideas at will.

- Find new ways to make money.

- Create new business opportunities.

- Manipulate and modify ideas until you come up with the most innovative and powerful ideas possible.

- Create new products, services, and processes.

- Improve old products, services, and processes.

- Develop solutions to complex business problems.

- Revitalize markets.

- See problems as opportunities.

- Become more productive.

- Be the "idea person" in your organization.

- Know where to look for the "breakthrough idea."

- Become indispensable to your organization.

Thinkertoys do not *render* the creative experience, they *suggest* it. To illustrate, let us imagine me drawing a rabbit on a blackboard. You say "Yes, that's a rabbit," although in reality there is nothing on the blackboard but a simple chalk line. The rabbit appears because you have accepted my motion that the space within the line suggests a rabbit. The line limits the content by suggesting a *significant form.*

I must stress that it is not enough to read the book—to create your own ideas, you have to *use* the techniques. Try to explain the joy of skiing to a bushman who has never left the desert. You can show him some skis and a picture of a snowy mountain, and perhaps get some of the idea across. However, to fully realize the concept of skiing our bushman *must* put on the skis and head down a mountain. If you merely read these techniques, you will have no more than a suggestion of how to get ideas. You'll be like the bushman standing in the desert, staring at a pair of skis and a photo of the Matterhorn, with a small notion of what skiing might be.

Each Thinkertoy is a specific technique for getting ideas to solve your challenges. Each chapter contains a blueprint that gives precise instructions for using the technique and an explanation of why it works—including anecdotes, stories, and examples of how real heroes used each technique to produce ideas and breakthroughs. I call them heroes because they left behind a mark, a sign, an idea, an enterprise, a product, or a service that reminds us of their innovation.

I also use illustrations, puzzles, charts, and hypothetical examples to demonstrate how various techniques work. Some of these hypothetical examples present usable ideas for new businesses, products, and services. These ideas are the gold beneath the river of words continually rushing past.

Each chapter begins with an inspirational quote from *The Art of War* by the legendary master, Sun Tzu. Sun Tzu wrote his extraordinary book in China more than 2,400 years ago, but his principles are as applicable to creativity in business as in warfare. Long a classic for Japanese businesspeople, his book is now required reading at many leading international business schools. From Tokyo to Wall Street, business leaders quote and apply the principles of Sun Tzu.

This new edition contains new Thinkertoys "Lotus Blossom," and "True and False," updated examples, and an entirely new group-brainstorming section with several new techniques.

A friend of mine, Hank Zeller (an executive, entrepreneur, inventor, and poet), once described creativity this way: "When you realize that you just came up with an idea that betters anything that has been done, well, your hair stands up on end, you feel an incredible sense of awe; it's almost as if you heard a whisper from God."

INITIATION

The first chapter in this section, "Original Spin," will help you overcome your fears, doubts, and uncertainties about creativity. The second, "Mind Pumping," provides exercises to help you start acting like an "idea person." To be creative, you have to believe and act as if you are creative.

Look at the illustration below. It appears to be two straight lines, but you can create a third line. To do this, tilt the book away from you so that it is perpendicular to your eyes. Position it so that the cross point is in front of you. Cross your eyes slightly to focus on the cross point. Do you see the third line? (It should look like a short pin sticking up out of the page.)

If you believe you are creative and act as if you are creative, you will begin to create ideas, like the third line, out of anything.

The worth of the ideas you create will depend in large part upon the way you define your problems. The third chapter, "Challenges," shows how to word problem statements so that the final statement has the feel of a well-hit golf ball.

ORIGINAL SPIN

"To secure ourselves against defeat
lies in our own hands."

SUN TZU

When you are depressed, your thoughts are quite different than when you are happy. When you feel rich and successful, your thoughts are quite different than when you feel poor and unsuccessful. Similarly, when you feel you are creative, your ideas are quite different than when you feel you are not.

Scientists have established that physiological responses can be consciously altered. You can condition yourself to trigger a particular chemical pattern in your brain that will affect your attitudes and your thinking in positive ways. This chapter contains some very simple exercises that will help you overcome your fears, doubts, and uncertainties, affirm your self-worth, and cultivate a creative attitude.

Nothing is more harmful to a positive creative attitude than fears, uncertainties, and doubts (FUDS); yet, most people let FUDS control their lives.

It is much more productive to learn to control your FUDS, to transform destructive negative attitudes into a new, positive reality. To do this, simply acknowledge the negative feelings and then focus your energies on what you want to substitute for them.

Suppose you are driving along and your oil pressure gauge comes on, warning you that your car is overheating. This is a negative indicator. However, you don't ignore it, nor do you become paralyzed with fear. You simply stop at a service station, have it corrected, and drive on.

Following this incident, you do not look at the oil pressure gauge continuously when you're driving, allowing the gauge to monopolize your thoughts. To do so would mean slow and erratic driving, if you had the courage to drive at all. So it is with your fears and doubts. You need to acknowledge them, and then replace them with positive thoughts.

Prescott Lecky, a pioneer of self-image psychology, developed a method that consisted of getting a subject to see that some negative concept of his was inconsistent with some other deeply held belief. Lecky believed that humans have an inherent need for consistency. If a thought is inconsistent with other, stronger ideas and concepts, the mind will reject it.

Lecky found that there were two powerful levers for changing beliefs and overcoming fears, convictions that are strongly felt by nearly everyone. These are:

1. The belief that one is capable of doing one's share, holding up one's end of the log, exerting a certain amount of independence.

2. The belief that there is something inside one that makes one equal in talent and ability to the rest of the world, and that one should not belittle oneself or allow oneself to suffer indignities.

One of his patients was a salesman who was afraid to call on top management clients. Lecky asked him, "Would you get down on all fours and crawl into the office, prostrating yourself before a superior personage?"

"I should say not!" the salesman replied.

"Then why do you mentally crawl and cringe? Can't you see that you are doing essentially the same thing when you go in overly concerned with whether or not he will approve of you? Can't you see you are literally begging for his approval of you as a person?"

The important thing to remember is that you do not have to change your personality or your life, or somehow make yourself into a new and better person in order to understand and replace your negative thoughts.

General George Patton was once asked if he ever experienced fear or uncertainty before battle. He replied that he often experienced fear before, and even during, a battle, but the important thing was "I never take counsel of my fears."

TICK-TOCK

Tick-Tock is a very powerful exercise based on Lecky's work that is designed to help you overcome your fears, doubts, and uncertainties. In Tick-Tock you write out your fears, confront them head-on, and then substitute positive factors that will allow you to succeed.

1. *Zero in on and write down those negative thoughts that are preventing you from realizing your goal.* Write them under "Tick."

2. *Sit quietly and examine the negatives.* Learn how you are irrationally twisting things and blowing them out of proportion.

3. *Substitute an objective, positive thought for each subjective, negative one.* Write these under "Tock."

Following are two examples of Tick-Tock exercises with sample negative and positive thoughts. The first addresses the fear of presenting a new idea to management; the second, the fear of producing a new product.

TICK-TOCK #1

TICK	TOCK
Presenting this idea is pointless. Management is more experienced and skilled than I am, and they probably thought of this before.	This is all or nothing thinking. The idea doesn't have to be a blockbuster—big endings come from small beginnings. Reverse roles; if I owned the company, wouldn't I want all the ideas I could get? I will write down all my self-doubting thoughts and refute them.
The idea is so nontraditional I'll be a laughingstock if I suggest it.	Even if the idea is rejected, people respect and admire those who are creative in their work and who are constantly trying to improve the current situation. No pain, no gain. The riskier the idea, the greater the potential for rewards.

I never had a new idea in my life. My best chance is not to take chances.

I assume my negative feelings necessarily reflect the way things are: I feel it, therefore it must be true. My real problem is a false image of myself: Would my company have hired me if they were as negative about me as I am?

My last idea failed miserably and Tom's didn't. I'm afraid to take another chance.

I exaggerate the importance of things (my failure, Tom's success). Thomas Edison once said that the only road to success was through failure. The only crime in life is never having tried. Instead of trying not to be wrong, try to be right.

TICK-TOCK #2

TICK

TOCK

I'll never be able to do it.

Just do a little bit at a time and get started. There's no reason I have to do it all on a crash schedule.

I'll probably screw it up and fail miserably.

It doesn't have to be perfect. I might learn something, and imagine how I'll feel when it's finally finished. I have a good track record of doing things well. If I concentrate on the project, my attitude will improve.

I can't discipline myself. I have no self-control. I won't be able to manage my time on my own.

I must have self-control because I've done well in other things. Just work on it as best I can as long as I can. I have as much self-control as anyone I know. The project is so important and the benefits so tangible that time management will be more fun than a problem.

What's the point in doing all that work? I'll never find a company to market it.

I have no way of knowing that. Give it a try. Some company will be interested. Besides, you can learn things even if someone rejects it. Where there is a will there is a way. If I believe in it, others will as well. It's a question of finding the right company.

At first, the figures above look strange and meaningless. Because you are mentally conditioned to look at black shapes and figures, you ignore the white shapes in between the black ones. However, if you focus on the white shapes, you can see the words "FLY" and "WIN." The white shapes become dominant and the black ones recede in importance.

In Tick-Tock, your negative thoughts will recede like the black shapes as your positive thoughts become dominant. Once you have used Tick-Tock for some time, you will find yourself mentally replacing negative thoughts with positive ones "on cue," so to speak. When you experience doubts or fears, you will automatically use them as a signal to look for the "white" thoughts.

HOW TO SPIN THE ORIGINAL SPIN

Years back, a group of scientists visited a tribe in New Guinea that believed their world ended at a nearby river. After several months, one of the scientists had to leave, which involved crossing the river. Safely across the river, he turned around and waved. The tribesmen did not respond because, they said, they didn't see him. Their entrenched beliefs about the world had distorted their perception of reality.

The CEO of a major publishing house was concerned about the lack of creativity among his editorial and marketing staffs. He hired a group of high-priced psychologists to find out what differentiated the creative employees from the others.

After studying the staff for one year, the psychologists discovered only one difference between the two groups: The creative people believed they were creative and the less creative people believed they were not. Like the

New Guinea tribesmen, those who felt they were not creative had a distorted perception of reality. These employees had lost their original spin.

The psychologists recommended instituting a simple two-part program designed to change the belief systems of those who thought they were not creative. The CEO agreed, and within a year, the uncreative people became many more times creative than the original creative group. Once their attitudes changed, they began to pay attention to small and large challenges and to flex their creative muscles in extraordinary ways. The following year, this group generated many innovative programs and blockbuster books. These people regained their original spin and began to transform themselves and the world around them.

The first part of this extremely effective program addressed self-affirmation; the second part dealt with creative affirmation.

SELF-AFFIRMATION

To increase your self-affirmation, get in the habit of remembering your successes, your good qualities and characteristics, and forgetting your failures. It doesn't matter how many times you have failed in the past; what matters is the successful *attempt*, which should be remembered and reinforced. A successful salesperson, for example, must be willing to fail in closing an order several times before succeeding once.

Success breeds success. Small successes are stepping-stones to greater ones. The first exercise is to write and maintain a self-affirmation list.

Record all the things you like about yourself—your positive qualities, characteristics, and traits. Include the successes you have had in every area of your life: work, home, school, and so on. Keep adding to this list as you think of more things and as you accomplish more. Acknowledging yourself, your abilities, and your own unique qualities will encourage you to get moving.

If you make a practice of remembering your successes and good personal qualities and paying less attention to your failures, you will begin to experience more success than you would have thought possible. Imagine a person learning to hit a baseball. At first, he will miss the ball many more times than he hits it. With practice, his misses will gradually diminish, and the hits will come more frequently. If mere repetition were the key to improved skill, his practice should make him more expert at missing the ball than hitting it. However, even though the misses outnumber the hits, he hits the ball more successfully because his mind remembers, reinforces, and dwells on the successful attempts rather than the misses.

CREATIVE AFFIRMATION

The second technique the psychologists used is a deceptively simple yet incredibly powerful technique that uses written affirmations to cultivate and reinforce the belief that you are a creative person.

Human beings act, feel, and perform in accordance with what they *imagine* to be true about themselves and their environment. What you imagine to be true becomes, in fact, true. Hold a given picture of yourself long and steadily enough in your mind's eye and you will become that picture. Picture yourself vividly as defeated and that alone will make victory impossible. Picture yourself vividly as winning and that alone will contribute immeasurably to success.

To visualize yourself as creative, affirm that you believe it to be true. An affirmation is a positive statement that something is already so. It can be any positive statement, general ("I am creative") or specific ("I am always in the right place at the right time, engaged in the right activity in order to get ideas"). Take a few minutes and write down several different affirmations about your creativity.

Now, take one of these affirmations and write twenty variations of it, using the first, second, and third persons. For example, "I, Michael, am a creative person. Michael is a creative person. Michael, you are a creative person." "I'm truly creative. Michael is the most creative person in the group. You, Michael, are gifted with creativity," and so on.

As you write, take your time and really ponder each word *as you write it.* Keep changing the wording of the affirmations.

Whenever you feel negative thoughts, write them on the other side of the page, or on a separate piece of paper. For instance, you might write, "Michael has not had a new idea in two years. Others do not feel Mike is creative. Michael is too dull to think up a good idea. I'm too old to be creative. I'm not educated enough to come up with good ideas." Then, return to writing your positive affirmations.

When you're finished, look at the negatives. These are your obstacles to being creative. Nullify the negatives by writing additional, specific affirmations to address the negatives. For the negatives above, you might write, "Michael has new ideas every day. Others do not know Michael well enough to make a judgment. Michael is an exciting person, not a dull one. Most inventors and big idea people do not have much formal education," and so on.

Write your affirmations about being creative every day for five days. During this period, the negatives will almost certainly stop; at that point just continue writing the positive affirmations, until you no longer feel the need.

Read the following words.

TAE CAT

Anyone can see that these letters spell out "THE CAT," right? But look more closely. If you examine the "H" and the "A," you will see that they are identical. Your perception of the word was influenced by your expectations. You expected to see "THE" and not "TAE," and "CAT" and not "CHT." This expectation was so strong that you influenced your brain to see what you expected.

In the same way, when you expect to be creative you will influence your brain to be creative. Once you believe you are creative, you will begin to believe in the worth of your ideas, and you will have the persistence to implement them.

SUMMARY

Each one of us must affirm our own individual creativity. Although many facets of human creativity are similar, they are never identical. All pine trees are very much alike, yet none is exactly the same as another. Because of this range of similarity and difference, it is difficult to summarize the infinite variations of individual creativity. Each person has to do something differ-ent, something that is unique. The artist, after all, is not a special person; every person is a special kind of artist.

CHAPTER TWO

MIND PUMPING

"Anciently the skillful warriors first made
themselves invincible and awaited the enemy's
moment of vulnerability."

SUN TZU

Tibetan monks say their prayers by whirling wheels on which their prayers are inscribed, spinning the prayers into divine space. Sometimes, a monk will keep a dozen or so prayer wheels rotating, like the juggling act in which whirling plates are balanced on top of long thin sticks.

The monk may be thinking about dinner, his religious future, or something else while he is spinning his prayer wheel. Similarly, there are priests who go through the motions of celebrating Mass without feeling a connection to the liturgy.

When the monk and priest assume the role of "religious person" and make it obvious to themselves and others by playing that role, their brains will soon follow. It is not enough for the monk or priest to have the *intention* of being religious: the monk must rotate the wheel; the priest must say the Mass. If one acts like a monk, one will become a monk. If one goes through the motions of being a priest, sooner or later, one will become emotionally involved in religion.

If you act like an idea person, you will become one. It is the intention and going through the motions of being creative that counts.

If you want to be an artist, and actually go through the motions of being one, you *will* become at least an adequate artist. You may not become another van Gogh, but you will be much more of an artist than someone who has neither had the intention nor gone through the motions. There is no way of knowing how far intention and action can take you. This world offers no guarantees, only opportunities and vicissitudes. When you reach for the stars you may not get one, but you won't come up with a handful of mud either.

This chapter contains eleven exercises that will encourage you to behave like an idea person.

IDEA QUOTA

Give your mind a workout every day. Set yourself an idea quota for a challenge you are working on, such as five new ideas every day for a week. You'll find the first five are the hardest, but these will quickly trigger other ideas. The more ideas you come up with, the greater your chances of coming up with a winner.

Having a quota will force you to actively generate ideas and alternatives rather than waiting for them to occur to you. You will make an effort to fill the quota even if the ideas you come up with seem ridiculous or far-fetched. Having an idea quota does not stop you from generating more ideas than the quota, but it does ensure that you generate your minimum.

Set an Idea Quota

Get Tone

Don't Be a Duke of Habit

Feed Your Head

Do a Content Analysis

Make a Brain Bank

Be a Travel Junkie

Capture Your Thoughts

Think Right

Keep an Idea Log

Thomas Edison held 1,093 patents. He was a great believer in exercising his mind and the minds of his workers and felt that without a quota he probably wouldn't have achieved very much. His personal invention quota was a minor invention every ten days and a major invention every six months. To Edison, an idea quota was the difference between eating beefsteak or a plateful of Black Beauty stew.

Ripley's—**Believe It or Not!**

The above puzzle is somewhat like your mind because every time you look at it you see something new. What are the entire contents?

Most probably you found some letters and numbers. If I told you your quota was to find all twenty-six letters of the alphabet and the numerals

0 through 9, chances are you would search the puzzle until you located them all. And you will find them all because they are all there. Similarly, you can stretch your mind to find ideas to fill idea quotas.

GETTING TONE

Fighter pilots say, "I've gone tone" when their radar locks onto a target. That's the point at which the pilot and plane are totally focused on the target. "Getting tone" in everyday life means paying attention to what's happening around you.

How many f's are in the following paragraph?

The necessity of training farmhands for first class farms in the fatherly handling of farm livestock is foremost in the minds of farm owners. Since the forefathers of the farm owners trained the farmhands for first class farms in the fatherly handling of farm livestock, the farm owners feel they should carry on with the family tradition of training farmhands of first class farms in the fatherly handling of farm livestock because they believe it is the basis of good fundamental farm management.

Total number of f's ___

If you've got tone, you found thirty-six f's. If you found less, you probably ignored the f's in the word "of." In the latter case, you are probably thinking, "Of course, it was right in front of my eyes the whole time."

Ordinarily we do not make the fullest use of our ability to see. We move through life looking at a tremendous quantity of information, objects, and scenes, and yet we *look* but do not *see*.

Paying attention to the world around you will help you develop the extraordinary capacity to look at mundane things and see the miraculous. Really paying attention to what you see will enable you to develop a kind of binary vision, with which you perceive what others see, but notice something unexpected as well.

Did you see anything unexpected in the below illustration? If not, look again.

An idea can be found anywhere. Maybe it's up in the hills, under the leaves, or hiding in a ditch somewhere. Maybe it will never be found. But what you find by paying attention, whatever you find, will always lead to something.

TINY TRUTHS

This exercise is designed to help you pay pure attention to the world around you. It was developed by Minor White, who taught photography at MIT.

Select a photograph or picture that gives you pleasure, the more detailed the better. Get comfortable and relax. Set a timer or alarm for ten minutes. Look at the photograph or picture until the timer goes off, without moving a muscle. Stay focused on the image. Do not allow your mind to free-associate. Pay attention only to the image in front of you. After the timer goes off, turn away from the image and recall your experience. Review the experience visually rather than with words. Accept whatever the experience is for what it is. After your review and your experience becomes kind of a flavor, go about your everyday work, trying to recall the experience whenever you can. You'll begin to experience tiny truths that you can find only by paying pure attention. Recall the experience frequently and recall it visually. Some think these tiny truths are the voice of God.

DUKES OF HABIT

Dukes of Habit must always do things the same way, must have everything in its place, and are at a loss if something violates their routines. Because everything in their lives is precisely folded, labeled, and placed in neat little cubbyholes, Dukes of Habit are limited problem-solvers. Don't be a Duke of Habit.

Deliberately program changes into your daily life. Make a list of things you do by habit. Most of the items will probably be those little things that make life comfortable but also make it unnecessary for you to think. Next, take the listed habits, one by one, and consciously try to change them for a day, a week, a month, or whatever.

- Take a different route to work.

- Change your sleeping hours.

- Change your working hours.

- Listen to a different radio station each day.

- Read a different newspaper.

- Make new friends.

- Try different recipes.

- If you normally vacation in the summer, vacation in the winter.

- Change your reading habits. If you normally read nonfiction, read fiction.

- Change your break habits. If you usually drink coffee, drink juice.

- Change the type of restaurants you go to.

- Change your recreation. Try boating instead of golf, and so on.

- Take a bath instead of a shower.

- Watch a different television news broadcaster.

FEEDING YOUR HEAD

Creative thinkers read to feed their minds new information and ideas. As Gore Vidal put it, "The brain that doesn't feed itself eats itself."

Here are some ideas to pump your mind when you read:

Select carefully. Before you read a book ask: "How good an exercise for my creative mind will this provide?" Make the most of your reading time by sampling broadly and reading selectively.

Take notes. In Albert Paine's biography of Mark Twain, Paine wrote: "On the table by him, and on his bed, and on the billiard-room shelves, he kept the books he read most. All, or nearly all, had annotations—spontaneously uttered marginal notes, title prefatories, or comments. They were the books he read again and again, and it was seldom that he had nothing to say with each fresh reading."

Outline. Outline a book before you read it, or read the first half, stop and write an outline of the latter half. Imagine what you will find before you read the table of contents or the book. This was George Bernard Shaw's favorite exercise; it will provide good, strenuous exercise for your imagination.

Read biographies. Biographies are treasure-houses of ideas.

Read how-to books on any subject. Exercise your mind by manipulating the ideas of others into new ideas. Read books on crafts, automobiles, carpentry, gardening, and so on. These books give you tools with which you can create unique ideas and products.

Read magazines on varied subjects. Walt Disney relied on the *Reader's Digest* for many of his ideas. He was quoted as saying: "Your imagination may be creaky or timid or dwarfed or frozen at points. The *Digest* can serve as a gymnasium for its training."

Read nonfiction. When reading nonfiction books, practice thinking up solutions to any problems presented in the book before the problem is solved. This was one of John F. Kennedy's favorite exercises.

Think. Think as you read. Search for new solutions to old problems, changes in business, trends in foreign countries, technological breakthroughs, connections, and parallels between what you read and your problems.

John Naisbitt, author of *Megatrends* and chairman of the Washington, D.C.–based Naisbitt Group, has been very successful in employing a method of trend spotting called "content analysis." He adapted this notion from methods used in a book he read about the Civil War. The historian who wrote the book, in turn, adapted content analysis from an article he had read about the CIA's intelligence-gathering methods. The CIA patterned it after methods used by the Allies in World War II. Allied forces discovered the strategic value of reading newspapers smuggled out of small German towns. These papers sometimes carried useful stories on fuel, food, and other items. Similarly, a small group of Swiss intelligence officers were able to figure out German troop movements by reading social pages to see where famous German officers were mentioned.

CONTENT ANALYSIS

Here's how to do your own content analysis:

- Scan your junk mail before you discard it. What trends in advertising, marketing, new products, and new values can you discern?

- Let your junk mail collect for a month or two before scanning it. Patterns and trends are more readily apparent, because you can see the repetitive nature of emerging trends.

- When you're on the road, read the local newspapers and shopping news giveaways. What inferences can you make about the local economy? Is it growing or declining? What new business opportunities do you see? What opportunities are transferable to your home town? What are the area's values, attitudes, and lifestyles?

- Actively observe popular culture. Watch network and cable TV, rent videos, read popular magazines and books, go to movies, and listen to popular songs. What are people interested in? What values and lifestyles are portrayed? Who are the popular heroes? Why are they heroes?

- Think about how your job has changed. What is in your "in" basket as compared with its contents this time last year? Has the corporate emphasis changed? Do you have more paperwork or less? More meetings or fewer? Where is the company heading? Talk to the people you work with for clues to the ways work attitudes, values, and commitments are changing.

- Attend as many business conferences, seminars, and lectures as you can.

- Listen to a different radio station every week to get a variety of perspectives. Who is the market for the station? What are they addressing? Who listens? Who advertises? Why?

- Make it a practice to scan the week's television schedule, and then tape the programs that interest you. When you're in the mood for television, watch the taped programs instead of whatever's on.

Your own content analysis will be infinitely more valuable to you than any of the available services, some of which charge clients $25,000 a year to provide them with this type of information. When you perceive trends and patterns of interest, begin to pump your mind for ideas, opportunities, and business possibilities. Look for connections and relationships between your content analysis and your business challenges.

BRAINBANKS

Collect and store ideas like a pack rat. Keep a container (coffee can, shoe box, desk drawer, or file folder) of ideas and idea starters. Begin collecting interesting advertisements, quotes, designs, ideas, questions, cartoons, pictures, doodles, and words that might trigger ideas by association.

When you are looking for new ideas, shake up the container and pull out two or more items at random to see if they can somehow trigger a thought that might lead to a new idea. If not, reshuffle and eventually you'll come up with some intriguing combinations of useful ideas.

The other day I shook up my Brainbank and pulled two clippings: One was about a man who invented a new coffin that is cheaper and more durable than the others on the market. The other was about a man who started a video camera rental service. Free-associating with death, funerals, videos, rentals, and so on, I hit on what might be a viable enterprise: Video tributes to the deceased. Do short videos of scenes from the deceased's life that could be made by super-imposing photographs over peaceful land-scapes.

TRAVEL JUNKIE

Be a travel junkie. Whenever you're feeling stale and bored, go to a store, trade show, exhibition, library, museum, flea market, craft show, old folks' home, toy shop, or high school. Pick up something at random and create connections and relationships in your mind with the object and your prob-lem. Wander around with an open mind and wait for something to catch your attention. It will. Your mind is like vegetation. It flourishes in one soil or climate and droops in another.

George Smith made candy on a stick in the early 1900s. Competition was fierce. He tried hard to find a new marketing twist to differentiate his stick candy from others. One day, he decided to take a break and went to the race track. One of the finest racehorses of the day was racing, and he bet a sub-stantial amount of money on it. The horse won. The name of the horse was Lolly Pop. Smith named his stick candy "lollipops" and made candy history.

CAPTURING IDEA BIRDS

Ralph Waldo Emerson once wrote: "Look sharply after your thoughts. They come unlooked for, like a new bird seen in your trees, and, if you turn to your usual task, disappear."

You have to record your own ideas, as, so far as I know, there is no store that sells Cliffs Notes on your past thoughts. If you think it, write it. In the figure to the left, the "target" shape is the black figure above the design. Find the target shape in the design and stare at it for a few seconds. When you stare at it in the design, the target shape will blink out of your conscious perception.

Just as the target shape disappears right before your eyes, your thoughts will disappear unless you write them down.

Psychologists have demonstrated that we are able to keep only about five to nine pieces of information in our mind at a time. We have all had the experience of looking up a phone number, then being distracted before dial-ing and forgetting the number in a matter of seconds. What is happening is that new information is bumping out older information before your mind can ready the older information for long-term storage in your memory.

In general, short-term memory can hold items fairly well for the first few seconds. After about twelve seconds, however, recall is poor, and after twenty seconds, the information will disappear entirely, unless you keep repeating it to yourself or write it down. Writing signals your brain that this piece of information is more crucial than others and should be stored in your long-term memory.

John Patterson, president of National Cash Register, was a fan of Napoleon. Patterson rode horseback with his executives every day at 5 A.M. He demanded that they maintain a "little red book" to record daily activities, thoughts, ideas, and so on. He ruthlessly fired many an employee who failed to maintain a notebook. He died in the midst of his business travels while scribbling in his little book.

Interestingly, one sixth of the major U.S. companies were headed by ex-NCR employees between 1910 and 1930. Among the disenchanted former NCR employees was Tom Watson, founder of IBM.

THINK RIGHT

Consciously work to make your thinking more fluent and more flexible (fluency means the number of ideas, flexibility refers to creativity). Making lists is a powerful way to increase your thinking fluency, as it forces you to focus your energy in a very productive way. To illustrate this, take a few minutes to think about possible uses for the lubricant WD-40. You probably came up with some ideas, but you almost certainly had a little trouble focusing, you probably censored some thoughts, and came up with only the most obvious uses.

Actually *listing* possible uses for WD-40 will help you to feel more focused and interested, and to come up with a greater number of ideas. Giving yourself a time limit will make you even more productive. But fluency is not enough—you must also be flexible.

If your list included such uses as "quick lubrication, loosen rusted things, lubricate bicycle chains," and so on, you demonstrated fluency, but you listed the ordinary expected uses of the product. You are flexible if your list contained such unusual entries as:

- Loosen jammed garbage disposals.
- Spray on birdhouse poles to keep animals away from the nest.
- Bait for mousetraps.
- Prevent deterioration of musical instrument strings.
- Fish bait.
- Restore used typewriter ribbons to make blacker impressions.
- A car safety product. Keep it in your glove compartment to unstick car doors in case of bad accidents.

Flexibility in thought means the ability to see beyond the ordinary and conventional roles. It means you are more improvisational and intuitive, can play with context and perspective, and focus on *processes* rather than *outcomes.*

Psychologist J. P. Guilford, a pioneer in the study of creativity, believed the following exercise helps exercise thinking fluency and flexibility, and enhances the ability to organize such complex projects as plots for novels, scientific theories, plans for new business organizations, or the building of any system which is interrelated and interconnected.

Play this game with friends. See who can get the most sentences in five minutes.

Write four-word sentences from the four letters of a given word:

I	don't	enjoy	apricots
Irritated	dogs	eagerly	anger

IDEA LOG

The idea log is one of the CIA's favorite techniques for recording information. There is a written log for each problem, which is used to record ideas, facts, thoughts, questions, and so on. This enables the agent to instantly focus on all the ideas, comparisons, interrelationships, and data relating to a given problem.

Maintain an idea log. Each section could be devoted to separate aspects of your business and personal life. Sections could include: marketing, product, selling, corporate, personal, services, special projects, and new business possibilities. There are many organizers and personal planners on the market these days, but it's much more fun, creative, and useful to design your own. Experiment with different methods of capturing ideas before you decide which is best for you.

Reviewing your recorded ideas periodically is a good way to titillate your imagination. Each time you review them, you will begin to search out connections between a recorded idea and your present situation or experience.

Suppose you are chewing gum to relieve stress and an idea occurs to you: Why not create a gum to measure stress? You record it in your idea log and review it from time to time. A few months later you read in a magazine that the body's pH can indicate health. While reviewing your idea log, an idea pops up: Develop a gum that uses the body's pH factor to measure health. The user would chew it for three minutes. If it turns dark pink, they're healthy. If it turns green, they should go home and go to bed.

SUMMARY

Effective ways to pump your mind for ideas are:

1. Set an idea quota.
2. Get tone.
3. Don't be a Duke of Habit.
4. Feed your head.
5. Do a content analysis.
6. Create a Brainbank.
7. Be a travel junkie.
8. Capture your thoughts.
9. Think right.
10. Keep an idea log.

Pumping your mind is like making a path through tall grass. Originally there is no path, yet as you walk the same way each time, one appears. In the same way, you may have no ideas at first, yet as you exercise your mind using these techniques, ideas appear.

CHAPTER THREE

CHALLENGES

"He who knows when he can fight and when
he cannot will be victorious."

SUN TZU

Imagine five brilliant entrepreneurs sitting down to consider new ideas. They can't get started until someone proposes something. But where does the proposal come from? How do they decide what problem to solve? Who decides the focus? How do they determine their goals?

If they try to come up with new ideas without having a specific goal, they could consume an infinite amount of time with no purpose. It would be like trying to climb these stairs—moving up and up and up forever, without purpose.

Before you start looking for ideas, you need to know what your goal is. This chapter will help you to identify worthwhile business problems and convert them into specific challenges to be solved using Thinkertoys.

A problem is nothing more than an opportunity in work clothes. A successful businessperson pays attention to problems, converting the problems into opportunities and deciding which opportunities are worth pursuing. These opportunities become productive challenges.

Anyone can learn how to pay attention. As a focusing exercise, select a color at random and spend an entire day looking for items that are that color or contain it. For instance, if you choose red you will discover an incredible number of red objects: cars, books, clothes, houses, fire trucks, chimneys, shoes, hats, paintings, and so on. Familiar objects will become new again, reds will become richer, and you will find that your perspective toward "red" has been dramatically changed. By tuning in "red" and tuning out other colors, you allowed yourself to understand the color red more deeply.

Consider the illustration in the margin.

This figure was drawn in 1900 by Joseph Jastrow, a psychologist. He drew the figure so that it can be viewed with equal validity as a duck or rabbit. When the face looks right it is a rabbit; when it looks left it is a duck. You tend to see the whole rabbit or the whole duck depending on which animal you select to focus on. It is difficult to concentrate and see both at the same time, rather than constantly shifting images.

Unless you set your business problems down in writing, your attention is constantly shifting and you become indecisive about what, if anything, you should focus on. Listing problems is a way for you to decide which ones are worth solving. It transforms a body of information into a set of components that can be restructured, checked, and searched.

Start keeping a journal of problems that you find to be personally interesting and that would be worthwhile to resolve. The following questions may help you get started:

- What would you like to have or to accomplish?
- What business idea would you like to work on?
- What do you wish would happen in your job?
- What business relationship would you like to improve?
- What would you like to do better?
- What do you wish you had more time to do?
- What more would you like to get out of your job?
- What are your unfulfilled goals?
- What excites you in your work?
- What angers you at your work?
- What misunderstandings do you have at work?
- What have you complained about?
- What changes for the worse do you see in the attitudes of others?
- What would you like to get others to do?

- What changes would you like to introduce?
- What takes too long?
- What is wasted?
- What is too complicated?
- Where are the bottlenecks?
- In what ways are you inefficient?
- What wears you out?
- What in your job turns you off?
- What would you like to organize better?
- In what ways could you make more money at work?

Following are typical business challenges:

- What creative suggestions can I make about new product ideas?
- How can I cut costs and increase production?
- How can we better differentiate our product from all others?
- What new product is needed? What extension of a current product's market?
- How can I sell 20 percent more than I am at present?
- What new selling techniques can I create? Can I reduce the cost of our current selling techniques?
- How can I become indispensable to my company?
- How can we better handle customer complaints?
- How can we improve the role service plays in the sale of our products?
- How can our advertising better communicate about our goods and services?
- Is it possible to encourage everyone in our organization to actively look for ways to better differentiate our products?
- What procedures could we institute that would reduce unnecessary paperwork?
- What awards would be more meaningful to employees?
- How can we become more customer-oriented?
- Is it possible to change our corporate image?

- In what ways might we out-perform the competition?
- Which of our products can we make into silver bullets? (A silver bullet is the leading product or service in a particular industry.)

In the following illustration, there are two sets of parallel lines. The lines appear to form a contoured border between them. Either set of lines can be seen as covering the other. Yet, in reality, there is no border between the two sets. There is nothing there. This illusion is created because our minds try to make the gaps between the lines into something meaningful.

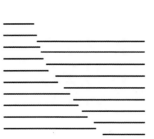

In the same way, the mere act of writing a challenge may trigger your mind to create something meaningful to fill in the gaps and solve it. A retired police detective who was looking for a business opportunity listed problems that were related to police work. One problem he listed was the difficulty in proving the identity of a stolen or kidnapped baby. Just writing the challenge provoked him to think of an idea for a new business venture: a DNA bank. His bank stores DNA samples for parents who are worried about identifying their children in case of a kidnapping or a baby swap. It costs $200 for collection and eighteen years of storage.

BUGS

Ideas sometimes grow out of irritation, like the pearls that grow when an oyster is irritated by grains of sand inside its shell. One creative soul was bugged by his inability to remember important dates such as anniversaries, birthdays, and so on. He was always a day late with presents. He made this bug into a challenge and created a novel product: vacuum-packed canned roses to be stored and used for emergencies.

After you make your "bug list," select the challenges that you find most interesting. Remember that a worthwhile problem for one person may very well be boring to another. An accountant and salesperson will not likely be stimulated or challenged by the same problem; indeed two people in the same discipline may not be challenged by the same problem. Only you can identify the kind of challenges that will stimulate and drive you.

Take the challenge of sliced bread. Few people in the early 1900s were bugged by slicing their own bread, but one of them was Otto Frederick Rohwedder. He invested sixteen years of his life and all of his money in inventing an automatic bread slicer, despite poor health, lack of enthusiasm from the industry, and financial ruin. In 1930, Continental adopted his slicer for Wonder Bread, and by 1933, about 80 percent of bread purchased was presliced. Rohewedder said he was not driven by money (he never became rich) but by the challenge of creating a workable bread slicer and an aversion to slicing his own bread.

BENEFITS

"Unhappy is the fate of one who tries to win his battles and succeed in his attacks without cultivating the spirit of enterprise, for the result is a waste of time and general stagnation."

SUN TZU

It's important to give yourself a compelling, personal reason for coming up with new ideas to solve your challenges. Weigh each challenge for personal benefits before you commit yourself. The best ideas come from those hungry for success and those who cultivate the spirit of enterprise.

Thomas Edison learned the importance of realizing a personal benefit from his work early on. His first invention was an automatic vote recorder for Congress. When he presented the invention to a Congressman, he was told that efficiency in lawmaking was the last thing on Congress's agenda. From that point on, Edison would often state that the only reason he invented was to make a lot of money. He didn't have the time, energy, or interest to modify the world to fit his inventions.

Before you decide which challenge to resolve, make a list of the benefits that may be gained if you are successful in developing a creative solution. What are the direct benefits: money, pleasure, recognition, property, and so on? What are the indirect benefits: new skills, knowledge, attitudes, etc.? Do the benefits outweigh the costs in terms of your time and energy? Which challenges would be the most rewarding to resolve? What problems or situations do you want to accept personal responsibility for solving?

If you feel that it is not necessary to realize any personal benefits before you dedicate yourself to solving a challenge . . . just lean your head sideways and watch the sawdust pour out of your ear.

After you decide what challenges are most interesting and likely to yield solid benefits, it is important to *accept* the challenge. To accept a challenge means to accept responsibility for generating ideas as possible solutions to the problem. The more you accept responsibility and dedicate yourself to generating ideas, the higher your probability of reaching an innovative solution.

There are different levels of commitment to different problems. Some problems need total dedication, others may need little effort. Whenever I think of total dedication, I'm reminded of a story I once heard about a samurai who had the duty to avenge his overlord's murder. When he had cornered the murderer and was about to dispatch him with his sword, the man spat in the warrior's face. The warrior sheathed his sword and walked away.

Why? Because the spitting made him angry, and if he had killed that man in anger it would have been a personal act. He had accepted the responsibility to do another kind of act, an impersonal act of vengeance.

After you decide what challenges are interesting and will yield you solid benefits, it is time to state those challenges in the most useful way possible. This will allow you to most effectively use Thinkertoys to generate creative solutions.

YOUR CHALLENGE STATEMENT

"A victorious army wins its victories before
seeking battle."

SUN TZU

The more time you devote to perfecting the wording of your challenge, the closer you will be to a solution. Conversely, the less time you take to define and center the challenge, the greater the chances for a not-so-great idea. You might end up with an idea that is as practical as a book about cattle ranching written by a cow.

One need only look at records from the U.S. Patent Office to find humorous examples of ideas generated by challenges that were not quite centered. These include: a golf ball that sends out smoke signals when it lands to help its owner find it, a diaper for parakeets, an alarm clock that squirts sleepers in the face, a fishing line for removing tapeworms from the stomach, and a machine that imprints dimples on the face.

Shape and center your challenge. Whenever I center a challenge, I think of sumo wrestling. Sumo wrestlers are those great big Japanese wrestlers. During the greater part of the wrestling contest, the two wrestlers are settled in a squat position, measuring each other. They assume a pose, hold it for awhile, then break, walk around, and assume their positions again. They repeat this act a number of times and then bang! They grab each other, one of the two hits the mat, and the bout is finished.

During all those rounds of squatting and posturing, they are sizing each other up and searching for that center in themselves from which all action springs. The only protection for a sumo wrestler is to be in a perpetual state of centeredness, ever ready for the sudden attack and immediate response.

Similarly, when you have a problem, you can write a challenge statement, study it for awhile, then leave it, change it, stretch and squeeze it, and restate it until you feel that the challenge is centered. Then, like the sumo wrestler, you are ready.

You center your challenge with questions. Questions help you look at challenges from different perspectives. Sometimes a different perspective will stretch your eyes wide open. How many cubes can you count in the figure in the margin?

It is possible to count six or seven stacked cubes, depending on whether the black diamonds are viewed as the tops or bottoms of the cubes. What changes is not the picture you are looking at but your perception of it. Questions can help change the perception.

BLUEPRINT

To center a challenge:

1. *Write it as a definite question, beginning "In what ways might I . . . ?"*

2. *Vary the wording of the challenge by substituting synonyms for key words.*

3. *Stretch the challenge to see the broader perspective.*

4. *Squeeze the challenge to see the narrow perspective.*
    (a) Divide it into subproblems.
    (b) Solve the subproblems.
    (c) Keep asking "how else?" and "why else?"

To start with, it's helpful to coin problems in a particular way. Write the problem you want to solve as a definite question. Use the phrase "In what ways might I . . . ?" to start a problem statement. This is something known as the *invitational stem* and helps keep you from settling on a problem statement that may reflect only one perception of the problem.

Write several different problem statements using the invitational stem "In what ways might I . . . ?" Each different statement will encourage you to look at the problem from a new perspective, and will point your thinking toward new possibilities.

Imagine you are the person in the illustration below. Your challenge is to tie together the ends of the two strings suspended from the ceiling. The strings are located so you cannot reach one string with your outstretched hand while holding the second. The room is bare, and you have only the things with you that you have in your pocket today. How do you solve the problem?

Initially, you might state the problem as: "How can I get to the second string?" However, you would then waste your energy trying to get to the second string, which is not possible. If, instead, you state the problem in a different way: "In what ways might the string and I get together?" you will likely come up with the solution—to tie a small object (such as a key, ring, watch, or belt) to the end of one string and set it in motion like a pendulum, then grab it while still holding the second string in your hand.

VARY THE WORDS

A simple technique to help you achieve different problem statements is to use synonyms or substitutes for key words in the challenge statement. The first step is to examine a particular challenge statement and identify the key words within it.

The product manager of OV'ACTION of Lievin, France, faced the following challenge: "In what ways might I develop a unique food product?"

He changed "unique" to "surprising" and "develop" to "transform" and restated the challenge to: "In what ways might I transform a product into a surprising food?"

He thought of things that might surprise him and then about how food products could surprise consumers in similar ways. For instance, one thing that would surprise him would be to see a familiar object in an odd shape, such as an airplane shaped like a cow. Similarly, he would be surprised to see a familiar food product in a strange and different shape, such as a banana shaped like a loaf of bread, tomatoes in the shape of pyramids, or square potatoes. These thoughts led to his idea: a square egg.

He developed a precooked egg cube with a yolk in the middle which has a shelf life of twenty-one days and can be reheated in a microwave oven (unlike conventional eggs, which explode).

Making a few simple word changes may provide the stimuli for new ideas. It's like injecting a few raisins into the tasteless dough of a challenge.

STRETCHING THE CHALLENGE

The samurai warrior was trained to keep his senses open to all possibilities. With his attention focused as broadly as possible, a samurai was more likely to detect a surprise attack or sudden movement than when his attention was focused analytically on a single object or way.

To keep your mind open to all possibilities, stretch your challenge by asking "why?" Asking "why?" will help you identify your general objective and allow you to challenge your assumptions. This, in turn, enables you to redefine and shape your challenges.

Suppose your challenge is: "In what ways might I sell more IBM computers?"

Step one: Why do I want to sell more IBM computers? "Because our overall computer sales are down."

Step two: Why do I want to sell more computers? "In order to improve our overall sales volume."

Step three: Why do I want to increase our sales volume? "In order to improve our business."

Step four: Why do I want to improve our business? "To increase my personal wealth."

Step five: Why do I want to increase my wealth? "To lead a good life."

Now the challenge can be reshaped in a variety of ways including:

"In what ways might I sell more computers?"
"In what ways might I increase my overall sales volume?"
"In what ways might I improve my business?"
"In what ways might I increase my wealth?"
"In what ways might I lead a better life?"

The idea is to look for the appropriate level of abstraction, the best viewpoint from which to gather ideas. A phrase such as "increase my wealth" allows your thinking to embrace far more opportunities than "sell more computers." You could negotiate for higher commissions, go into another career, get a part-time job, make some investments, sell other products, and so on.

By coining your challenge as broadly as possible, you put yourself on the top of a mountain from which you can view all possible approaches to the top. If you don't look at all the possible approaches, you may preclude yourself from seeing the best route to the top.

The shipping industry provides a useful example of the consequences of not looking at all approaches to solving a problem.

In the 1950s, experts believed that the ocean-going freighter was dying. Costs were rising, and it took longer and longer to get merchandise delivered. This increased pilferage at the docks as goods piled up waiting to be loaded.

The shipping industry formulated their challenge as: "In what ways might we make ships more economical at sea and while in transit from one port to another?"

They built ships that were faster or required less fuel, and reduced crew size. Costs still kept going up, but the industry kept concentrating its efforts on reducing the specific costs related to ships while at sea and doing work.

They were doing things right, but they weren't doing the right thing. They were about as effective as an expert salesperson who spends all her energy, time, and talents trying to sell veal door-to-door.

A ship is capital equipment and the biggest cost for the capital equipment is the cost of *not working,* because interest has to be paid without income being generated to pay it. Finally, a consultant stretched the industry's challenge to: "In what ways might the shipping industry reduce costs?"

This allowed them to consider *all* aspects of shipping, including loading and stowing. The innovation that saved an industry was to separate loading from stowing, by doing the loading on land, before the ship is in port. It is much quicker to put on and take off preloaded freight. They decided to concentrate on the costs of *not working* rather than *working,* and reduce the amount of time a freighter does not work. The answer was the roll-on, roll-off ship and the container ship.

This simple solution was the direct result of reframing the challenge. The results have been startling. Freighter traffic has increased fivefold in the last thirty years, and costs are down by 60 percent. Port time has been reduced by three quarters, and with it, congestion and theft.

SQUEEZING THE CHALLENGE

Once you have a broad idea of what you are trying to find, narrow the objective from the general to the specific by squeezing it. This makes your challenge easier to solve by reducing the area within which problem-solving takes place. Imagine trying to find an address, knowing only that it was somewhere in Montreal. If you knew that it was west of Old Montreal, it would be easier to find. If someone told you it was within walking distance of the Hotel Bonaventure, it would be still easier to find. So it is with challenges. You set your own limits within which to search for ideas.

To squeeze a challenge and ascertain its strengths, weaknesses, and boundaries, ask who, what, where, when, why, and how.

Who helps you identify individuals and groups who might be involved in the situation, have special strengths or resources or access to useful information, and who might gain from a resolution of the problem.

What helps identify all the things, objects, and items involved in the situation, the requirements, difficulties involved, rewards, and advantages and disadvantages of formulating a resolution.

Where considers the places, locations, and focal points of the problem.

When probes the schedules, dates, and timeliness of the situation.

Why helps you reach an understanding of your basic objective.

How helps you recognize how the situation developed, actions that may have been attempted or are now occurring, and steps that might be taken.

A design company framed their challenge as: "In what ways might we design a unique and convenient trash container?" To squeeze the challenge, they asked these questions:

"Who can help us design the container?"
"What material should we use?"
"Where can we get other materials?"
"When should we make it?"
"How can we make it more convenient?"
"What is a unique form?"
"Why will a new container be superior to existing ones?"

The subproblems become:

"In what ways might others help us design a better container?"
"In what ways might we make containers out of other materials?"
"In what ways might we obtain other materials?"
"In what ways might we schedule the project?"
"In what ways might we make containers more convenient?"
"In what ways might we design a unique container?"
"In what ways might we make our containers superior?"

These subproblems inspired the company to create an innovative product: the convertible trash can. This convertible can is made of recyclable plastic and is stored flat. Instructional graphics, locking tabs, and a quick-releasing system allow the user to turn flat sheets into cylindrical containers in seconds. The container is better-looking than other containers and devours less of the Earth's resources.

Squeezing the Challenge Further

Once you have asked these questions, go one step further—ask "how else?" and "what else?" You can almost always squeeze more out of your challenge.

O. M. Scott & Co., a leader in lawn-care products, sells seeds, fertilizer, pesticides, and so on. At one time, they were a small seed retailer in competition with corporate giants such as Sears, Roebuck and Co. and Dow Chemical. Their products were good, but no better than the competition's.

Scott's general challenge was: "In what ways might we improve our market share?" They narrowed this to several specific challenges and then settled on one: "In what ways might we differentiate our products from the others?"

All the lawn-care products were basically similar. All claimed to be "scientific," and described in meticulous detail how much of the stuff should be applied, given soil conditions and temperatures. All conveyed to the customer that growing a lawn is a precise, controlled scientific process. Customers did not seem to pay much attention to brand names.

Scott's salespeople asked their customers how the company could separate itself from the pack. The customers talked about their frustration in trying to plant their lawns in a precise and controlled way. Scott focused on this frustration and brainstormed ways to solve it. The challenge now became: "In what ways might we alleviate customer frustrations with planting?"

Asking "how else?" and "what else?", they came up with ideas ranging from more friendly directions to gardening classes for customers. Then they hit on the idea that made millions: a simple, mechanical gadget called the Scott Spreader. This small, lightweight wheelbarrow has holes that can be set to allow the proper quantities of Scott's products to pass through in an even flow. Before the Scott spreader, no lawn-care supplier had given the customers a tool to *control* the process. Scott designed its product line around the Spreader and, overnight, the small seed retailer became the market leader in lawn care.

Here's a challenge that seems to have no solution—certainly no obvious one. In the illustration below, remove three matches to leave four.

How can six minus three equal four? Just because the answer isn't obvious doesn't mean it's not there. By asking: "How else can I make a four?" and "What else is a four?" you can solve the challenge. Remove the matches at the top, bottom, and right, and now the answer is obvious.

CHAPTER FOUR

THINKERTOYS

In order to get original ideas, you need to be able to look at the same information everyone else does and organize it into a new and different pattern. This is *active thinking*.

Here is an equation of Roman numerals, made with ten matches. It is incorrect. Can you correct the equation without touching the matches, adding new matches, or taking away any matches?

$$XI+I=X$$

To solve this problem, you have to break away from the obvious way of looking at things. If you look at a situation from only one perspective, it's like drawing a boundary around the way you think and working only within that boundary. You can solve this problem by looking at it in a new way. To make the equation correct, turn the book upside down.

How would you describe the figure in the margin?

Most people describe it as a square of smaller squares and circles or as alternate rows of squares and circles. Few people will spontaneously see it as columns of alternate squares and circles. This is because we tend to passively organize similar items together in our minds. Once it's pointed out that it can also be viewed as columns of alternate squares and circles, we, of course, see it.

To go beyond the boundaries in your mind, you need to become an active thinker, to organize information into new patterns. It is the formation and the use of new patterns of information that gives rise to new ideas.

Take two accomplished waffle-makers whose waffles are equal in quality and price. One is a passive thinker, the other active. For some reason, people stop buying waffles. The passive thinker does nothing and goes out of business; the active thinker fashions the waffle into a cone and creates a whole new product: the ice cream cone. A passive thinker is unable to move beyond the given information to new ideas, while an active thinker is constantly organizing information into new ideas.

Thinkertoys provide concrete techniques to help you become an active thinker. Thinkertoys reflect linear *and* intuitive thinking, both of which are necessary for optimum creativity. The basic difference between the two is that the linear Thinkertoys structure existing information while the intuitive toys generate new information using insight, imagination, and intuition.

We have two eyes, two ears, two hands, and two minds. Our left brain thinks in terms of words and symbols while our right brain thinks in terms of images. Linear Thinkertoys are for the left brain, intuitive Thinkertoys for the right brain.

The following chart summarizes some of the major differences between left-brain and right-brain functions:

LEFT BRAIN	RIGHT BRAIN
dealing with one thing at a time	integrating many inputs at once
processing information in a linear fashion	holistic perception or thinking
	seat of dreams
operating sequentially	awareness without definition
writing	seeing whole solutions at once
analyzing	seeing similarities
idea-linking	intuition
abstracting	insight
categorizing	gut feeling
logic	synthesizing
reasoning	visualizing
judgment	visual memory
mathematical	recognizing patterns
verbal memory	relating things to the present
using symbols	

The left side is the side used more by writers, mathematicians, and scientists; the right side by artists, craftspeople, and musicians. Remembering a person's name is a function of the left-brain memory while remembering their face is a function of the right brain. Reading books on how to play golf is a job for the left brain, while getting a "gut feel" for the golf swing is a job for the right brain.

Imagine a long passenger train traveling down a railroad track. One person is staring straight ahead at the train as it passes him. He sees that part of the train that is passing in front of him, from car to car. First, the engine, then the first car, the second car, and so on. If he has good peripheral vision, he might glimpse parts of those cars that have already passed him by and parts of those cars which have yet to pass.

Another person views the same train from an airplane high above. She sees the whole train all at once, from beginning to end. This is the difference between the two sides of our brain. The left brain processes pieces of information sequentially, one by one, bit by bit. The right brain processes information all at once, holistically, intuitively.

GUIDELINES

I do not recommend working through this book from start to finish, reading one Thinkertoy at a time, as though it were a textbook. You can best profit by *playing* with these toys, in your own unique style, to stimulate ideas from your imagination. Invent your own singular method for using them. You might be tempted to just use the one or two Thinkertoys you like best, but playing with a variety will be more productive.

If you pick just one, you might choose a perfectly adequate technique for getting ideas, but that does not mean there cannot be a better way. In school, when you add a column of numbers, you get a sum. If you have the right answer, you move on to the next problem.

Many people carry that idiom over into creative thinking. As soon as they have an answer, they stop thinking. They are satisfied with the first answer that comes along. Reality, though, is different from arithmetic. Some answers are better than others: They cost less, afford more status, are made better, easier to use, more aesthetic, are easier to install, or whatever. There is no reason for supposing that the first answer is the best one.

One day I set out for my favorite restaurant. Some friends set out from the same place at the same time and got there long before I did. I asked them what route they had taken. They explained that they had taken the obvious route: They had turned down an alley that led them directly to the restaurant.

My own route had always seemed the best way to go, so I had never looked for another one. I was not even aware of the *possibility* of a better route. I had driven by that alley several times but never explored it. After all, I knew the best way to go. Because I never explored the alley, I never found out how useful it was. At the entrance to an unlikely approach, there is usually nothing to indicate that it is worth exploring, and yet it may lead to something useful. So it is with creative techniques. Unless you investigate them, you will never discover their usefulness.

The second reason for using a variety of different techniques is to cultivate a creative attitude. A good actor plays many different parts, and plays each to the fullest, depending on which mask he is wearing. A good actor will take pride in being versatile, in being able to play many different types in comedies and tragedies. The more parts he plays, the more accomplished he becomes. The varied experiences give depth to the actor's performance.

In the same way, you need to take pride in your skill as a creative thinker. The ability to use *all* the techniques and to carry through the thinking that goes along with them will give depth to your creativity. Once you have experienced all the Thinkertoys, you can call up any one of them to help you with a particular problem. Some of these toys are like the reverse gear on a car. It's there, but you rarely use it—you seldom see people driving their cars down the road in reverse. On the other hand, one needs to have it and know how to use it for maneuverability whenever you're stuck and can't move forward.

The key is to *use* the Thinkertoys. Merely reading and not using them is like dropping a rose petal down the Grand Canyon and waiting for the echo.

Following are some ways to use Thinkertoys:

Work with one particular Thinkertoy at a time. Use it over and over again until you are thoroughly familiar with the technique. Spend several hours or even several days.

Select one linear and one intuitive Thinkertoy to take advantage of both sides of your brain. The left one handles logic and language while the right side excels at nonverbal tasks. Research into the thought processes of highly creative people reveals that they utilize both sides of their brains.

Select Thinkertoy at random. Write the Thinkertoy titles on slips of paper and put them in a container. When you have a challenge, shake the box and randomly retrieve the name of the toy to use.

Thinkertoys produce an enormous quantity of ideas, and quantity is a key to creativity. Alex Osborn, a pioneer of creativity research, said: "Quantity! Quantity! And more Quantity! Is the order of the day." And he added, "The more sights you take, the more likely you are to hit port." The writer Stendahl said, "I require three or four cubic feet of ideas per day, as a steamboat requires coal."

Thinkertoys generate so many good ideas that you will feel like you're in a candy store and you want to sample every piece of candy. Of course, if you tried, you would get sick to your stomach. You can't try all your ideas either, so you'll need guidelines to help sort through and judge them.

1. *Inventory all the ideas in the sequence in which they occurred.*

2. *Browse through the list.* As you do, you will find that you are subconsciously prioritizing the ideas. If you have difficulty prioritizing, try the technique described in *Worrywillie's Guide to Prioritizing.*

3. *Develop criteria for judging the ideas.* They should be ideal criteria, regardless of how impossible they might seem to fulfill. These criteria, of course, depend upon the specific challenge and will vary according to your objectives. The criteria to judge a new sales promotion will differ from those used to judge a shoe design. A bonus program will not be evaluated the same way a negotiations program will. And so on.

   Some key questions to ask when developing criteria are:

   • What standards might be applied to these ideas?

   • How might we determine the strengths and weaknesses of the ideas?

   • Which criteria are essential? Desirable? Optional?

   • How might we best compare or analyze the ideas?

   • Which criteria will best help us to refine and develop ideas?

4. *Use judgment and intuition to choose the best ideas.* Using your criteria, you should be able to funnel the huge quantity of ideas into a select few. Do not allow yourself to be wholly analytical. Your intuition may tell you when an idea that does not meet your criteria is, nevertheless, so powerful that it is the one to adopt.

   Use a simple classification scheme to label ideas:

   excellent
   likely—needs refinement
   possible chance—needs improvement
   50/50—could go either way
   long shot—remote

   You may never choose to back a long shot or a 50/50 idea; however, if you list and classify them, you have the choice of rejecting or improving them. If you do not list them, you have no choice in the matter at all.

5. *Take your best ideas and get feedback.* Use the techniques described in *Murder Board.*

PART ONE

—

LINEAR
THINKERTOYS

Group A

This group reorganizes known information in different ways by listing, dividing, combining, or manipulating it to give you new entry points for solving problems. Proceeding from these entry points, you can jump from one idea to another until you find the one you need. Just as we use stepping-stones to move across a river, we can use ideas to move across a challenge.

FALSE FACES

Technique: Reversal.
Profile: How to find ideas by reversing conventional assumptions.

SLICE AND DICE

Technique: Attribute listing.
Profile: How to get new ideas from a challenge's attributes.

CHERRY SPLIT

Technique: Fractionation.
Profile: How to get ideas by dividing a challenge into two or more components and then reassembling them in new and different ways.

THINK BUBBLES

Technique: Mind mapping.
Profile: How to map your thoughts so as to spark new ideas.

SCAMPER

Technique: Questions.
Profile: How to manipulate what exists into something different.

FALSE FACES

"All warfare is based on deception."

SUN TZU

In the illustration at right, figure A shows two lines of equal length bounded by arrow-like angles. In figure B, the arrow-like angles are reversed on one of the lines, which changes our perception and creates the illusion of a shorter line. It's not shorter; measure it and you will find it is equal in length. The lines haven't changed; your perception of them has.

In figure A, the angles at the end of the lines seem to open up a potentially limited space. Reversing the angle seems to close off and limit the area, which changes your perception of the length of the lines.

A simple reversal of angles dramatically changes what we see in the illustration. The same perceptual changes occur when we reverse our conventional thinking patterns about problems and situations. When Henry Ford went into the automobile business, the conventional thinking was that you had to "bring people to the work." He reversed this to "bring the work to the people" and accomplished his goal by inventing the assembly line.

Suppose you built a house using a "yard" stick that was actually an inch short. If you assumed that it was a full yard and used it to measure everything you built, then everything would be wrong, and your ceilings, doors, and windows would be too low. If you had started by questioning the measuring stick, there would have been no problem. It is the same with all problems: If you start with incorrect assumptions, your solutions will be poorly constructed.

Sometimes assumptions seem so basic, so fundamental, that we never think to challenge them. Consider the illustration on the next page. We assume that the far-away figure, which looks as large as a nearby one, must, in fact, be larger because things are supposed to grow smaller as they move

A

B

away from us. Yet this assumption doesn't hold up. Measure the figures with a ruler and you'll find that they are all the same size.

Assumptions are maintained by the hug of history. Yet, history does not guarantee their validity, nor does it ever reassess their validity. At times, an assumption presents a false face that we mistake for something immutable; a truth that cannot be challenged.

Try to link the nine dots below with no more than three straight lines which will cross through all nine dots, without lifting your pencil.

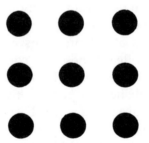

A surprising number of people will make two assumptions: (1) you must not extend beyond the outside dots, and (2) the lines must pass through the center of each dot. Neither of these "rules" was mentioned above, and once you challenge those assumptions, the problem is easily solved (see p. 47).

Whenever Thomas Edison was about to hire a new employee, he would invite the applicant over for a bowl of soup. If the person salted his soup before tasting it, Edison would not offer him the job. He did not hire people who had too many assumptions built into their everyday life. Edison wanted people who consistently challenged assumptions.

Problems are often salted with assumptions that hinder creativity. Suppose you tell an architect that you want a certain kind of knob on the door between the dining room and kitchen so that it can be easily opened and shut. This illustrates the assumption that the answer to traffic between the two rooms *is* a door, rather than a redefinition of the space, or of the design, or of how we prepare and eat food. The assumption that a knob is the solution precludes numerous other possibilities.

I put so much emphasis on challenging assumptions to show that any assumption can be challenged. For example, in regard to the illustration on the previous page, many people assume you cannot link all nine dots with one straight line. You can, and you can do it in several different ways: One way is cut out the dots, line them up in a straight line, and then draw a line through it (below); another is to take a large brush, dip it in paint and swipe it across all the dots.

Obviously, many things have to be taken for granted, and the purpose is not to pretend that one has the time to challenge every assumption, but instead to show nothing is sacrosanct. Once you truly realize this, you are open to all sorts of discoveries. Imagine diving into a lake that everyone assumes is freezing and discovering balmy, warm water. Until you jump, you will never know for sure.

BLUEPRINT

To reverse a challenge:

1. *State your challenge.*

2. *List your assumptions.*

3. *Challenge your fundamental assumptions.*

4. *Reverse each assumption.* Write down the opposite of each one.

5. *Record differing viewpoints that might prove useful to you.*

6. *Ask yourself how to accomplish each reversal.* List as many useful viewpoints and ideas as you can.

For a long time it was assumed that people must be stationary and wired into machines for medical personnel to monitor their body's vital signs, such as heart rate, breathing, body temperature, presence of hazardous gases, and so on.

A group of U.S. Navy and marine doctors challenged this assumption and brainstormed for ways to get real-time information about the vital signs of wounded marines on the battlefield. The information could be telecommunicated back to physicians at mobile hospital units. Medics, physicians, and triage units could then save more seriously wounded warriors. The challenge was how to monitor the vital health signs of mobile marines in combat.

The navy funded the original research, which was conducted at Georgia Tech. Dr. Sundaresan Jayaraman and Sungmee Park were assigned the project and explored the synergy between textile engineering and computing. Working together, they conceptually blended garments and computers into what they called the Smart Shirt.

The Smart Shirt is a T-shirt wired with optical and conductive fibers with sensors woven into the design of the shirt. It is a garment that functions like a computer. It monitors heart rate, breathing, respiration, body temperature, presence of hazardous gases, and a host of vital functions alerting the wearer or medic of the nature of the problem. The data flows to a personal status monitor that transmits to a remote medical triage unit behind the battle lines. The unit transmits advice back to the medic on how to best treat and transport the wounded marine.

The Smart Shirt represents a quantum leap in health-care monitoring, producing accurate, real-time results. The potential applications for the technology beyond military applications are boundless. This military innovation has enormous potential for applications in telemedicine, monitoring of patients in postoperative recovery, and monitoring of astronauts, athletes, firefighters, law enforcement personnel, chronically ill patients, elderly persons living alone, and infants. All this, and the shirt can be laundered, too.

REVERSE ASSUMPTIONS

Reversing your assumptions broadens your thinking. You may often find yourself looking at the same thing as everybody else, yet seeing something different. Many creative thinkers get their most original ideas when they challenge and reverse the obvious.

Alfred Sloan took over General Motors when it was on the verge of bankruptcy and turned it around. His genius was to take an assumption and reverse it into a "breakthrough idea." For instance, it had always been assumed that you had to buy a car before you drove it. Sloan reversed this to mean you could buy it while driving it, pioneering the concept of installment buying for car dealers.

He also changed the American corporate structure by challenging the conventional assumptions about how organizations were run. He quickly realized that GM's haphazard growth was stifling its potential. He reversed the basic assumption that major companies are run by an all-powerful individual, creating a new theory that allowed for entrepreneurial decision-making, while still maintaining ultimate control. Under Sloan, GM grew into one of the world's biggest companies, and his reversal became the blueprint for the modern American corporation.

Reverse some of your basic assumptions about business. For instance, you might start with the idea that "A salesperson organizes the sales territory," then reverse it to "The sales territory organizes (controls) the salesperson."

This reversal would lead you to consider the demand for new salespeople as territories become more complex. A salesperson with a large territory may be too well "controlled" by it to react to new accounts and sales possibilities.

Another reversal might be: "A salesperson *dis*organizes the sales territory." This would lead to a consideration of how to make salespeople more efficient. You could add telemarketing support personnel, in-office follow-up systems, and so on, to organize the territories for salespeople.

Harry Seifert, CEO of Winter Gardens Salads, used reversal to cook up a winning recipe for productivity. Instead of giving employees a bonus *after* the busy times of the year, he gives them their bonus *before* the busiest time of the year.

Just before Memorial Day, when they have the largest demand for coleslaw and potato salad, Sierfert dishes out $50 to each of his 140 employees to arouse their enthusiasm for filling all of the holiday orders as efficiently as possible. "Because employees are trying to achieve a goal," he observes, "they don't feel like they are being taken advantage of during the intense periods." Production has risen 50 percent during the bonus period.

How To?

After you reverse your assumption about a challenge, ask yourself how to accomplish the reversals. You are not necessarily looking for one right answer, but for a different way of viewing existing information.

Consider the challenge of motivating city dwellers to recycle their paper products (newspapers, magazines, and cardboard). The basic assumption is that people give paper products to a pickup person for recycling.

Reverse it to giving paper products to people. How could doing this promote recycling?

The idea: The pickup person hands out a certain number of rolls of toilet paper or boxes of tissue, according to the weight of the material he collects. By giving as well as receiving, you motivate people to recycle their used paper products.

Suppose you want to start a new restaurant and are having difficulty coming up with ideas. To initiate ideas, try the following reversals:

1.   List all your assumptions about your subject.

     Example: Some common assumptions about restaurants are:
     A.   Restaurants have menus, either written, verbal, or implied.
     B.   Restaurants charge money for food.
     C.   Restaurants serve food.

2.   Reverse each assumption. What is its opposite?

     Example: The reverse assumptions would be:
     A.   Restaurants have no menus of any kind.
     B.   Restaurants give food away for free.
     C.   Restaurants do not serve food of any kind.

3.   Ask yourself how to accomplish each reversal. How can we start a restaurant that has no menu of any kind and still have a viable business?

     Examples:
     A.   A restaurant with no menu.
          Idea: The chef informs each customer what he bought that day at the meat, fish, and vegetable markets. He asks the customer to select items that he or she finds appealing and creates a dish with those items, specifically for that customer.
     B.   A restaurant that gives away food.
          Idea: An outdoor cafe where customers pay for time instead of food. Use a time stamp and charge by the minute. Selected food items and beverages are free or sold at cost.
     C.   A restaurant that does not serve food.
          Idea: Create a restaurant with a unique decor in an exotic environment and rent out the location. People bring their own food and beverages (picnic baskets, etc.) and pay a service charge for the location.

4. Select one and build it into a realistic idea. In our example, we decided to work with the "restaurant with no menu" reversal. We'll call the restaurant The Creative Chef. The chef will create the dish out of the selected ingredients and name the dish after the customer. Each customer will receive a computer printout of the recipe.

Reversals destabilize your conventional thinking patterns and free information to come together in provocative new ways. For example:

- Drivers control the parking time of their cars. Reverse this to cars control parking time. This triggers the idea of parking anywhere as long as you leave your lights on.

- Dentists have dental tools. Reverse this to dentists do not have dental tools. How can a dentist do dental work without tools? This provokes the idea of patients buying their own tools, which dentists store in sterile compartments to help prevent the spread of disease.

- Travelers pay for lodging while traveling. Reverse this to travelers do not pay for lodging. The public library system is a great success in giving people access to books and information for free. Why not use the same model to give people a place to stay for free? Set aside land in different cities where people are allowed to stay for free. You basically get a "land library card" that allows you to stay on a piece of land for a certain amount of time. This will help the homeless and those who wish to travel cheaply.

- Parents have to pay for toys. Reverse this to toys are free. Again, use the library model, lending out puzzles, games, video games, high-tech toys, educational toys, and so on to children with membership privileges. Kids could use the toys for a few weeks before they are returned to the library. This would provide a variety of continual stimuli for the child without the need for a closet full of unwanted toys.

- A chair has height. Reverse this to a chair is flat. This inspires the idea of a piece of thick padding material that you could lay over something else, maybe a large rock or downed tree, to create a chair. In effect, you could place the pad over anything in nature to create a chair.

- All games require competition. Reverse this to come up with a game that requires cooperation. Say two boys of different ages and skill levels are playing badminton. The older boy is much better than the younger one and wins every game. The younger boy is discouraged and refuses to play. Since this spoiled the fun for the older boy, it posed the problem of how to keep the younger boy playing? A conventional thinker would suggest giving the older boy a handicap or exhorting the younger to be a good loser. But through reversal, we can change the game into a cooperative game by making the goal seeing how long the two boys can keep the bird going back and forth.

Suppose my challenge is: "In what ways might I create a new business for airports and train stations?"

My basic assumptions are:

- Airports and train stations are for people who are traveling from one point to another.

- Planes and trains are constantly arriving and departing.

- People depart rapidly.

I reverse these assumptions to:

- Airports and train stations are for people who are *not* traveling.

- Planes and trains are *not* arriving and departing.

- People are *not* departing rapidly.

I now have a new perspective on the challenge. Perhaps I could create a business to serve people caught by bad weather, strikes, missed trains or planes, or those who have long delays or layovers and want to rest—people who, for some reason, are delayed in their travels. They would need lodging but would not want or be able to leave the terminal.

The idea: A capsule hotel that would provide basic amenities in modular, prefab, Pullman-style sleeping compartments that could be stacked two or three high. Each capsule would come with a TV, radio, alarm clock, and reading light. A community shower would be available to all guests. The front desk would be staffed twenty-four hours a day and would carry razors, soap, toothpaste, toothbrushes, and so on. The price for a twenty-four-hour stay would be 50 percent cheaper than airport hotels and would also have low hourly rates, perhaps $10 an hour. Such hotels are already in use in Japan and are quite popular.

The capsules would be easy to clean and maintain. Because they are modular, they could be easily moved between locations. They could also be leased to cities as temporary lodging for the homeless or for people who are forced out of their homes by fires and floods.

The figure on the next page is known as Schroeder's staircase. It will appear right side up even when turned upside down.

Assumptions can also appear right side up when turned upside down, and this may lead to a new idea. Consider the assumption that banks loan money to people to buy land. Reverse this to people loaning land to banks. How might this work? What ideas can you think of?

One idea: People who have unused land could enter into an agreement whereby they loan the land to the bank to develop. The bank would figure out the finances, hire the builder, and rent and manage the property; the owner would get a biannual dividend from the bank for the use of the property. At the end of an agreed-upon period, the property would revert to the owner. By reversing a basic assumption, you could realize a mutual profit with a bank by "lending" them your land.

SUMMARY

Imagine a cage containing five monkeys. Inside the cage, hang a banana on a string and place a set of stairs under it. Before long, a monkey will go to the stairs and start to climb toward the banana. As soon as he touches the stair, spray all the monkeys with ice-cold water. After a while, another monkey makes an attempt with the same result—all the monkeys are sprayed with ice-cold water. Pretty soon, when another monkey tries to climb the stairs, the other monkeys will try to prevent it.

Now, turn off the cold water. Remove one monkey from the cage and replace it with a new one. The new monkey sees the banana and will want to climb the stairs. To his surprise, all of the other monkeys attack him. After another attempt and attack, he knows that if he tries to climb the stairs he will be assaulted.

Next, remove another of the original monkeys and replace it with a new one. The newcomer goes to the stairs and is attacked. The previous newcomer takes part in the punishment with enthusiasm.

Again, replace a third monkey with a new one. The new one goes to the stairs and is attacked. Two of the four monkeys that beat him have no idea why they were not permitted to climb the stairs, or why they are participating in the beating of the newest monkey.

After replacing the fourth and fifth monkeys with new ones, all the monkeys that have been sprayed with ice-cold water have been replaced. Nevertheless, no monkey ever again approaches the stairs. Why not? Because as far as they know that's the way it's always been around here.

Don't be a monkey. Challenge all assumptions.

SLICE AND DICE

"When he is united, divide him."

SUN TZU

Imagine renovating a house with many rooms. Each of the rooms is part of the function of a house, and we tend to think of one "house" instead of a building composed of many different rooms.

Each room, however, is separate from the others, and we may think of them, accordingly, as separate entities: bedrooms, bathrooms, garage, living room, den, kitchen, and so on. Regarded this way, they are separate attributes that together constitute a house.

To change the nature of the house, you do not blow it up and start building a new and different one. It is much more productive to shift your focus from the one "house" to the many separate "rooms" and improve or change one room at a time. By changing a few rooms, you can convert a large house made up of many rooms into a mansion.

Every problem is a house with many rooms. To stimulate new ideas, identify and list the various attributes of a problem and work on one attribute at a time.

Imagine that the box in the margin represents your challenge, with each square representing an attribute. Divide the box into as many squares as you can. What is your final total?

Some people will see sixteen, or perhaps seventeen (if they counted the square which contains the smaller ones), squares; others will see more, and a few will see all thirty. The more you slice and dice your challenge, the more attributes you will be able to improve or change. Try to be as comprehensive as possible—if you omit something, you won't be able to bring it back later. Quantity is more important than quality at this point.

People define attributes differently. When listing the attributes of a problem, think of them simply as its components, and make a general list without worrying about how correct it is. Trusting yourself will make your solutions unique and may produce an idea that will shake you down to your kneecaps.

Some common ways to describe attributes are descriptive, process, function, social, price, and ecological.

Common *descriptive* attributes are: substance, structure, color, shape, texture, sound, taste, odor, space, and density.

Common *process* attributes are: marketing, manufacturing, selling, function, and time.

Common *social* attributes are: responsibilities, politics, and taboos.

Common *price* attributes are: cost to manufacturer, wholesaler, retailer, and consumer.

Common *ecological* attributes are: positive or negative impact on the environment.

The attributes of a pencil might be listed as: used for writing, yellow, lead, eraser, sharp, hexagonal, has printing on it, and is cylindrical.

The attributes of a challenge to pay for a corporate acquisition might be: amount of payment, time of payment, type of payment, security, source of financing, management responsibilities, corporate politics, press relations, time to close the deal, and employee relations.

ATTRIBUTES OF A SCREWDRIVER

Consider the attributes of a common screwdriver.

1. Round.
2. Steel shank.
3. Wooden handle.
4. Wedge-shaped end.
5. Manually operated. A twisting motion provides power.
6. Used for tightening and loosening screws.

To invent a better screwdriver, focus on each specific attribute and try to improve it. Look at each attribute or component and ask "How else can this be accomplished?" or "Why does this have to be this way?"

AB Bacho Tools of Sweden studied the screwdriver handle. They discovered that most craftspeople use both hands to turn a screwdriver even though the handle isn't designed for it. So, they developed a screwdriver handle with space for both hands, called the Bacho Ergo screwdriver, and what they call the "ergo" concept soon extended to their entire tool line. Since then, Ergo tools have gone on to win design prizes and have even been shown in museums. Bacho claims that redesigning the lowly screwdriver handle allowed them to maintain a strong position in the tool market.

We usually describe an object by listing its functions. The way we use something is not inherent in the object itself—it grows out of experience and observation. A screwdriver's primary function is to tighten or loosen screws. To discover new applications and ideas, you need flexibility of thought.

In the illustration to the right, the lone dot attracts your attention because it seems different somehow. We tend to assume that items that happen to be close together will have more in common than those which are distant. By separating the attribute "steel shank" from the screwdriver's other attributes, you are able to get some distance from the other attributes and focus on it without being influenced by them. The more you are able to focus on a specific attribute, the more likely you are to think flexibly and discover alternative ideas.

By examining "steel shank" as a separate attribute, we can move away from our stereotypic label of a screwdriver and come up with new applications. Possible other uses could include: weapon, probe, pointer, plug, pipe bowl cleaner, head and back scratcher, shoehorn, paint-can opener, measuring tool, tool to remove paper jams from copiers, scraper, prying device, telephone dialer, tapping tool, mini-dowel, and so on. Can you think of more uses? How might economic considerations affect possible uses? How about aesthetic considerations?

BLUEPRINT

1. *State your challenge.*

2. *Analyze the challenge and list as many attributes as you can.*

3. *Take each attribute, one at a time, and try to think of ways to change or improve it. Ask "How else can this be accomplished?" and "Why does this have to be this way?"*

4. *Strive to make your thinking both fluent and flexible.*

Many years ago, bicycle manufacturers improved bicycle design by examining the following attributes:

1. Frame.
2. Handlebars.
3. Pedals.

4. Brakes.

5. Tires.

6. Chain.

7. Drive sprocket.

They improved each attribute of the bicycle, including the following:

1. Lightweight frames made out of new materials.

2. Racing handlebars replacing traditional handlebars.

3. Pedals with straps and grips.

4. Hand brakes replacing axle brakes.

5. Lightweight, solid tires replacing inflatable ones.

6. Chains with clamps to make changing them easier.

7. Sprockets that provided ten gears.

If you tried to improve the bicycle by thinking of a bike as a whole entity, you may have left something out of consideration. What if they had improved everything but the tires? Of course, mountain bike manufacturers have improved on most of these items, as well as some new ones such as twenty-six gears, reinforced frames, and oval (instead of circular) chain rings. What have *they* left out?

Read the following:

Since the words "I love Paris in the springtime" are very familiar to most people, they fail to notice that the word "the" appears twice. However, if you concentrate on reading one word at a time, you automatically see the second "the." In the same way, Slice and Dice forces you to methodically rotate your attention to each attribute, one at a time.

Even trivial attributes sometimes provide the clue to a solution. Everything has meaning, no matter how small or seemingly insignificant. Even tiny pine needles have a clean fresh smell. Tiny improvements in a thousand places can lead to an innovation in almost any product or service. When you pay attention to attributes and improve them one by one you build a wave of ideas, drop by drop.

U.S. Precision Lens Co. developed a sophisticated new plastic projection TV lens. Happy with the item's sales, they went on to other things. Tethered to their original idea for the lens, they depleted the idea's capital by not trying to refine or improve it.

In Japan, Matsushita Electric "sliced and diced" the lens into its various attributes. Discovering that the original plastic was ill-suited for laser-based products such as DVDs and CD-ROM, they focused on improving that one simple attribute.

Lenses in general were the bottleneck in cost and performance for many laser-based products, so Matsushita worked quietly and methodically to make one small improvement in the U.S. Precision Lens Co. lens. In 1986, they unveiled it: an aspheric lens made of glass. Smaller and more precise than the original lens, it slashed manufacturing costs by 90 percent—another classic triumph brought about by improving one component of an already successful product. It was also another case of a U.S. company overlooking its own creative capital.

When you are invited to a banquet, you take what is set before you. If you demanded that your host serve a special fish or perhaps a certain type of bread, you would be deemed rude and absurd. Take your challenge as it is served to you, and slice and dice it into separate pieces or attributes with the sharp knife of your mind.

The Boatmen's National Bank of St. Louis was looking for better ways to advertise their cash-management services. They divided all their services into attributes and discovered that one of those attributes—their early reporting of checks clearing a company's account—was unique. So they made this the focus of a major ad campaign.

Rather than sending out another brochure, they mailed boxes containing English muffins, jars of jelly, a knife, and a napkin to 1,400 prospective customers. The accompanying message read, "While you're having breakfast, Boatmen's already has available to you the information you'll need about your checks at the opening of the business day." This innovative campaign produced leads that were as warm as toast.

Which figure is the widest of the above?

They are the same size. However, as the number of subdivisions increases, the squares appear to become progressively wider. (This is known as the Opel-Kundt illusion and was first demonstrated in 1895.)

In the same way, when you subdivide a challenge into many separate parts, the nature of the challenge does not change. However, your perception of it does. It is this expansion of consciousness that leads to new ideas.

A frozen-fish processor was concerned that his product tasted bland. He tried everything to keep the fish fresh-tasting, including keeping them in fish tanks right up to processing. Nothing worked; the fish remained listless. To find a solution, he listed the attributes of a fish, including:

Lives underwater

Has gills and fins

Constantly moves to escape from predators

Cold-blooded

Changes color out of water

He looked at each attribute separately, trying to find ideas to solve his problem. Finally, he hit upon the solution: He put a small shark in the tank with the fish. The fish kept moving to escape being eaten and retained their vitality and thus their fresh flavor.

His challenge did not change, but by subdividing it into attributes, he expanded his consciousness to include predators, which proved to be the key to his solution.

Sometimes listing and then *clustering* related attributes will inspire an idea. The owner of a fast-food franchise had trouble with employee turnover. The majority of his employees were teenage students.

He sliced and diced the attributes of students into:

They go to school	Young
Like instant gratification	Parental supervision
Pride in grades	Like money
Competitive	Seek parental approval
Developing a work ethic	Seek teacher approval
Worried about future	Thinking about college
Seek recognition	Working to buy things

He focused his attention on the following cluster:

Pride in grades	Competitive
Work ethic	Recognition
Money	Parental approval
Teacher approval	College

The idea blared out at him from behind the cluster of attributes, honking like a saxophone for his attention.

The idea: A bonus plan based on grade-point averages. Any student who works for a whole semester and earns a 2.5 to 3.0 GPA is awarded a fifteen-cent-per-hour bonus for all hours worked that semester. The ante would be upped to 25 cents per hour for students earning better than 3.0.

The cost is marginal, probably less than 5 percent of his payroll costs for the time period. The advantages are many:

- Students are encouraged to work for the entire semester.

- The bonus attracted better students, who tend to be better workers.

- Guidance counselors and teachers do his recruiting for him, recommending his restaurant to students looking for work.

- Parents encourage their children to work at his place.

- Great PR for the restaurant. He gets free newspaper and television coverage.

SUMMARY

Sometimes ideas are just new information grafted onto an attribute and spliced with another thought. Two Manhattan psychotherapists contemplated some of the common attributes of their patients (shy, busy, housebound, and so on). These patient attributes sparked a new idea—counseling by mail. They launched a new enterprise designed to provide mail-order therapy for shy, busy, or housebound people.

A first-class idea person can slice and dice challenges into separate, simple attributes and then combine them into new, more complex structures, just as stars do.

CHAPTER SEVEN

CHERRY SPLIT

"Who can determine where one ends
and the other begins?"

SUN TZU

Sometimes the solution to a problem lies within the problem itself. Cherry Split allows you to take a challenge apart and then reassemble the parts into new ideas. It's titled "Cherry Split" after the first example of its use diagrammed in this chapter.

Giving a child a complete model fort is giving him a place where his ideas go to die—he has little choice but to use it as is. However, if you give him a set of building blocks, he can create any number of new and unique structures.

Cherry Split divides a challenge into separate blocks which you can reassemble in different ways to create any number of alternative ideas.

Do you see a square in the following illustration?

There is no actual, printed square. Yet, by splitting a target into halves, we can perceive a square where none exists (the curved sections end abruptly at what we perceive as the edges of a square). In the same way, by splitting attributes, we can shape and reshape components of a problem into ideas where none existed before.

1. *State the essence of your challenge in two words.* For instance, if your challenge is "In what ways might I improve my sales of Canon copiers?", the two-word phrase that captures the essence of your challenge is: "Selling copiers." In the example that follows, the challenge is "In what ways might we improve the methodology of picking cherries?"; the two-word phrase is "Cherry picking."

2. *Split the challenge into two separate units.* In the diagram, note how "cherry" and "picking" are handled.

3. *Split each attribute into two* more *attributes.* For instance, "cherry" is split into "delicate" and "separate," "picking" is split into "remove" and "transport."

   Do not worry about the correctness of the split; no two people will split attributes in the same way. One person will look down a street and see an indescribable beauty in the shadows, the light, the brick walls, the dark porches, and the grayed snowbanks. Another person will see only rubble. You have to define attributes for yourself, taking your clues where you find them.

4. *Continue splitting the attributes until you feel that you have enough to work with.* In the cherry example, I split "delicate" into "damaged" and "blemished," "separate" into "selecting" and "closeness to each other," "remove" into "touch and hold" and "picking," and "transport" into "ground" and "boxes."

5. *Examine each attribute for ideas.* The wonder of this method is that big ideas can dwell in the most insignificant attribute just as the flavor of an entire ocean is contained in one drop.

6. *Try reassembling the attributes.* New combinations can induce new perspectives and new ideas. Splitting a challenge into several attributes is like removing a dividing panel from between chambers of very hot and very cold air: New forces rush together, creating new ideas.

CHERRY PICKING PROBLEM

Challenge: "In what ways might we improve the methodology of picking cherries?"

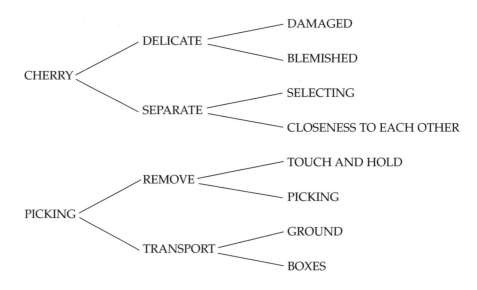

As our illustration shows, we split our challenge into the following attributes:

delicate	selecting
separate	closeness to each other
remove	touch and hold
transport	picking
damaged	ground
blemished	boxes

You could focus on just one attribute, such as "delicate," and decide to create a new type of cherry with stronger skin, to better withstand human handling.

You might reassemble attributes, such as "remove," "selecting," and "picking," and then look for a new way to accomplish these three attributes. One idea might be to shake the trees by hand and catch the fruit in large nets to minimize bruising.

Or, you might put "touching and holding," "selecting," "picking," and "transporting to the ground" together. Free-associating from this combination of attributes, one could come up with the idea of a hydraulic lift which would raise the cherry pickers up to the cherries. Picking by lift would help to minimize the number of times fruit is handled, thus reducing damage.

The separated attributes encourage rearranging of information, provoking you to search out new ways of doing things. It does not matter how many of the attributes you use or how you link them when you generate ideas. It's just a way to add a few more ball bearings to your imagination.

CUSTOMER SERVICE PROBLEM

Imagine a company has a problem with customer service. We might separate out the attributes of customer service in the following manner:

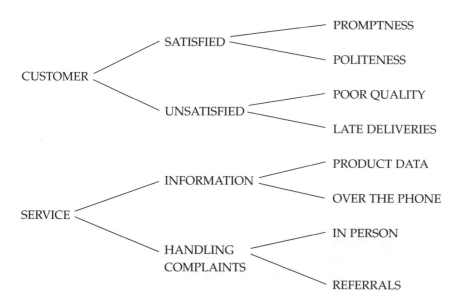

CUSTOMER
— SATISFIED
— PROMPTNESS
— POLITENESS
— UNSATISFIED
— POOR QUALITY
— LATE DELIVERIES

SERVICE
— INFORMATION
— PRODUCT DATA
— OVER THE PHONE
— HANDLING COMPLAINTS
— IN PERSON
— REFERRALS

You could focus on one attribute, "politeness," and think of ways to incorporate more politeness into your customer service program. One idea might be to have everyone in the company perform one five-minute act of exceptional courtesy per day.

You might connect "information," "over the phone," and "unsatisfied customers," and suggest that customer service reps call unsatisfied customers, collect information about their dissatisfaction, write a report containing detailed suggestions for improvement, and distribute it to the people involved in the problem.

Or, you might connect "unsatisfied customers," "late deliveries," "information," and "over the phone," and suggest that customer service reps call to inform customers about possible late deliveries and give them daily updates. The idea here would be to alert the customers to problems before they themselves became aware of them.

Cherry Split allows you to replace the inhibiting unity of a fixed problem with the more creative situation of working with several attributes in a variety of ways, generating so many combinations that you'll have to brush them away from your face.

Let's try one more example. A sports magazine publisher's challenge was "In what ways might I extend the market for my sports magazine?"

He cherry split the challenge:

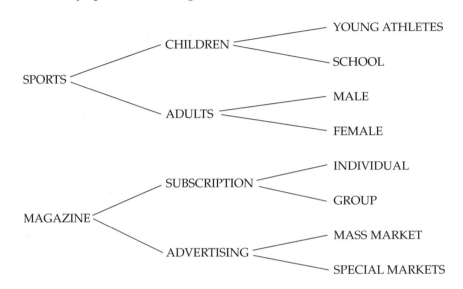

By putting "sports," "magazine," "children," "school," and "young athletes" together, he came up with the idea of modifying his adult sports magazine to appeal to kids. He plans to add a few special features to the basic magazine, such as a monthly profile of outstanding young athletes. The company intends to sell subscriptions through schools and to provide free subscriptions to underprivileged kids as part of the Kids Literacy Program, which distributes magazines to schools and provides teaching guidelines. The children's version will attract an ever-larger crop of readers who will be likely to subscribe to the adult version in a few years.

GROUP EXERCISE

To use Cherry Split as a group exercise, present a challenge to a group and ask them to split it into as many attributes as possible. List the attributes as they are suggested, and keep going as long as anyone has ideas for further splitting. It doesn't matter if some of the suggestions overlap, but do ask anyone who volunteers a seemingly similar attribute to explain how it's different. If they believe it offers something new, go ahead and list it.

Ask each member of the group to reassemble the attributes into a new way of looking at the challenge. Start with one person's idea and ask the rest of the group to build on it, until you've exhausted all possibilities. Then go on to the next person and repeat the process again and again, until you're satisfied that you have drawn out as many creative ideas as possible.

A few years ago, a beer company was looking for new products to sell. In a group exercise, they split the challenge into clusters of attributes. Here is one of the clusters:

distribution network	flavored
rural	six-packs
liquid	spring water

This particular cluster led to an idea for a new product: a line of bottled water. At present, bottled water is distributed to urban areas nationally but is less available in rural communities. The beer company, with its established distribution network, found that they could penetrate the rural market.

The water comes from the same mountain springs as water used in its beer. They sell the water plain and flavored in six-packs.

The obviousness of this particular beer company selling bottled water became apparent only when executives studied the challenge and fractionated it into the particular attributes of selling beer.

SUMMARY

Cherry Split enables you to break apart a challenge into separate pieces. When you do this, you begin to see new material that had once been part of something else. When you first try to fit the pieces back together, you will be like a child fitting together his first model fort—awkward and slow, but when a piece slips into a proper slot, ideas begin to jump and take shape like coveys of startled birds into the air.

THINK BUBBLES

"Order of disorder depends upon organization."

SUN TZU

When you look at the ceiling in an auditorium, you might say that the *lights* are on, or you might say that the *light* is on. In the first case, you are placing emphasis on the individual bulbs, in the second you are emphasizing their output. The important thing is not the *emphasis* but the *process,* the light.

When you map a challenge, you can emphasize either individual thoughts or the challenge as a whole. In making a mind map, emphasis is not important—the *process* is. It provides a way to communicate with your mind.

Think Bubbles is a graphic technique for organizing your thoughts. It creates an actual, physical picture of the way your mind blueprints a challenge. Think Bubbles allows you to record, store, and manipulate information about a challenge in a variety of ways, as well as letting you see relationships between different parts of the problem.

How would you describe the figure below?

● ● ● ●   ● ● ● ●   ● ● ● ●

They are twelve separate and unrelated dots. However, because of the way they are organized, we perceive them as three separate *groups* of dots. In fact, it is almost impossible to see them any other way. By organizing the dots into groups, one can give them a new identity.

This is what happens when you take your separate thoughts and organize them on paper by mapping them—the thoughts are immediately given a new identity. This new identity can be evaluated, developed, and resolved if resolution proves possible: altered or discarded if it does not. Once you project your blurred mental images onto paper, the process of idea evolution can really begin.

Because the map is designed to help you communicate with yourself, it's okay if the relationships between items are confusing to everyone but you. Similarly, your map can be as messy as you like, so long as you can read it. Some maps look like they were slapped down on paper by the testy tail of a barnyard animal. With practice, you will form and refine a method of mind mapping that is uniquely your own. What matters is that it makes sense to you, the creator.

BLUEPRINT

The mapping process usually goes like this: When you are caught with a challenge that defies solution, map out your impressions and thoughts about it. Study the map. If no ideas come after prolonged study, you will probably feel uneasy. In that case, put the map away for a few days. When you return to it, you will find that your mind is more focused on the challenge, and you will usually experience a moment of insight. This should be followed by a period of concentrated thought, during which the insight unfolds into a complete idea. Although maps can and should be highly individualized, all mind maps share five basic characteristics:

1. *Organization.* Mapping presents information organized in the way you think it. It displays the way your mind works, complete with patterns and interrelationships, and has an amazing capacity to convey precise information, no matter how crudely drawn.

   You can make your map of think bubbles as simple or as complex as you want. You can use large paper, a blackboard, or anything you like. You can group related ideas of equal importance horizontally and use connecting arrows to denote special relationships or color code different types of relationships. The visual, flexible nature of mapping makes it extremely useful as a device to help us see, express, and think about complex problems.

   You can readily add to the map later—and should be prepared to, as your first map will rarely produce an idea that meets all of your criteria.

2. *Key words.* Ignore all irrelevant words and phrases and concentrate only on expressing the essentials, and what associations these "essences" excite in your mind.

3. *Association.* Make connections, links, and relationships between seemingly isolated and unconnected pieces of information. These connections open the door to more possibilities. You can feel free to make any association you wish, without worrying whether or not others will understand you.

    An entrepreneur looking for new products mapped out various ideas. The map reminded him of analysis, which reminded him of psychotherapy, which reminded him of Sigmund Freud. He wrote "Sigmund Freud" and drew a bubble around it. The bubble reminded him of a pillow, and that association inspired his idea.

    The idea: He's manufacturing a pillow with Freud's picture on it, and marketing it as a tool for do-it-yourself analysis.

4. *Clustering.* The map's organization comes close to the way your mind clusters concepts, making the mapped information more accessible to the brain. Once your ideas are clustered, try to adopt the viewpoint of a critic seeing the ideas for the first time. This allows you to test your associations, spot missing information, and pinpoint areas where you need more and better ideas. Mind mapping is an idea generator. It does *not* supply raw material, so your map may show areas where you need to collect more information.

5. *Conscious involvement.* Making the map requires you to concentrate on your challenge, which helps get information about it transferred from short-term to long-term memory. In addition, continuous conscious involvement allows you to group and regroup concepts, encouraging comparisons. Moving think bubbles around into new juxtapositions often provokes new ideas.

Suppose my challenge is: "In what ways might I better market my consulting services?"

I write the essence of the challenge, "marketing consulting services," in the center of the page and draw a bubble around it. Then I free-associate another thought about the challenge. I write it. I draw a bubble around it and draw a line connecting it to the original. I continue to write whatever comes to mind, drawing bubbles and connecting related think bubbles with lines. The resulting map appears on page 70.

The clusters of bubbles stimulate the following ideas to help me market my consulting services:

1. *Marketing through referrals by former clients and nonclients,* such as bankers and trade association executives.

2. *Personal marketing:* Personal cold-call selling, writing personal letters, and joining professional organizations.

3. *Nonpersonal marketing:* Direct mail, public relations, publishing, and advertising.

4. *Targets of influence.* This would include other professionals who serve the same clients, decision makers in client organizations, managers and directors of trade and professional associations, and leaders of industry.

5. *Targets of opportunity.* This includes former clients with new needs, potential new clients, and targeted market niches.

The marketing plan I get from the map is to market my services through referrals and both personal and nonpersonal marketing. In addition, the map shows me where more and better information is needed, specifically on targets of opportunity.

The vice president of a light bulb company wanted to increase sales. He wrote "light bulbs" in the middle of a page and connected it with a *process,* "lighting," and a *system,* "4,000 distributors." He wrote down what came to mind, drew bubbles, and made connections.

His initial map appears on page 71.

The key concepts featured on his initial map were:

1. Attributes of light bulbs: lifespan, lighting, colors, and decoration.
2. Markets: industrial, institutional, and retail.
3. 4,000 distributors to reach his present markets.
4. Energy management to conserve costs.
5. "Decoration management," to enhance lighting quality.

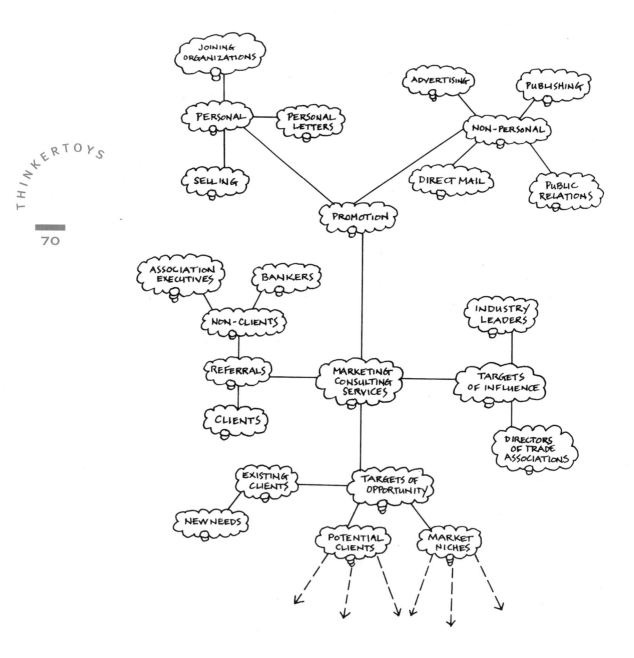

The map became increasingly complex as he worked on it over time, and prompted him to think about his business in various new ways. The bubble that produced the final idea was the one containing "energy management."

The idea: He created an energy management division, which bypassed the distributors and focused on industrial and institutional markets, allow-

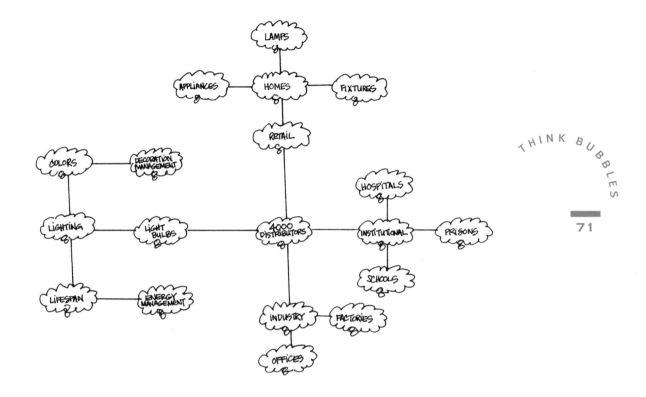

ing clients to cut energy costs. As a consequence, the company closed massive orders for light bulbs. He put it this way: "The map led to a cascade of ideas that motivated us to act and create a whole new division."

SUMMARY

Mapping a challenge or an idea allows you access to a certain mental spark: It flares up in the mind, is conducted to the hand, flows to the paper, and bursts into a tiny fire that, when seen, closes the circle by traveling back into the eye and farther into the subconscious.

Sometimes these tiny fires become the very ideas that you need to resolve your challenge; sometimes they need to be tended and fueled with more information before they flare into ideas. And, sometimes, these tiny fires smolder for days, weeks, or months before they blaze. However, if you take no action when that spark flares up in your mind, its spark burns out, turns cold, and is forgotten.

SCAMPER

> "He who can modify his tactics in relation to his
> opponent, and thereby succeed in winning,
> may be called a heaven-borne captain."
>
> **SUN TZU**

Manipulation is the brother of creativity. When your imagination is as blank as a waiter's stare, take an existing item and manipulate it into a new idea. Remember that everything new is just an addition or modification to something that already existed.

You will note that SCAMPER is much longer than any other chapter in this book. This is because it is actually a collection of nine techniques for transforming any object, service, or process into something new. Much of this Thinkertoy is devoted to specific examples, which may be skimmed or skipped. You should, however, pay close attention to the nine techniques; as you read about them, try asking yourself how TV, suitcase, hamburger, home mortgage, or any other object or process can be improved. Ideas will appear almost involuntarily.

Can you transform the rabbit on the next page into a duck?

If you have trouble doing this, manipulate the page by turning it a quarter-turn to the left—suddenly, the duck takes form. You can also manipulate existing ideas and products into new things.

The new thing can then be changed into still other new things. To limit yourself to your first idea is a disaster for your imagination. The best way to get a good idea is to get as many ideas as you can. Any particular way of looking at things is just one of many other possible ways.

If you had a bag filled with thousands of white marbles and just one ruby one, the odds of anyone picking out that ruby marble would be very low. If you kept adding ruby marbles, the chances of picking one would keep increasing. Generating alternative ideas is as solid and positive a procedure as putting more ruby marbles into the bag. You still may not get a ruby marble, but it never hurts to increase your odds. There is nothing to lose when you generate alternatives, and everything to gain.

Several things happen when you search out alternative ideas:

1. One of the alternative ideas may solve your problem.

2. An alternative idea may help you rearrange the components of your problem, thereby solving it indirectly.

3. The alternative might prove to be a better starting point.

4. One alternative might be a breakthrough idea that has nothing to do with the problem at hand. When that happens, when you get this kind of breakthrough, your hair stands on end, your mouth goes dry, and you want to stand up and holler. Alexander Graham Bell found *his* breakthrough while he was trying to invent a hearing aid; he invented the telephone instead. Ray Kroc was trying to develop a market for his Multimixers when he discovered "fast food"—a concept that would change America's eating habits.

5. You may generate a number of alternatives and then return to your original idea. Compiling numerous alternative ideas in no way prevents you from using the most obvious approach, but it makes the decision to use it much more meaningful. Instead of being chosen because it seems the only option, it is chosen after it becomes apparent that it is the *best* one.

How many different answers can you think of to the question: "What is half of thirteen?" Of course, the obvious answer is six and a half. However, see how many other possible answers you can come up with before you read further.

There are six alternatives: Halving the *numeral* 13 gives you 1 and 3 ($^1/_3$). Halving the *word* "thirteen" gives you 4 . . . letters on each side. Converting 13 into Roman numerals and halving it one way gives you 11 and 2 (XI/II). Halving it a different way gives you 8 (XIII).

Alternatives are provocative; they force you to overcome your clichéd patterns of thinking. After reading this chapter, you will find yourself walking down the most unlikely pathways, because you know that they often lead to surprising insights and ideas—ideas as startling as finding a trout swimming in your morning cereal.

SCAMPER is a checklist of idea-spurring questions. Some of the questions were first suggested by Alex Osborn, a pioneer teacher of creativity. They were later arranged by Bob Eberle into this mnemonic.

Substitute something.

Combine it with something else.

Adapt something to it.

Modify or **M**agnify it.

Put it to some other use.

Eliminate something.

Reverse or **R**earrange it.

To use SCAMPER:

1. *Isolate the challenge or subject you want to think about.*

2. *Ask SCAMPER questions about each step of the challenge or subject and see what new ideas emerge.* Asking the questions is like tapping all over the challenge with a hammer to see where the hollow spots are.

Consider the challenge: "In what ways might I improve my selling techniques?" First, identify all the stages in the selling process (i.e., prospecting, presenting, overcoming objections, closing, follow-up, paperwork, time management, and so on.) Then, ask SCAMPER questions to generate a wide variety of ideas about reshaping and manipulating each stage of the selling process.

For instance, let's say you have decided to isolate "prospecting." Now apply SCAMPER to that one step. Ask yourself:

- What procedure can I *substitute* for my current one?

- How can I *combine* prospecting with some other procedure?

- What can I *adapt* or copy from someone else's prospecting methods?

- How can I *modify* or alter the way I prospect?

- What can I *magnify* or add to the way I prospect?

- How can I *put* my prospecting *to other uses*?

- What can I *eliminate* from the way I prospect?

- What is the *reverse* of prospecting?

- What *rearrangement* of prospecting procedures might be better?

Prod your imagination with SCAMPER questions, and then continue asking "How can . . . ?" "What else . . . ?" "How else . . . ?" If you do this for each stage of the selling process, you will generate the maximum number of ideas for improving your selling techniques.

Suppose a paper clip manufacturer wants to improve his product. He would start looking for ideas by asking:

- What can be *substituted* in the clip?

- What can I *combine* the clip with to make something else?

- What can I *adapt* to the clip?

- How can I *modify* the clip?

- What can I *magnify* or add to the clip?

- What *other uses* can I find for the clip?

- What can be *eliminated* from the clip?

- What is the *reverse* of clipping?

- What *rearrangement* of the clip might be better?

One manufacturer *substituted* plastic for metal, *added* color, and produced plastic clips in various colors so that clipped papers could be color-coded, thereby creating *another use* for clips.

Applying SCAMPER to a Hamburger

Ray Kroc was a middle-class high-school dropout, a former piano player, and a real-estate salesman who sold paper cups for seventeen years. In his fifties, Ray Kroc left the paper cup business and hit the road selling a little machine called the Multimixer, which could make six milkshakes at a time.

One day in 1954, a hamburger stand in California ordered eight Multimixers. Curious, Kroc drove his dusty little car out to investigate. He was stunned by the volume of business that Dick and Maurice McDonald were doing. They had unwittingly hit on the concept of fast food—homogenized, predictable items that are quick and easy to prepare. The McDonalds had simplified, economized, and minimized the hamburger stand.

Kroc and the McDonalds formed a partnership that allowed Kroc to find new sites, and open and run them. What followed was *not* instant success but obstacles and challenges. Ray Kroc became a billionaire because he identified the right challenges and manipulated existing information into new ideas to solve them.

Following are some of the challenges he faced and how the SCAMPER principles helped to shape his ideas.

SUBSTITUTE

Problem: The McDonalds proved to be lethargic business partners. Kroc was worried that they might sell out to someone who didn't want him around.

SCAMPER Solution: Substitute a different partner. Kroc was cash poor, but he was determined to buy out the McDonalds. Kroc raised the $2.7 million asking price from John Bristol, a venture capitalist whose clients (college endowment funds) realized a $14-million return on their investment. The next substitution was to go public, which he did in 1963, making many investors rich.

COMBINE

Problem: Ray Kroc's first hamburger stand was planned for Des Plaines, Illinois, but he couldn't afford to finance construction.

SCAMPER Solution: Combine purposes with someone else. He sold the construction company half-ownership in return for constructing his first building.

ADAPT

Problem: Ray Kroc was interested in developing a new twist on the food business, but he lacked ideas.

SCAMPER Solution: Adapt someone else's idea. Kroc was amazed at the volume of business the McDonalds were doing by selling a hamburger in a paper bag here, a helping of french fries there. Kroc's big idea was adapting the McDonalds' simple merchandising methods to create a new concept—fast food.

MODIFY

Problem: The french fries made in Kroc's first stand in Illinois didn't taste like the originals; they were tasteless and mushy. He tried the McDonalds' recipe again and again, to no avail. A friend finally solved the mystery—Kroc stored his potatoes in the basement, while the McDonalds kept theirs outside in chicken-wire bins, exposed to desert winds that cured the potatoes.

SCAMPER Solution: Modify the storage area. Kroc cured the potatoes by installing large electric fans in the basement.

MAGNIFY

Problem: A number of franchise owners wanted to expand the basic menu.

SCAMPER Solution: Magnify the burger and add new items to the menu. He created the popular Big Mac by way of a $10 million "Build a Big Mac" contest. Later additions included the Egg McMuffin, Filet-o-Fish, and Chicken McNuggets.

PUT TO OTHER USES

Problem: Kroc needed to develop other sources of income.

SCAMPER Solution: Put McDonald's to use in the real estate business. Kroc's company would lease and develop a site, then re-lease it to the franchisee, who would have to pay rent as well as franchise fees. Today, 10 percent of the company's revenue comes from rentals. In the 1960s, Kroc also bought back as many of the original sites as he could. While this policy initially accrued huge debts, it gave McDonald's the upper hand against competitors, who periodically faced massive rent hikes.

ELIMINATE OR MINIFY

Problem: Hamburger patty distributors packed their burgers in a way that was efficient for them, but that also meant McDonald's employees had to restack them to keep the bottom patties from getting crushed.

SCAMPER Solution: Eliminate the problem. Kroc refused to do business with packagers unless they shipped fewer burgers in each stack. Employees no longer had to restack burgers, saving McDonald's time and money. He also eliminated the middleman by buying entire crops of Idaho Russet Burbank potatoes.

Rearrange

Problem: Kroc wanted to differentiate his establishments from the competition.

SCAMPER Solution: Rearrange the architecture. Kroc changed the original red-and-white, box-shaped prototype into the Golden Arches and added drive-throughs in the 1970s.

Asking SCAMPER Questions

Even the hot dog, as we know it, is the result of asking the right question at the right time. In 1904, Antoine Feutchwanger was selling sausages at the Louisiana Exposition. First he tried offering them on individual plates, but this proved too expensive. He then offered his customers white cotton gloves to keep the franks from burning their fingers. The gloves were expensive, too, and customers tended to walk off with them. Antoine and his brother-in-law, a baker, sat down to figure out what inexpensive item could be added (**modify**) to the frankfurter to prevent people from burning their fingers. His brother-in-law said something like "What if I baked a long bun and slit it to hold the frank? Then you can sell the franks, and I can sell you the buns. Who knows, it might catch on."

When the lines at the left are combined to form the figure on the right, we can no longer perceive the original two patterns without great effort. Instead, we see a continuous wavy line running through a series of bars.

By manipulating the lines, we have created something new out of already-existing items. With SCAMPER, you also take something that already exists and do something to it. Then you do something else to it. You keep doing something to it until you invent an original idea that can exist on its own. In group problem-solving sessions, SCAMPER questions can get ideas flowing and direct the group's imagination.

Following are more than one hundred SCAMPER questions and a collection of examples that show how SCAMPER has fostered innovation. The examples range from ancient to modern, from individuals to corporations, and from gimmicks to breakthrough ideas. The questions blink in and out like fireflies throughout the history of innovation, from the creation of flying doggie snacks to the restructuring of corporate America with junk bonds.

SUBSTITUTE

You can substitute things, places, procedures, people, ideas, and even emotions. Substitution is a trial-and-error method of replacing one thing with another until you find the right idea. Scientist Paul Ehrlich tried well over five hundred colors before he found the right one to dye the veins of laboratory mice, making many new experiments possible.

To find ideas using substitution, ask:

- What can be substituted? Who else? What else?

- Can the rules be changed?

- Other ingredient? Other material?

- Other process or procedure?

- Other power?

- Other place?

- Other approach?

- What else instead? What other part instead of this?

WHAT CAN BE SUBSTITUTED?

A Starbuck's store manager played around blending different beverages, substituting one for another, over and over until she came up with a concoction that she had her staff sample. They loved it, so Starbucks tested it throughout southern California with great success. They named it the Frappuccino, and today it is a ready-to-drink venture with Pepsi-Cola that is a $500-million business unto itself.

Fireplace logs made out of coffee was the brainchild of Rod Sprules, who experimented with various ingredients and processes in an effort to make environmentally friendly logs. By combining used coffee grounds with candle wax compressed into a log shape, he invented a clean-burning, high-energy fuel product.

WHO CAN BE SUBSTITUTED?

A Japanese company came up with a unique service by asking "Who else could fulfill this need?" A Japanese wedding reception is considered a failure if no executives or bureaucrats attend. So, a company was created to provide plausible stand-ins. For instance, at one wedding, an actor played the part of an executive from the bride's company: He gave a five-minute speech full of praise for the excellent job she was doing at the office. The groom knew it was a sham, but neither his parents nor his new in-laws figured it out. At another wedding, the company provided seventy-five of the groom's eighty guests.

WHAT CAN BE SUBSTITUTED FOR CASH?

One entrepreneur figured out how to substitute smart cards (cards with embedded integrated circuitry) for coins in parking meters. Drivers load value onto smart cards; when they park, they activate the card with the correct zone code and display the card in their windshield, which acts as an in-car parking meter. Drivers then deactivate the card when they leave, so the card deducts payment for the exact amount of time used. Parking attendants verify the correct payment through a handheld reader, which can also report traffic and parking information back to the city's central data system. Since the system is cashless, it also cuts down on theft.

WHAT MATERIAL CAN BE SUBSTITUTED?

Some people have had tattoos surgically removed, which is a painful, expensive process. Others have tried to use cosmetics to cover and hide them. Instead of cosmetics, one company has developed a microskin. Microskin is a cosmetic skin that can be used to hide tattoos, birthmarks, or other skin imperfections.

Discarded cell phones are a growing environmental problem. British researchers have devised biodegradable polymer casings for cell phones that can simply be tossed into a compost heap for fertilizing flowers. Better still, the casing contains a seed that will begin germinating after the phone is recycled, blossoming into the flower of your choice. The research is being conducted by engineers and agricultural specialists at the University of Warwick and PVAXX Research and Development.

WHAT PLACE OR SCENARIO CAN BE SUBSTITUTED?

The FBI wanted to close down an international smuggling ring that smuggled drugs, counterfeit money, and counterfeit cigarettes into the country. Their plan was to round up all the criminals on one day to prevent the felons from escaping. They put together an elaborate ruse with two undercover agents, one male and one female, who had worked with the smugglers for several years. The two agents staged a fake engagement and a few months later invited the smugglers to their fake wedding on a yacht named Royal Charm docked near Atlantic City. Invitations were sent out, a date was given, and RSVPs were received from different points around the world. They were assured transportation would be provided to the yacht from a warehouse decorated in festive ribbons. The felons, dressed in tuxedos and fashionable gowns, were arrested one by one as they arrived at the warehouse. The arrests led to the seizure of $52 million of counterfeit cigarettes, $25 million in counterfeit bills, and $25 million in drugs (ecstasy, methamphetamines, and Viagra). By choosing the right place, the FBI rolled up one of the largest and most sophisticated smuggling rings in one day.

WHAT OTHER APPROACH CAN BE USED?

A unique approach to selling music is to just ask the customers to hum the song. Researchers with the Fraunhofer Institute for Digital Media Technology have teamed with Musicline.de, the German record industry's joint Internet platform, to develop a system called Query by Humming to consumers equipped with a PC, sound card, microphone, and Internet access. Is there a song you want to buy but you don't know what it's called? After you've recorded a simple fifteen-second "la-la-laaaaa-la-la" sample, Query by Humming compares it with a database of some two million songs and displays the ten most likely matches—along with links to artist information and sites where you can purchase the song. Further development of the system will allow searches by musical instruments. The system could be a boon for record stores and radio stations hoping to help music lovers find their favorite tunes.

WHAT OTHER FORMAT CAN BE USED?

Paul Sagel invented Crest's teeth-whitening strips, called Whitestrips, which has been one of the most successful new product launches in Procter &

Gamble's history. The key moment in selling this radical innovation came when Sagel had to pitch the product to the company's senior management.

P & G had a standardized presentation procedure for pitching ideas, but he changed the format in two ways. First, he brought in the parts to his prototype and built it right there, on the spot, to show how simple it was. Second, a few days before the meeting, he had his teeth whitened. They glowed. Sagel was his own prototype!

COMBINE

Much creative thinking involves synthesis, the process of combining previously unrelated ideas, goods, or services to create something new. The printing press was created when Gutenberg combined the coin punch with the wine press. Gregor Mendel combined mathematics and biology to create the new science of genetics.

Look at the illustration below. Hold the book level and place a pencil about halfway between yourself and the figure, and focus on the pencil's point. Your eyes will gradually cross, and the two figures will eventually combine to form a three-dimensional pyramid. You can also see this effect when you focus on a point between the two figures and slowly bring the book toward the tip of your nose.

A three-dimensional pyramid came into being when two individual objects merged. In the same way, an idea can become something else by annexing its neighbor.

To combine, ask:

• What ideas can be combined?

• Can we combine purposes?

• How about an assortment?

• How about a blend, an alloy, an ensemble?

- Combine units?

- What other article could be merged with this?

- How could we package a combination?

- What can be combined to multiply possible uses?

- What materials could we combine?

- Combine appeals?

WHAT MATERIALS CAN BE COMBINED?

A Hungarian architect combined cement with optical fiber to create a new type of concrete that transmits light. It has the strength of traditional concrete but, thanks to an embedded array of glass fibers, the material displays a view of the outside world, such as the silhouette of a tree. The shadows on the lighter side will appear as sharp outlines on the darker one. Even the colors remain the same. The special effect of these combined materials creates the general impression that the thickness and weight of a concrete wall will disappear.

WHAT UNITS CAN BE COMBINED?

A new multipurpose communications and entertainment center in the kitchen could also help busy families keep secure. The iCEBOX, developed by Salton Inc.'s Beyond Connected Products division, is a multimedia device with flip-down monitor on which families can play DVDs, watch television, surf the Internet, order groceries, and download recipes for the family chef. The device also allows for closed-circuit video monitoring: A parent in the kitchen can monitor visitors at the door or the kids anywhere in the house or yard.

WHAT IDEAS CAN BE COMBINED?

Examine any idea you come up with to see if it could be combined with other ideas to create something even better. In the mid-1880s, new technology enabled George Eastman to develop a cellulose film that weighed almost nothing and was impervious to the rough handling that could damage heavy glass photographic plates. The idea by itself was a great one . . . and then Eastman designed a lightweight camera to use with the new film. This combination made Eastman Kodak the world leader in photography within ten years.

WHAT PURPOSES CAN BE COMBINED?

Auto designers combined movements of helicopters and automobiles into a fully functional vehicle that literally goes sideways, its wheels turning up to 45 degrees in the same direction.

Suppose you combined the household toilet with devices that perform urinalysis and measure blood pressure, pulse, temperature, and body weight? A Japanese company has done just that. It's called the Smart Toilet, and it can display the user's results on a built-in monitor.

What would happen if you combined the power of persuasion with food or music? One marketing study showed that subjects who were given a snack of peanuts and Pepsi-Cola were more likely to be persuaded by a written message than subjects who went snackless. In another study, subjects were more influenced by messages that were accompanied by folk music than by ones that were unaccompanied. It's no accident that the people in charge of "selling" presidential candidates tend to include pleasant background music in every television commercial.

A sake brewer in Fukushima, Japan, has combined classical music with his product's fermentation. He claims that the sake's flavor has improved since he began playing the music, and he is now marketing Mozart Sake.

WHAT PRODUCTS CAN BE COMBINED TO MULTIPLY PURPOSES?

Product designers at Sheaffer Pen created the Prelude MPI pen, which joins a pen and highlighter into one. The company calls it a writing tool. Pop off the cap, and it's a ballpoint pen. Twist the black band and a yellow highlighter tip emerges around and past the ballpoint.

A Japanese hosiery company is embedding millions of microcapsules of vitamin C and mineral-rich seaweed extract in every pair of pantyhose. The capsules supposedly burst when the pantyhose are worn and the nutrients are absorbed into one's skin.

WHAT RESOURCES CAN BE COMBINED?

Researchers are working on multifuel automobiles. To obtain maximum efficiency and meet stronger environmental standards, vehicles will use combinations of various fuels, such as reformulated gasoline, electricity, and natural gas. Vehicles may carry more than one type of fuel, with an onboard computer that will conduct ongoing analyses of travel conditions to calculate fuel mixtures for maximum fuel efficiency and performance.

ADAPT

One of the paradoxes of creativity is that in order to think originally, we must first familiarize ourselves with the ideas of others. Thomas Edison put it this way: "Make it a habit to keep on the lookout for novel and interesting ideas that others have used successfully. Your idea needs to be original only in its adaptation to the problem you are working on." Many cultural historians agree with Edison in that a whole host of new objects and ideas are based on objects and ideas already in existence. Adaptation is a common and inescapable practice in creativity. Even the "Star Bangled Banner," which was written in defiance of England, was essentially the same as a popular tune sung in English pubs.

To become an expert at adaptation, ask:

- What else is like this?

- What other idea does this suggest?

- Does the past offer a parallel?

- What could I copy?

- Whom could I emulate?

- What idea could I incorporate?

- What other process could be adapted?

- What else could be adapted?

- What different contexts can I put my concept in?

- What ideas outside my field can I incorporate?

WHAT IDEA CAN BE ADAPTED?

How about a restaurantplex? People go to the theater multiplex to see the latest hot movie, but when what they want to see is sold out, they wind up seeing their second or third choice. Having multiple theaters in one place means people don't drive home without seeing a movie, and thus sells a lot more tickets. Apply that idea to restaurants. Diners might go to a restaurant multiplex with a particular restaurant in mind, but they'd know that even if that restaurant is too busy, a fine meal is probably assured. There could even be a central line for the next available restaurant.

Think of all the "of-the-month" clubs that were spawned by the Book-of-the-Month Club. One of the newest is the Panty-of-the-Month Club, which delivers designer silk panties once a month, gift-wrapped and perfumed.

WHAT PROCESS CAN BE ADAPTED?

After watching *Spider-Man,* researchers at the University of Manchester played with the idea of developing adhesives that would help people climb and cling to vertical surfaces. They brainstormed by considering ways that animals, reptiles, insects, and birds attach themselves to plants and trees. They were most intrigued by geckos, which have tiny hairs on the soles of their feet that allow them to climb slick surfaces. The researchers adapted this feature into an adhesive that mimics geckos' feet, demonstrating the feasibility of self-cleaning, reattachable dry adhesives. These artificial micro-hair adhesives are being developed into gecko gloves, which will enable humans to climb vertical walls as easily as a gecko or Spider-Man.

WHAT DIFFERENT CONTEXTS CAN THE CONCEPT BE PUT IN?

In the figure below, the inner circles are the same size. However, the one on the left appears larger because the *context* in which it appears influences what you see. When you place any subject in a different context, your imagination can stimulate new ideas.

WHAT BEHAVIORS CAN BE ADAPTED?

A group of product designers turned their attention to how people clean their bathrooms. They were fascinated with the little tricks and rationalizations that facilitate the process of cleaning a bathroom. One designer, while on vacation in Puerto Rico, watched the hotel housekeeper use a flat broom to reach high up into her shower's murkier corners. The designer copied the concept and developed the Mr. Clean Magic Reach, a bathroom cleaning system with a telescoping pole. The owner of the Mr. Clean brand expects to sell 150 million Magic Reaches a year.

CAN THE CONTEXT BE ADAPTED FOR A DIFFERENT MARKET?

In 1956, a couple of brothers named Jacuzzi, who sold water pumps for farm use, designed a special whirlpool bath as a treatment for their cousin's arthritis. They did little with this new product until 1968, when Roy Jacuzzi put the concept in a different context—the luxury bath market—and bathrooms were never the same again. The Jacuzzi sold like crazy across the country, from California to the White House.

WHAT IDEAS CAN BE ADAPTED FROM NATURE?

Medical doctors working with geneticists have discovered a way to use fireflies to fight cancer. The gene that activates a firefly's bioluminescence is inserted into cancer cells, causing them to glow. A photosensitizing agent is added, making the cells produce toxic substances and causing them to self-destruct. This principle is already used in photodynamic therapy, which uses bursts of light to attack tumors. Inserting the light source directly into the cells makes it possible to attack tumors deep in the body without using an outside light source that could damage healthy tissue on the way.

WHAT MATERIAL CAN BE ADAPTED?

In New Mexico, a research project is under way to adapt jimsonweed, poisonous to humans, to help clean up heavy-metal pollution in the environment.

MAGNIFY

Americans tend to believe that bigger is better. People often perceive objects they value highly as being larger than objects they value less. Bruner and Goldman, in 1947, did a study demonstrating that poor children perceived coins to be much larger than rich children did.

Which tree above attracts your attention?

Notice how your attention is automatically attracted to the large tree. This is why magnification is often used in advertising and equipment design.

Search for ways to magnify, add to, or multiply your idea, product, or service.

- What can be magnified, made larger, or extended?

- What can be exaggerated? Overstated?

- What can be added? More time? Stronger? Higher? Longer?

- How about greater frequency? Extra features?

- What can add extra value?

- What can be duplicated?

- How could I carry it to a dramatic extreme?

WHAT FEATURES CAN BE ADDED?

A New Zealand company added a sensor to packaged fruit. The sensor changes color by reacting to the aroma released by fruit as it ripens. The sensor is initially red and graduates to orange and finally yellow. By matching the color of the sensor with their eating or storing preferences, customers can accurately choose fruit by their ripeness preference.

A freelance designer working on improving the ordinary blanket invented an ingenious new product. The Light Sleeper is a pillow and duvet that uses light to awaken sleepers gently. You set the time you want to be awakened, and the bedding slowly brightens with light that simulates the dawn. By adding electronics to textiles, the designer created electroluminescent textiles and a product that could replace noisy, jarring alarm clocks. The technique could benefit people with seasonal affective disorder, simulating natural light to release hormones that help relieve depression.

WHAT CAN BE EXAGGERATED?

How can beer be exaggerated? Sam Adams created an "extreme" beer named Utopia, which is 25 percent alcohol. It's therefore the strongest beer in the world. It comes in a kettle-shaped bottle reminiscent of the copper brewing kettles used by brew masters for hundreds of years. It's a sipping beer that has been aged in single-use bourbon casks, giving it a rich flavor.

CAN IT BE MADE ENORMOUS?

To promote the cheese industry, the state of Wisconsin created the world's largest cheese, a 40,060-pound cheddar they rolled from city to city on a publicity tour.

WHAT FUNCTIONS CAN BE ADDED?

Designers Matt Grossman and Ryan Lightbody at Purdue University added another wheel to training bikes. Called a "shift bike," the training bike uses two rear wheels that help a child balance at slow speeds. Speeding up moves the wheels closer, shifting the balance from the bike to the tyke.

Chef Homaro Cantu, owner of Moto, created herb-stuffed silverware that enhances the olfactory experience of a dish. He's also experimenting with food levitation. By injecting helium into froths and zapping smaller substances with an ion-particle gun, he hopes someday to float plate-free meals above the dining-room table.

CAN SOUND BE ADDED?

Long-distance air travel could become safer thanks to sound-triggering sensors in seats. Passengers on extended flights are at risk of deep vein thrombosis—blood clots that develop in the legs when people sit still too long. The clots can break loose, lodge in the heart or lungs, and kill the passenger. Now, a smart airline chair developed in Britain can sense when someone's been sitting too long and issue a get-up-and-move-around warning.

A Japanese company added a microchip to the base of the condom and created the "singing" condom. It plays "Love Me Do" by the Beatles.

CAN IT BE BUILT UP?

A & B Hydroponics have developed the first rotating vertical hydroponic system that will produce crops such as strawberries, tomatoes, flowers, mushrooms, and herbs vertically. The rotating system produces more vegetables and fruits per square meter than ever before.

CAN IT BE OVERSTATED?

Carter-Wallace Inc., is now marketing condoms that are 20 percent larger than the standard "one size fits all." The brawny Magnum condom may just be the best marketing ploy ever. After all, what man in his right mind would ask for one of the smaller brands?

HOW CAN IT BE MORE FREQUENT?

IKEA, the Swedish furniture chain, found a way to expand its retail traffic by renting Christmas trees. "The spirit of Christmas can't be bought, but for $10 you can rent it," the IKEA ad said. For $20 ($10 for the rental and $10 for the deposit) you could rent a Douglas fir in New York City, where trees go from $50 and up. After the holidays, customers return the trees and IKEA mulches them for their gardens or donates them to the community. The customers also received a coupon for a free four-year-old Blue Spruce sapling to help save the environment. Customers can pick up their tree in the first week of April. Just by being extra nice to its customers, IKEA made it worthwhile to visit one of its stores three separate times.

WHAT WOULD ADD EXTRA VALUE?

Aromatherapy is a popular fashion in the home, encompassing bath and shower products. Standard and luxury toilet paper makers realized that by adding scent and design to toilet paper they could increase its value. Manufacturers are also adding prints to toilet paper, to make it more attractive to consumers. The Elleair range of toilet paper from Daio is available in a number of different prints, such as rose or lavender, to match the scents. Color is also being added to standard toilet rolls, so that consumers can match the color schemes of their bathrooms.

MODIFY

At one time, the Ford Motor Company controlled 60 percent of the automobile market. Then General Motors asked some questions about modification and came out with a philosophy that stated, "A car with every shape and color for every purse and purpose." Henry Ford responded with "Any customer can have a car painted any color so long as it is black." Ford's sales slumped, and by the 1940s he had just 20 percent of the new car market. GM, by modifying its products to the market, had taken the lead.

What can be modified? Just about any aspect of anything. Even a perfect square can be modified by a circular background to appear bent when it is not.

To modify your ideas, ask:

- How can this be altered for the better?

- What can be modified?

- Is there a new twist?

- Change meaning, color, motion, sound, odor, form, shape?

- Change name?

- Other changes?

- What changes can be made in the plans? In the process? In marketing?

- What other form could this take? What other package?

- Can the package be combined with the form?

How Can It Be Modified for Another Purpose?

Just about any aspect of anything can be modified. For example, the ordinary ice cream cone came about when a merchant modified his product's form and purpose. Ernest Hamwi was trying to sell paper-thin Persian waffles at the 1905 World's Fair. It was hot, and for days he watched people walk past his little stand to a nearby ice-cream stand. When that stand ran out of dishes, Hamwi brought some hot waffles over. He fashioned the waffles into cones, let them cool, and served ice cream on top of them.

How Can It Be Modified for the Better?

The franchise business has become so competitive that many companies are having trouble finding qualified franchisees. Heavenly Hot Dogs has modified the design of their hot-dog stands so that they can be operated from a wheelchair. They are also designing other mobile units that can be driven by disabled people. The response has been overwhelming, and the CEO expects that handicapped people will soon account for 50 percent of the company's total franchisees. Also, Heavenly discovered that it can take a tax write-off of $35,000 of the $60,000 required to adapt the carts. Handicapped entrepreneurs are also eligible for low-interest loans and priority locations at military sites and government buildings.

In What Other Form Should It Be?

Insulin needles are somewhat disconcerting to both users and observers. Battelle Institute brainstormed for different ways to disguise the needle and ended up with the HumaPen, which is a reusable insulin injection pen. The attractive, user-friendly device looks like an expensive pen, so it can be used discreetly in public. The pen uses existing insulin cartridges and needles, is easily loaded, and has an easy-to-read dosage display, which is an important feature for many people with diabetes.

What if you designed a Christmas card that would have a reuseable postcard as the picture? This could be sold to corporations, politicians, and anyone who wants to present an image of efficiency.

The circus business was in a downward spiral before Cirque du Soleil opened its doors in 1984. It was becoming increasingly difficult to get adults to pay to go to the circus, and it was getting harder every year. But by modernizing the form of the circus and shifting the focus to performance, Cirque du Soleil changed the meaning of what a circus is and created a multibillion-dollar business in the process.

How Can the Shape Be Modified?

Designers at Moen have revolutionized the shower by changing the shape of the water flow. Most traditional showerheads provide a fixed ring of water. The Moen showerhead provides a moving, swirling stream that completely surrounds you. This technology delivers larger water droplets containing more heat, giving you a warmer shower with less water.

A simple thing like changing the shape of a business card can reap big dividends. Phil Pies of Max Pies Furniture hands out business cards with one rounded corner—the cards say, "25 percent safer than most other business cards." Clients not only keep the card but they also show it to others in their travels.

How Can It Be Given a New Twist?

Everyone is talking about the price of gas these days. A major oil company is developing plans for prepaid gift cards with a new twist. The gasoline gift card provides free gas up to a predetermined limit, much like a phone card. The cards expire within six months of purchase. Speculators who believe gasoline prices will be lower within a few months will purchase the cards at the present price and hold them for a few months before using them. If they're right, they've created their own discount plan.

How Can the Packaging Be Modified?

Paint cans are heavy, hard to carry, hard to close, hard to open, hard to pour, and no fun. Yet they've been around for a long time, and most people assumed there had to be a reason they were so bad. Dutch Boy realized there was no reason, and that the can could be an integral part of the product. They introduced an easier-to-carry, easier-to-pour, easier-to-close paint jug. The new Twist & Pour paint container is a packaging innovation. You pop the cover and use the packaging itself as the paint pan for the roller. No mess, no bother. You look at this paint container and you have to wonder why it took so long for someone to come up with the idea. Not only did the new packaging increase sales but it also got Dutch Boy more distribution (at a higher retail price).

How Can Standard Procedures Be Modified?

Famous Supply Company, a building-products distributor in Akron, Ohio, changed the standard benefits plan to create "wellness dividends." They increased the deductible from $100 to $150 and required workers to pay a monthly premium for medical coverage: $25 for individuals and $50 for families. Each year, workers who haven't submitted any claims recuperate two-thirds of their premiums. The system has made employees more conscious about their medical bills and their health. That, in turn, has enabled Famous Supply to keep health-care costs below the national average.

HOW CAN ATTITUDES BE CHANGED?

Can you persuade people to try new things by changing your approach? A marketing group that was attempting to create a demand for grasshoppers as a gourmet food conducted some test marketing in which they tried to get Americans to eat the insects. They first tried using a relaxed and friendly spokesperson who presented his arguments in a pleasant manner. Few people tried the grasshoppers, and those who did disliked them. Next, they tried a spokesperson who was cold, distant, and hostile. Remarkably, more people tried and liked the grasshoppers.

HOW CAN THE MARKETING BE CHANGED?

3M's famous Post-it pads almost bit the dust because the marketing people relied on advertisements and brochures, which did not generate much interest, to introduce the new product. Then general sales manager Joe Ramey noticed that people who started playing with the pads couldn't stop. Ramey immediately convinced the company to modify its marketing approach and give free samples away to as many people as possible. The result was that the Post-it became one of 3M's all-time champion products.

PUT TO OTHER USES

These questions will first help you find an idea, product, or service and then they will help you imagine what else can be done with it. George Washington Carver, the famous botanist-chemist, found more than three hundred uses for the lowly peanut, because he never stopped looking.

In the illustration on the next page, the middle figure can be seen either as "13," if you read it top to bottom, or as "B," if you read from left to right. Every subject takes its meaning from the way it is used.

Creative people can take just about anything and make something useful out of it. In 1857, Joseph Gayetty took ordinary unbleached manila hemp paper and had his name watermarked on each sheet. He marketed it as "Gayetty's Medicated Paper—a perfectly pure article for the toilet and for the prevention of piles." In this new context, pure manila hemp paper became the first toilet paper.

12

A 13 C

14

History is full of inventions, innovations, and products that developed from something else. Post-it pads, Silly Putty, and vulcanized rubber were all developed by people attempting to make something else. Bright entrepreneurs would willingly stand at street corners, hat in hand, begging passersby to drop their unused ideas into it.

To find other uses, ask:

- What else can this be used for?

- Are there new ways to use it as is?

- Other uses if modified?

- What else could be made from this?

- Other extensions? Other markets?

HOW ELSE CAN IT BE USED?

A Chicago salesperson, Ed Newton, sold incentive products that companies award to top salespeople or give to employees during the holidays. His sales were dismal. Customers were always asking for products his company did not have. He tried to get his company into special orders, but his bosses declined. He hated walking away from such obvious potential business, so he quit and went into business for himself. Instead of handing over a catalog and asking them for an order, he would ask them what they would really like to give their employees. He also offered his own ideas. Customers then greeted him as a consultant rather than a salesperson, and his new company was off and running.

WHAT CAN BE DONE WITH THE WASTE?

A chicken rancher wondered what else he could do with chicken feathers. He worked with researchers at the U.S. Agricultural Research Service and found that chicken feathers could help save trees by taking the place of wood pulp in various products. Replacing half the wood-pulp content of composite paper with chicken feathers means only half as many trees are needed. Feather fiber is finer than wood pulp and can collect more spores, dust, dander, and other particles, thus dramatically improving the air in homes and offices. Feathers could also be used to make strong, less-dense plastic composites for car dashboards, boat exteriors, and similar products.

Goodyear Tire & Rubber Company has a pollution-free heating plant in Jackson, Michigan, that uses discarded tires as its only fuel. Similarly, Firestone has shown that a ton of tires can yield 150 gallons of oil and 1,500 cubic feet of heating gas. This process could eliminate the ecologist's nightmare of billions of tires littering the landscape. Only 9 percent of tires are recycled at present, it's illegal to burn them, and landfills are getting scarce.

Rubber bands are now made from old surgical tubing. Garbage is compressed into construction blocks or processed in polyactic acid that becomes new garbage bags. Sawdust is sold as compressed fire logs. Slag is used as soil conditioner. And petrochemical waste is the basis for Silly Putty.

WHAT OTHER USES CAN IT HAVE AS IS?

You know those mesh bags that fruit and onions come in? You can reuse them at the beach for collecting shells and holding suntan lotions and other small items that might get lost in the sand. And if you rinse them off in the water, they'll be dry before you get home.

Metal surgical pins and joints found in the ashes of cremated bodies are to be recycled under a new scheme in North Somerset, England. A councilman has introduced a plan to recycle the metal pins, plates, and artificial joints.

WHAT OTHER USES CAN IT HAVE IF MODIFED?

Medical waste has become a major problem for America. Currently, about 13,000 tons are generated each day by the nation's 6,800 hospitals. Most of it is incinerated, which involves high handling costs and the risk of releasing airborne pollutants. The high cost of handling and transporting waste has led some hospitals to dump it illegally, causing health scares when it washes up on beaches. Fortunately, Combustion Engineering of Stamford, Connecticut, has developed a way of disinfecting medical waste using modified microwaves that can be moved from site to site. The disinfected waste can then be compressed and deposited safely in landfills or burned without danger. The process takes only twenty minutes.

Why not use a shirt as a personal message board? An electronic company created a thin programmable LED sign that can be attached to a shirt. Personalized messages of up to thirty-two characters scroll continuously across the display, which could make it easy to communicate in a noisy room.

WHAT OTHER FIELDS COULD USE IT?

A conservative think tank took the concept of private ownership and applied it to a serious environmental problem. Their idea was to increase private ownership of elephants to help fend off poachers.

ELIMINATE

The original doughnut did not have a hole. According to one legend, a small boy who was watching his mother fry doughnuts noticed that the centers weren't thoroughly cooked. He took a fork and poked out the center, creating the pastry we know today.

Ideas sometimes come from minifying a subject. Through repeated trimming of ideas, objects, and processes, you can gradually narrow your challenge down to that part or function that is really necessary—or, perhaps, is appropriate for another use. For instance, if you omit the war-making functions from a tank and keep only the weight and caterpillar track, you create a tractor.

A	B	C	D	E
F	G	H	I	J
K	M	N	O	P
Q	R	S	T	U
V	W	X	Y	Z

Can you figure out what single-word Christmas greeting the design above conveys?

The Christmas message is "Noel" (no L).

Find things to reduce, eliminate, streamline, omit, and miniaturize by asking the following questions:

- What if this were smaller?

- What should I omit?

- Should I divide it? Split it up? Separate it into different parts?

- Understate?

- Streamline? Make miniature? Condense? Compact?

- Subtract? Delete?

- Can the rules be eliminated?

- What's not necessary?

What Can Be Streamlined?

NASA's three-hundred-pound spacesuit may be fine for working in weightlessness, but it just won't do for walking around on Mars. Consequently, NASA is supporting studies of new mobility technologies to streamline spacesuits for space travel. Dava Newman, an aerospace engineering professor at MIT, is developing a spray-on spacesuit. Her research group is working on the possibility of spraying a layer of polymer fabric over an astronaut, in a booth much like those used for spray-on suntanning. The "second-skin" suit could be augmented by temperature-control underwear, flexible joint attachments, and perhaps even an exoskeleton.

What's Not Necessary?

If computer monitors can shrink to almost nothing, why not keyboards? Two companies are working on developing virtual keyboards designed to accompany portable devices like PDAs, tablet PCs, and cell phones. A laser beam projects a glowing red outline of a keyboard on a desk or other flat surface. A sensor like those used in digital cameras monitors the reflection of an infrared light projected on the same spot. It can tell which "keys" you strike by the way the reflection changes. Eventually, such virtual keyboards will most likely be built into the gadgets they work with so that they disappear when not in use.

WHAT CAN BE OMITTED?

If you like water skiing but have trouble finding someone to drive the boat, forget the driver and go alone. The Solo is a boat designed to help you do just that. It's an eight-foot-long fiberglass boat with all the controls, including acceleration, turning, and a start-and-stop button, embedded in the tow handle. For added safety, the kill switch is activated when you drop the handle.

CAN IT BE MADE SMALLER?

William Shockley, Walter Brittain, and John Bardeen aren't household names, but the device they invented in 1947, the transistor, has made thousands of new products—from pocket radios to personal computers—practical and affordable.

A rancher in Mexico is breeding cows that weigh 25 percent less than the average cow yet produce the same amount of milk.

Scientists at UC Berkeley fashioned the smallest electric motor—three hundred times smaller than a human hair. The motor's gold paddle spins on an axis made from multiple carbon nanotubes, each nestled inside the other.

WHAT COULD BE DIVIDED OR SPLIT UP?

The glassware company Lenox was aware that most brides would like a set of good china but that a whole set is too expensive for any one person to give as a gift. They asked, "How can we divide a set so people can purchase just a few pieces?" They adapted an old idea, the bridal registry, so that the bride registers only Lenox china with a single merchant to whom she refers wedding guests. This simple idea—dividing a major purchase—has made Lenox the favorite "good china" maker and one of America's fastest-growing manufacturers.

HOW CAN IT BE MINIMIZED?

PID's new lamp omits the metal, plastic, or wood for a stand or base. Instead, the lamp supports itself on a helium-filled Mylar balloon. Reel out more tether for a high or low light. Depending on your needs, the LED lamp can be directed up for broad reflected light or down for more focused light. And with LEDs as your source, you can look forward to low energy usage and long bulb life.

Can It Be Understated?

In the illustration below, the inner squares are the same size. However, the one on the right seems larger.

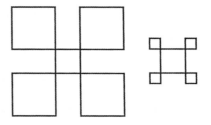

By understating the surrounding squares of the figure on the right, the inner square is made to seem larger than the one on the left.

Think of a product as an object surrounded by a cluster of advertising, marketing, and sales promotions and programs, like the squares that surround the figures in the illustration. Sometimes when these promotions and programs are understated, the quality of the product (the inner square) they surround is perceived to be greater than it is in reality.

For instance, compare the understated promotions of Rolls Royces with the overstated promotions of GM's cars. In reality, the actual value of a Rolls is not even close to what the average person perceives it to be. The average (modern) Rolls will last about as long as the average GM car (100,000 miles) and will have as many maintenance problems. But the ads work.

Rearrange

Consider the alphabet: ABCDEFGHIJKLMNOPQRSTUVWXYZ. These twenty-six marks have been arranged in countless ways to make you laugh, cry, worry, wonder, question, love, hate, and ponder. They've been rearranged to form the words in *Hamlet, Tom Sawyer,* the Bible, and the general theory of relativity.

Creativity, it could be said, consists largely of rearranging what we know in order to find out what we do not know. Rearrangement usually offers countless alternatives for ideas, goods, and services. A baseball manager, for example, can shuffle his lineup 362,880 times.

The puzzle that follows, which probably originated in Japan, can be solved quickly if you make the right rearrangement. Arrange eight toothpicks, as shown below, in the shape of a fish swimming to the left. Add a dime to represent the fish's eye.

The challenge: Can you move just three toothpicks, and the dime, to make the fish swim in the opposite direction? (The solution is found at the end of this section.)

Just as we can move the fish in different directions by rearranging the toothpicks, so can we create new ideas by rearranging existing information.

Ask:

- What other arrangement might be better?

- Interchange components?

- Other pattern? Other layout?

- Other sequence? Change the order?

- Transpose cause and effect?

- Change pace?

- Change schedule?

WHAT OTHER ARRANGEMENT MIGHT WORK BETTER?

Every elevator ride is basically a local one. The elevator stops maybe five, ten, or even fifteen times on the way to your floor. This is expensive transportation, and it's frustrating for people in the lobby waiting for elevators. The Schindler elevator company has come up with a better arrangement. When you approach the elevators, you key in your floor on a centralized control panel. In return, the panel tells you which elevator is going to take you to your floor. With this simple presort, Schindler Elevator Corporation has managed to turn every elevator into an express. Your elevator takes you immediately to the twelfth floor and races back to the lobby. This means buildings can be taller, they need fewer elevators for a given density of people, the wait is shorter, and the building can use precious space for people rather than for elevators

How Could the Schedule Be Changed?

What if you change the commission schedule? Create silver handcuffs, a deferred bonus plan. Set a specific goal for a salesperson who is generating, say, $100,000 in sales annually. For each year the person tops $110,000 in sales annually, the person will get a bonus of $2,500—but the bonus is only payable after the person has stayed with the firm for seven years. If the person hits their quota each year during that time, the company will pay out a $17,500 bonus plus interest. If the rep leaves before that, the company keeps the money.

How Could the Pattern Be Changed?

Timberland Travel Gear came up with a new pattern for shoes. Their line of shoes is modular. You can buy the shells (outers) separate from the chassis (footbeds). This allows the shells to be more flexible so they can be pressed flat to take up less space, reducing the volume and weight of footwear for travelers by 50 percent. Should one part of your shoe wear out, you no longer need to throw away the whole shoe. Just retain the good element and replace the other. This new pattern creates less waste, more utility, and more value.

How Could the Pace Be Changed?

What happens when salespeople change the pace of their presentation? Fast-talking salespeople are sometimes regarded with suspicion, but rapid speech may actually increase one's persuasiveness. One firm approached Los Angeles residents in parks and shopping malls and asked them to listen to a tape-recorded speech arguing that caffeine should be regarded as a dangerous drug. All subjects heard the same message, but half heard it at the slow rate of 102 words per minute, half at the fast rate of 195. The fast-talking communicator was viewed as being more knowledgeable and objective, and was more effective at changing the subjects' attitudes. Within limits, the faster you talk, the more likely people are to assume you know what you're talking about.

How Could Components Be Rearranged?

This question helped a young Japanese businessman make one of the fastest fortunes in the country's history. As recently as 1965, Japan had almost no paved roads outside of big cities. The country was rapidly adopting the automobile, and most citizens traveled at high speeds on roads that had hardly changed since the tenth century. They were scarcely wide enough for two cars to pass, with blind corners, hidden entrances, and junctions every few miles at which a half-dozen roads met at every conceivable angle. Accidents mounted at an alarming rate, especially at night. The press clamored for the government to do something, but paving the roads was going to take twenty years and a "drive safely" campaign had virtually no effect.

Then Tamon Iwasa took another look at the traditional highway reflector and realized that one could rearrange the little glass beads that serve as mirrors so that they could be made to reflect oncoming headlight *from* any direction *to* any direction. The government installed the Iwasa reflector by the hundreds of thousands, and the accident rate plummeted.

Fish Solution

Solution to the fish puzzle: Move the dime and three toothpicks as shown below.

Reverse?

Reversing your perspective opens up your thinking. Look at opposites and you'll see things you normally miss.

This figure was designed by Edgar Rubin in 1915 and can be seen as either a vase or a pair of faces. In the reversal method, one takes things as they are and reverses them to get more ideas.

Dr. Albert Rothenberg, a noted researcher on the creative process, has identified a process he terms "Janusian thinking," named for the Roman god Janus, who had two faces that looked in opposite directions. In Janusian thinking, two or more opposites or antitheses are conceived simultaneously, either as existing side by side or as equally operative, valid, or true. Dr. Rothenberg has identified traces of Janusian thinking in the works of Einstein, Mozart, Picasso, and Conrad. The way to use Janusian thinking is to ask, "What is the opposite of this?" and then try to imagine both opposites existing at the same time.

Questions to ask when using the reversal principle are:

- Can I transpose positive and negative?

- What are the opposites?

- What are the negatives?

- Should I turn it around? Up instead of down? Down instead of up?

- Consider it backwards?

- Reverse roles?

- Do the unexpected?

HOW CAN A FAILURE BE TURNED INTO A SUCCESS?

Whenever we attempt to do something and fail, we end up doing something else. As simplistic as this statement may seem, it is the first principle of creative accident. Reversing the question from "Why have I failed?" to "What have I done?" reverses the negative into a positive. Years back, Roy Plunkett set out to invent a new refrigerant. Instead, he created a glob of white waxy material that conducted heat and did not stick to surfaces. Fascinated by this unexpected material, he abandoned his original line of research and experimented with this interesting material, which eventually became a household product, Teflon.

WHAT NEGATIVE CAN BE REVERSED?

One of the negatives of owning nice clothes is the dry-cleaning bills. How can this be reversed? Is there a way to clean clothes without taking them to a dry cleaner? One entrepreneur was convinced there was, and he invented an appliance that removes wrinkles and odors for up to three items of clothing in about thirty minutes. It extends clothes' wearability between cleanings. Whirlpool bought the idea and predicts it has a potential market in hotels, offices, and airports.

An ice creamery in New York offers discounts pegged to the falling thermometer. The colder it gets, the cheaper the ice cream gets.

CAN THE SCHEDULE BE REVERSED?

Would it make sense to reverse the way farmers plough wheat fields by having them plough at night instead of during the day? Peter Juroszek and colleagues at the University of Bonn in Germany have found that strips of land ploughed at night grow five times fewer weeds. The seeds of most weeds need less than a millisecond's light for germination to begin, whereas the seeds of most crops can grow in complete darkness. Ploughing brings seeds temporarily to the surface before they are reburied. Wheat fields in particular grew so few weeds that pesticides are unnecessary.

CAN SERVICES BE REVERSED?

Let's go back into the past when doctors made house calls. Instead of going to the doctor, let's turn things around and do our own checkup at home. A personalized health monitoring system is being developed for home use. Soon consumers will have quality health monitoring in the comfort and privacy of their own homes. Circulatory, heart, and kidney testing will become as easy as home pregnancy tests. Using such a system, patients would transmit via the Internet their results to the doctor, who can then tell them what to do. Or the doctor may elect to send a medical van with professionals to administer more complicated tests or remedies.

WOULD THE OPPOSITE WORK?

Instead of selling something, sell nothing. A reclusive Australian designer dreamed up Invisible Jim, the toy no one can see. As the box describes him, Jim is "completely devoid of darting eyes" and boasts nongripping hands "as not seen on TV," and he can even wear a "camouflage" suit (sold separately). Pitched as an alternative greeting card, the item's retail price is about $3. The packaging—printed cardboard wrapped in a clear plastic cover—costs about 10 cents to make.

CAN THE PROCESS BE REVERSED?

Bicycle designers typically design the seat last. The Stylyx Bicycle was the first bicycle designed seat first. By starting from the end, Stylyx created a bicycle with a unique ergonomic design that reduces seat-related soreness and makes peddling easier.

Legos has developed a digital design suite where you design your project online, and then Legos makes the parts (plus a few extras) and sends them to you to build it. Thus, you start with your finished design and then build it with the parts.

CAN IT BE TURNED AROUND?

Once there were two furniture stores on Main Street in Elmira, New York. One day, one of the stores put up a sign reading "The Cheapest Furniture on This Street." The other responded with "The Cheapest Furniture in This Town." It continued to escalate:

". . . in this County."
". . . in this State."
". . . in America."
". . . in the Free World."
". . . in the World."
". . . in the Universe."

After a few days, the first store owner quietly reposted his original sign, "The Cheapest Furniture on this Street." He had realized that all he really needed to claim was that he was cheaper than his nearest competitor.

WHAT WOULD BE UNEXPECTED?

What would be your reaction if a trash can started talking? The Germans have created the first trash can that thanks people for not littering. It's hoped they will encourage people, in a pleasant way, to throw trash in the baskets and not on the street. The strategically located smart baskets, powered by solar cells, will be able to say "thank you" in three languages.

Reverse your perspective. Look at the following illustration. Is the airplane coming toward you or moving away from you?

Study it again; can you make it switch direction? If you can't see the plane coming toward you, imagine yourself looking down on it from above. If you can't see it flying away, imagine yourself under it watching it fly off to your left. Chances are that when you first looked at it, you saw it moving in one direction only. It took a few moments, but after some concentration, you experienced a new perception, a new way of looking at the plane. It is the same with ideas. If you take a few moments and concentrate, you can experience a new perception.

SUMMARY

All ideas are in a state of constant flux. There can be no such thing as an ultimate idea any more than there can be an ultimate poem that would make all further poems unnecessary or an ultimate symphony that would render all further musical composition redundant. Consider Leonardo da Vinci's masterpiece *Mona Lisa*. He worked on it for four years and was still trying to improve it until his death.

We look at the illustration and we immediately see a giraffe and then move on.

How many of us notice that the giraffe's skin is strange? It is striped. In fact, it has zebra stripes. Once we identify the giraffe, we assume everything about the giraffe is okay and question nothing. We think stereotypically.

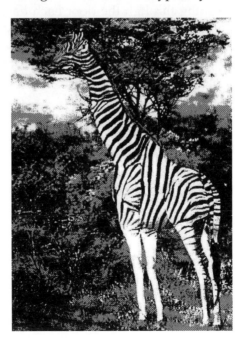

In workshops, I sometimes give a group a candle, some corkboard, and a box of tacks. The challenge is to fasten the candle on the wall so that it does not drip on the floor. Most participants have great difficulty coming up with the solution. However, when participants are given a candle, some corkboard, and the thumbtacks and the box separately, most solve the problem quickly because now they see the box as something more than a container.

In the first case, the box containing the tacks is subject to a particular association. Participants see it only as a container for tacks, not as a possible wall fixture for the candle.

When it is separated out, participants are quickly able to see how they could use it to solve the problem by tacking the box to the wall as a platform and placing the candle on top. The function of any object is not inherent in the object itself but develops from our observation of and association with it.

The workshop participants look at the box of tacks and do not see the details. And the details sometimes contain the germ of an idea that will lead to a creative breakthrough. Listing the parts or attributes of a subject will enable you to break your stereotypical notion of the subject as a continuous whole and to discover relationships that you likely would otherwise miss.

Imagine you wanted to improve the revolving door, the kind used in office buildings and department stores. You could list the attributes of a revolving door and then focus on each attribute one at a time by asking SCAMPER questions.

Possible attributes are:

- It has individual compartments.

- Pushing it manually creates the energy to move it.

- It's made of glass to see through.

- It needs one or more people pushing it around at a time.

The attribute *pushing it manually creates the energy* inspires one to think of ways to harness all the energy voluntarily created by thousands of people pushing through the door each day. This triggers the idea of *modifying* the revolving door to make electricity from the force of people pushing it around—that is, *putting the energy to some other use.* Separating the revolving door into attributes broke our typical notion of a revolving door and inspired us to think of a creative way to harness the door's potential energy.

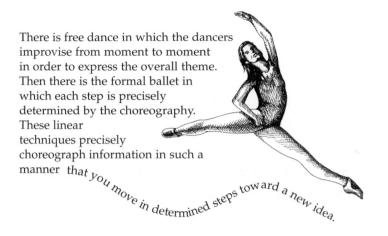

There is free dance in which the dancers improvise from moment to moment in order to express the overall theme. Then there is the formal ballet in which each step is precisely determined by the choreography. These linear techniques precisely choreograph information in such a manner *that you move in determined steps toward a new idea.*

Group B

TUG-OF-WAR

Technique: Force field analysis.
Profile: How to graph a challenge's positive and negative forces and then maximize the positives and minimize the negatives.

IDEA BOX

Technique: Morphological analysis.
Profile: How to identify and box the parameters of a challenge to quickly produce thousands of new ideas.

IDEA GRID

Technique: FCB grid
Profile: How to find new ideas and creative strategies using a grid to organize complex masses of information.

LOTUS BLOSSOM

Technique: Diagramming.
Profile: How to diagram obstacles and then use them to reach your goal.

PHOENIX

Technique: Questions.
Profile: How to use a checklist of problem-solving questions—originated by the CIA—to guide your thinking.

THE GREAT TRANSPACIFIC AIRLINE AND STORM DOOR COMPANY

Technique: Matrix.
Profile: How to create a key-word index and mix and match the key words in a matrix to produce new ideas.

FUTURE FRUIT

Technique: Future scenarios.
Profile: How to project a future scenario in order to take advantage of unexpected opportunities.

TUG-OF-WAR

"One defends when his strength is inadequate;
he attacks when it is abundant."

SUN TZU

A good football coach does not say, "There is one way all great football teams win games, and we must do it the same way." Rather, he tries to determine which positions on his team are strong and which are weak by testing and observing each individual football player. Then, he replaces the weaker players or teaches them to overcome or disguise their weaknesses. For example, if a defensive end is an ineffective pass rusher, the coach might teach him ways to trick the blocker. Only in this way can the coach bring his team's unique talents into play.

A football team has one goal: To win. To win, the coach will develop a strategy to maximize the team's strengths and minimize its weaknesses. For instance, if a team has a weak defense, his strategy might be to control the ball and keep his defense off the field; if the offense is weak, he might teach his team to keep the other team deep in their own territory. By being aware of the positive and negative aspects of his team, the coach most efficiently uses football knowledge to win games.

It is the same with challenges. You must be aware of the positive and negative forces operating in a challenge before you develop a strategy for solving it. Your strategy should allow you to take advantage of the positive factors while eliminating or diminishing the negative ones.

This Thinkertoy is modeled after *force field analysis,* a technique first developed by social psychologist Kurt Lewin. It allows you to see how positive and negative forces push and pull you toward a best case or worst case scenario.

Positive and negative forces won't sit still for a portrait. They are constantly vibrating, pushing and pulling. Tug-of-War is a frame on which you can fasten down these forces and study them. It can help you to:

1. Better define your challenge.

2. Identify strengths you can maximize.

3. Identify weaknesses you can minimize.

BLUEPRINT

1. *Write the challenge you are trying to solve.*

2. *Describe the best-case scenario and the worst-case scenario;* the best that can happen and the worst.

3. *List the conditions of the situation.* Conditions are anything that modifies or restricts the nature or existence of your subject. They are whatever requirements you perceive to be essential to solving a particular challenge.

4. *Note the "tug-of-war."* As you list the conditions, you will find the forces pushing you to the best case and those pulling you toward catastrophe. Pit each condition against its opposite on the continuum by specifying its push and pull powers.

In the example on the next page, the situation being analyzed is an individual's job security. The conditions listed for job security are: track record, customer relations, working with peers, energy level, creativity, leadership ability, and job dedication. Beside each condition are best-case and worst-case scenarios.

In the next illustration, assume the center represents the current situation, while the best- and worst-case scenarios are playing tug-of-war with the conditions of job security. The best case is promotion, the worst case is getting fired. Most of the conditions are being pushed toward the best case. However, two conditions, customer relations and creativity, are being pulled toward the worst case.

BEST-CASE SCENARIO (PROMOTION)	+	CENTER	−	WORST-CASE SCENARIO (FIRED)
SUCCESSES	← TRACK RECORD			FAILURES
LIKED			CUSTOMER RELATIONS →	DISLIKED
WELL-RESPECTED	← WORKING WITH PEERS			DISLIKED
INTENSE	← ENERGY LEVEL			LOW
HIGH			CREATIVITY →	LOW
CHARISMA	← LEADERSHIP ABILITY			NO CHARISMA
HIGH COMMITMENT	← JOB DEDICATION			ROUTINE

TUG OF WAR

CHALLENGE: WHAT IS MY PRESENT JOB SECURITY?

There are three ways to move a condition toward the best-case scenario.

1. Maximize your strengths.

2. Minimize your weaknesses.

3. Add more positive forces.

You might choose to further strengthen the positive forces: track record, working with peers, energy level, leadership ability, and job dedication.

To minimize weaknesses, reframe them as challenges:

"In what ways might I improve my customer relations?"

"In what ways might I improve my creativity?"

Finally, you could create new positive forces to further outweigh the negative ones; for instance, you might work on a new positive condition of report writing and add that force to your analysis.

TUG OF WAR				
CHALLENGE: PROBABILITY OF GETTING A MAJOR SALE				
BEST-CASE SCENARIO: (CLOSING THE SALE)	+	CENTER	−	WORST-CASE SCENARIO: (LOSING THE SALE)
SUPERIOR	← PRODUCT			INFERIOR
NONE			COMPETITION →	SUPERIOR
LOWEST	← CUSTOMER NEED		PRICE →	HIGHEST
REAL	← CUSTOMER KNOWLEDGE			LITTLE OR NONE
HIGH	← CUSTOMER'S BUDGET			POOR
ABLE TO BUY				NOT ABLE TO BUY
EXCELLENT			SALES PRESENTATION →	POOR
OVERCAME THEM	← ANSWERING OBJECTIONS			NOT ABLE TO OVERCOME
LIKED BY CUSTOMER			COMPATIBILITY WITH CUSTOMER →	DISLIKED BY CUSTOMER

The key is to work on the conditions. A clay pot sitting in the sun will always remain a clay pot. It has to go through the white heat of a furnace to become porcelain. This technique can give you insight into the "clay" of your challenge. However, you have to do something to it to make the "best case" happen.

Now let's consider the probability of a certain company getting a major sale. The best-case scenario would be closing the sale, the worst case would be losing the sale entirely.

Our negative forces are:

- Our competitors' products are perceived as superior.

- Our price is higher than alternative products.

- We gave a poor presentation.

- Our relationship with the customer could be better.

Our positive forces are:

- Our product is better than other comparable products.

- The customer has a real need for the product.

- Our customer is able and ready to buy.

- We answered and overcame all raised objections.

Our options are:

1. We can further strengthen our positive forces.

2. We can reframe the negative forces as challenges to be solved. For instance:
   "In what ways might our product be perceived as superior?"
   "In what ways might we add value to the product to further justify its price?"
   "In what ways might we make up for the poor presentation?"
   "In what ways might we improve our relationship with the customer?"

3. We can add more positive forces, such as customer service, packaged financing, bring in support personnel to help obtain the sale, and so on.

In Tug-of-War, maximizing strengths is the punch; minimizing weaknesses is the clever footwork. Consider how Steven Jobs and Stephen Wozniak created Apple computers. In 1976, their principal strength was a unique design for a personal computer; their principal weakness was an utter lack of capital—between them they had $1,300.

- Jobs maximized their principal strength by selling fifty as-yet-unbuilt computers to a string of computer hobby stores, based on their unique design.

- He minimized their weakness by securing credit to buy parts, based on sales of unbuilt computers.

- He added a positive force by using the profits gained from the sale of the first six hundred computers to start work on the enormously successful Apple II.

Apple went public at the end of 1980 and, after three weeks, its shares were worth more than Ford Motor Company shares.

SUMMARY

Once there was a man who died and found himself in Hell, with the road to Heaven blocked by a huge mountain. Although indignant that he was in Hell, the man assumed he could do nothing to change his situation and settled down to an eternity of suffering. He never discovered that the mountain was on wheels—to reach Heaven he needed only to push the mountain aside.

Once you identify the forces operating in your challenge, they become as negotiable as a mountain on wheels. You can either learn to live with the negatives by limiting your options and compromising your goals, or you can change their position and neutralize their impact.

CHAPTER ELEVEN

IDEA BOX

"In battle there are only the normal
and the extraordinary forces, but their
combinations are limitless;
none can comprehend them all."

SUN TZU

In poker, the highest possible hand is a straight flush—five cards in sequence in the same suit.

If you are allowed to keep the cards you wanted, discard others, and continue to draw cards as long as you wished, you would eventually draw a straight flush. Within a set number of cards there is a vast number of combinations, some good, others useless. The more combinations you create, the greater your likelihood of getting a winning hand. This is, in essence, the principle behind the Idea Box.

The Idea Box is modeled after the *morphological box,* credited to Dr. Fritz Zwicky. It is a way of automatically combining the parameters of a challenge into new ideas (parameter here means characteristic, factor, variable, or aspect). You choose the number and nature of the parameters for the challenge; what's important is to generate parameters and then list variations for each parameter.

Think of the parameters as card suits (hearts, spades, clubs, and diamonds), and the variations as the different cards within each suit. By coming up with different combinations of the variations of the parameters, you create new ideas.

1. *Specify your challenge.*

2. *Select the parameters of your challenge.* To determine whether a parameter is important enough to add, ask yourself, "Would the challenge still exist without the parameter I'm considering adding to the box?"

3. *List variations.* Below each parameter, list as many variations as you wish for that parameter. The number of parameters and variations will determine the box's complexity. Generally, it is easier to find new ideas within a simple framework than a complex one. For instance, a box with ten parameters, each of which has ten variations, produces 10 billion potential combinations.

4. *Try different combinations.* When the box is finished, make random runs through the parameters and variations, selecting one or more from each column and then combining them into entirely new forms. You can examine all of the combinations in the box to see how they affect your challenge. If you are working with a box that contains ten or more parameters, you may find it helpful to randomly examine the entire box and then gradually restrict yourself to portions that appear particularly faithful. It's like hunting for stars in a box.

Let's look at an example.

NEW LAUNDRY HAMPER

Situation: I'm a marketing director for a company that produces laundry hampers. The market has matured, and the company needs a new design to capture the customer's imagination. My challenge is: "In what ways might I improve the design of laundry hampers?"

Description: I analyze laundry hampers and list their basic parameters. I decide to work with four parameters (material, shape, finish, and position) and plan to use five variations for each.

Idea Box: I construct my box with the parameters on top, leaving five boxes beneath each parameter for the variations. To generate the variations, I ask myself:

IMPROVE DESIGN FOR LAUNDRY HAMPER			
	MATERIAL	SHAPE	FINISH	POSITION
1	WICKER	SQUARE	NATURAL	SITS ON FLOOR
2	PLASTIC	CYLINDRICAL	PAINTED	ON CEILING
3	PAPER	RECTANGLE	CLEAR	ON WALL
4	METAL	HEXAGONAL	LUMINOUS	CHUTE TO BASEMENT
5	NET MATERIAL	CUBE	NEON	ON DOOR

- What *materials* could be used to make hampers?
- What *shapes* can hampers be made in?
- What *finishes* can be used on hampers?
- What are the *positions* for hampers?

Under each heading I list five alternatives.

Idea search: The next step is to randomly choose one or more variations and connect them to create new possibilities. These random combinations may trigger new ideas or potential solutions.

After making any random runs through the box, one combination of variations for the parameters provoked an idea for a new design.

The idea: Using the random combination of net material, cylindrical, painted, and positioned on the door, I came up with a laundry hamper fashioned into a basketball-type net, approximately 40 inches long, attached to a cylindrical hoop and hung on a backboard that is attached to a door. This allows kids to play basketball with dirty laundry as they fill the hamper. When it is full, a tug on a drawstring releases the clothes.

Five alternatives for each parameter generates a possible 3,125 different combinations. If only 10 percent prove useful, that would mean 312 new ideas. In theory, a perfectly constructed Idea Box contains all of the possible solutions to a specified challenge. In practice, the box may be incomplete; a critical parameter or variation may not have been included. When you feel this may be the case, you should reconsider and adjust the parameters or variations accordingly.

NEW BUSINESS EXTENSION FOR CAR WASHES			
	METHOD	PRODUCTS WASHED	EQUIPMENT	PRODUCTS SOLD
1	FULL	CARS	SPRAYS	RELATED PRODUCTS
2	SELF	TRUCKS	CONVEYORS	NOVELTIES
3	HAND	HOUSES	STALLS	DISCOUNT BOOKS
4	MOBILE	CLOTHES	DRYERS	EDIBLE GOODS
5	COMBINATION	DOGS	BRUSHES	CIGARETTES

New ideas and inventions are merely new combinations of existing bits and pieces. The Idea Box snaps existing information together into provocative new patterns, and the ideas appear, almost by accident, out of nowhere. When the ideas appear, you'll grin like a kid who has caught his first fish.

NEW BUSINESS EXTENSION FOR CAR WASHES

A car wash owner fell on hard times. To survive, he needed to find a new market, a new market extension, or a new idea. He analyzed "washing" and decided to work with four parameters: method of washing, products washed, equipment used, and other products sold.

He constructed a box with the four parameters on top; under each parameter he listed five variations. Then he randomly chose one or two more items from each parameter and connected them to form a new business.

The random combination of self, dogs, brushes, stalls, sprays, dryers, and related products sparked the idea for a self-service dog wash. This dog wash has ramps leading to waist-high tubs where owners spray their pets, scrub them with brushes (provided free of charge), shampoo, and blow dry them. In addition, he sells his own line of dog products, such as shampoos and conditioners. Pet owners wash their dogs while their car is going through the full-service car wash.

In the figure below, we see the dot to which the arrow is pointing as part of the diagonal line, even though it is actually closer to the vertical line. We tend to ignore the relationship with the vertical line and see the dot *only* as a continuation of the diagonal one. This illustrates the principle of *common fate:* Events that *seem* to be continuous are likely to be seen as a single entity rather than as discrete events.

In much the same way, we tend to see the elements of a challenge as one continuous whole, ignoring even obvious relationships between its elements. The way we perceive things makes these relationships almost invisible, yet they often direct us to new ideas. The Idea Box allows us to see these relationships by separating a whole into parts and scrambling the parts.

NEW PRODUCTS FOR PUBLISHER

A publisher who is looking for new products decides to work with four parameters: kinds of books, properties of books, processes of publishing, and forms of information.

Under each parameter, he lists ten variations, allowing 10 x 10 x 10 x 10 or 10,000 possible combinations. Assuming a 10 percent yield of truly useful ideas, this gives him a possible 1,000 good ideas jumping over and around him like fleas.

Connecting how-to cooking book, odor, advertising, and premium, our publisher created a scratch-and-sniff cookbook for a major food company to use as a premium. All of the recipes featured the company's products, and each was accompanied by an illustration so that the reader could tell not just how the dish would look but how it would smell as well.

The publisher then connected nonfiction, social responsibilities, advertising, acquiring manuscripts, nontraditional distribution, and hardback to create a new publishing concept. He intends to pay leading authors $60,000 each to write one-hundred-page hardback books on socially responsible topics. He will sell advertisement space within the books to finance

IDEA BOX FOR PUBLISHING				
	KINDS	PROPERTIES	PROCESSES	FORMS
1	FICTION	SOUND (AUDIO BOOKS)	ACQUIRING MANUSCRIPTS	COFFEE TABLE GIFT BOOKS
2	NONFICTION	COLOR	MANUFACTURING	NEWSLETTER
3	CLASSICS	TEXTURE	MARKETING	ANTHOLOGIES
4	HOW-TO BOOKS (COOKING, HOME CARE, ETC.)	SOCIAL RESPONSIBILITIES	DISTRIBUTION TRADITIONAL OR NONTRADITIONAL	SOFTWARE
5	BUSINESS	ILLUSTRATIONS	WRITING SOFTWARE	HARDBACK
6	TEXTBOOK	SUBSTANCE: PAPER OR FLOPPY DISK	REMAINDERING	PAPERBACK
7	CHILDREN	ODOR	ADVERTISING	PREMIUM
8	RELIGION	EXERCISES, GAMES OR PUZZLES	TIME FROM MANUSCRIPT TO FINISHED PRODUCT	MAGAZINE
9	MYSTERY	TASTE	KNOWLEDGE OR ENTERTAINMENT	LOOSE-LEAF
10	SPORTS	SHAPE, LARGE, SMALL OR ODD STRUCTURE	DESIGN AND FORMAT	PACKAGED WITH OTHER PRODUCTS

publishing and printing, and distribute them free to 150,000 prominent people. The publisher will eventually sell the original book in stores and also sell reprint rights to paperback publishers, and license some of the books to foreign publishers.

MARKETING A BOOK

The same publisher had a several-year-old book of standard speeches that had a miserable sales record. He decided to find an innovative way to sell this book. After analyzing how books are marketed, he selected four parameters: packaging, distribution, promotion, and selling.

Under each parameter, he listed ten alternative variations and randomly played with the various combinations until he came up with a new idea.

He combined (see box next page) packaging as a function, to be distributed through other retail outlets, provide free articles to newspapers, and selling using own direct force and came up with the idea to package the book's speeches as scrolls in a cardboard can, called *Canned Speeches*. This new product was sold in office supply stores as well as standard retail outlets. The publisher then wrote and sent articles about this novel package to major newspapers, thereby getting a good deal of free publicity. A mediocre collection of standard speeches became a smashing bestseller.

In the publishing examples, we could generate a possible 1,000 combinations. The more imagination you use in thinking up parameters and variations, the more possible combinations you can create. For instance, suppose you choose five parameters with twenty alternative attributes. This would give you 20 x 20 x 20 x 20 x 20 or 320,000 possible combinations, all without spraining your brain.

Sometimes the best ideas are the result of fortuitous flux. Ideas large and small often occur as a result of a chance combination. An automobile salesman designed an Idea Box and played with it every day. One day he randomly connected odor, air-conditioning, operator-controlled, and new car smell.

This chance combination led to the idea of a fragrance-control system for cars. With a touch of a button, drivers can choose from jasmine, mint, a fresh leather smell, or perfume scents, all blowing through the air-conditioning system. The soft aromas will, according to the salesman, improve ride comfort. He intends to sell his patent to an automobile manufacturer.

SUMMARY

When you write a poem, you discover that the very necessity of fitting your meaning into a specific form requires you to search your imagination for new meanings. You reject certain ways of writing and select others, always trying to arrange the words in a new and imaginative way. Form is an aid to finding new meaning, a stimulus to discovering the essence you wish to express. Think how much more meaning Shakespeare infused in his plays because they were written in blank verse rather than prose, or into his sonnets because they were limited to fourteen lines.

Fitting your challenge in an Idea Box simplifies and condenses it in a similar way. It forces you to find new connections and new meanings; your imagination must leap to fill the gaps and make sense of the whole. Imagine a mime impersonating a man walking his dog. The mime's arm is

IDEA BOX FOR MARKETING A BOOK				
	PACKAGING	DISTRIBUTION	PROMOTION	SELLING
1	COVER: HARD OR SOFT	TRADITIONAL DISTRIBUTORS AND WHOLESALERS	ADVERTISING	DIRECT SALES FORCE
2	FLOPPY DISK	DISTRIBUTE WITH OTHER PUBLISHERS	BOOK REVIEWS	DIRECT MAIL
3	PACKAGE WITH OTHER ITEMS	DISTRIBUTE AT EXHIBITS AND CONVENTIONS	TALK SHOWS	SPECIAL SALES: PREMIUMS AND INCENTIVES
4	PACKAGE TO ADAPT TO SEASON	COMPUTER STORES	BONUS INSERTS, COUPONS	TELEMARKETING
5	GIFT ITEM	OTHER RETAIL OUTLETS	VIDEOS BASED ON THE BOOK	DOOR TO DOOR
6	SOLO OR SERIES	CHAIN STORES	TIE-IN WITH CHARITY	INDEPENDENT REPS
7	PACKAGE WITH POPUS OR DIE CUTS	DIRECT TO CONSUMER	FREE ARTICLES TO NEWSPAPERS	SELL TO SCHOOLS AND LIBRARIES
8	PACKAGE WITH BUILT-IN GIMMICK SUCH AS A BOOK HOLDER	THROUGH MANUFACTURER OF RELATED PRODUCTS	SEMINARS AND WORKSHOPS	SALES KITS
9	CREATE PACKAGE TO SERVE SOME FUNCTION SUCH AS A DOORSTOP	SELF	TIME DISCOUNTS	AUTHOR CONNECTIONS
10	PACKAGING AS AN ALTERNATIVE ADVERTISING VEHICLE	THROUGH HOME PARTIES	CONTEST	SELL FOREIGN RIGHTS

outstretched as though holding the dog's leash. As he jerks his arm back and forth you *see* the dog straining at the leash to sniff this or that. The dog and the leash become the most real part of the scene, even though there is no dog or leash. With the Idea Box, you may see a connection (the mime and his arm) that will provide the stimulus for your imagination to fill the gaps (the dog and the leash) and create a new idea.

CHAPTER TWELVE

IDEA GRID

"Therefore the skillful commander takes up
a position in which he cannot be defeated and
misses no opportunity to master his enemy."

SUN TZU

There is a vast order in the universe. Every time I throw a coin in the air, it returns and hits the floor. Because there *is* a vast order, things can be separated and understood. When NASA sends up four rockets one-half second apart, their afterimages are approximately simultaneous. We can say that we see four rockets "at the same time." This is the illustration of simultaneity. To see order, we attempt to comprehend spontaneously things that are non-spontaneous.

In the figure below, the two horizontal lines are the same length, yet the top one appears to be longer.

This is known as the Ponzo illusion and is explained by the fact that we attempt to comprehend the image as a whole and are led by our experiences to see the vertical lines as if they were railroad tracks receding in the distance. The only way to comprehend what is really there is to examine each line individually, as a separate "event."

The universe of business is also composed of separate events, yet we say things like "that is a good business" or "that market is solid," as though all of the events were appearing as a singular entity at the same time. To find opportunities, you need to look at the separate events that make up the universe of business and understand their relationships. An Idea Grid is designed to let you do just that.

BLUEPRINT

The basic grid is the FCB Grid, a powerful tool that enables one to compress large amounts of complex information. It was first developed in 1978 by Richard Vaughn, a research director of the worldwide advertising corporation Foote, Cone & Belding.

High involvement represents perceptions of expensive products such as cars and boats.

Low involvement represents less costly products such as ordinary household products.

Think represents verbal, numerical, analytic, cognitive products for which the consumer desired information and data. For example, automobiles, boats, computers, cameras, and so on.

Feel represents products that appeal to a consumer's emotional needs and desires, such as travel, beauty, cosmetics, and so on.

You place your product on the grid by researching both the product and its potential market. For instance, life insurance would fall in the High/Left quadrant, insecticide in the Low/Left, and costume jewelry in the Low/Right quadrant.

FCB GRID

	THINK	FEEL
HIGH INVOLVEMENT	1.	2.
LOW INVOLVEMENT	3.	4.

Once the product is placed, you have a powerful basis for generating ideas. You can read and understand the grid immediately because the visual language used in placement is intuitively understood. It's like seeing the ocean for the first time: You learn as much about the vastness of the ocean from your first moment's glance as you would in a month of study.

The FCB Grid allows you to:

- Identify holes in the market.

- Predict the demand for new product ideas.

- Formulate an advertising strategy.

- Reposition your business or product by:

    Positioning it so it is the minimum distance from the competition you want to master.

    Positioning it so it is the maximum distance from the competition for maximum differentiation.

    Leaving the position unchanged and attempting to change customer perceptions.

When using grids, keep your analysis simple, clear, and expressible in only a few lines. If your grid is elaborate and takes a lot of time to communicate, it will lose its meaning. Think of the grid as a piece of rope which takes on meaning only in connection with the things it holds together.

USING THE GRID TO GET IDEAS

People think of a balloon as a continuous solid skin that holds air. But if you look at the skin of a balloon with a microscope, you'll find that it is not continuous at all; it is full of holes. The balloon is a kind of net in which the holes are so small that the air molecules cannot get out. There is, in fact, no such thing as a continuous solid skin, or a "solid" or "continuous" anything in the universe.

So there certainly can be no such thing as a "solid" company, or a market with no holes, or a "solid" anything in business. One way to get new ideas is to locate the holes in a market, an industry, or a business. The Idea Grid makes this easy.

A major publisher was confronted with the challenge: "In what ways might we publish a unique book on gardening for children ages four to twelve?"

He first researched six major publishing firms in the usual ways—surveys, questionnaires, sales records, and so on—and discovered that the major books on gardening for children were, basically, reasonably priced, straight-forward, well-illustrated instructional books. He drew a grid and placed all six in various levels in the Low/Left quadrant as low involvement, thinking books.

He studied the grid and determined that his basic choices were:

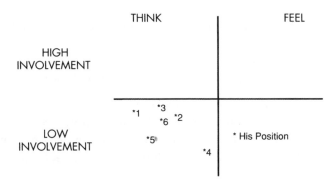

1. *Low/Left quadrant:* He could position his book against the existing books as a low involvement, thinking book.

2. *High/Left quadrant:* He could create a high involvement, thinking book, such as an encyclopedia or other reference book.

3. *High/Right quadrant:* He could create a high involvement, feeling book. Examples of this might include art books and books packaged with fairly expensive objects.

4. *Low/Right quadrant:* He could create a low involvement, feeling book, such as a coloring book or a book packaged with less expensive objects.

The publisher surveyed all the options and decided to focus on the Low/Right quadrant.

Using the grid to look for holes in the market, he found the idea he was looking for, floating like a flower in a bowl.

The idea: A coloring book titled *Growing Vegetable Soup.* The book describes a delicious vegetable soup, then leads the reader through the actual work: planting the seeds, watering, weeding, and digging up the

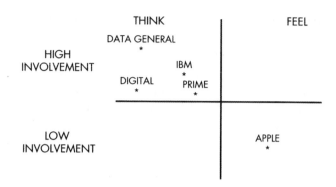

vegetables, and finally making the soup and eating it. The book was a best-seller.

USING THE GRID TO APPLY IDEAS

A new idea usually requires imagination and effort to get results. For instance, the essence of competition is differentiation; creating something better than and different from the competition. However, sometimes even an obvious functional difference doesn't sell unless you look for an imaginative application.

Look at Apple Computers. Their unbelievable success is not because of the product's small size or low price. After all, why would anybody buy a sophisticated piece of hardware that looked like a child's toy from some unknown company? There was no way Apple could claim superiority over IBM, Digital Equipment, Data General, or Prime, especially given the horror stories about the computer market at that time. Instead, Apple provided an imaginative application of their idea.

First, they graphed the computer environment as above.

Apple's genius was to avoid positioning themselves with the crowded cluster of giant competitors in the High/Left quadrant. Challenging these giants in their own quadrant would have been like challenging a school of piranhas to a game of water polo.

They avoided that position by not calling themselves a minicomputer or a microminicomputer. They did something different. They positioned themselves in the Low/Right quadrant as far away as possible from the giants and developed a marketing and advertising strategy that emphasized:

- A new and entirely different computer intended for the average person rather than computer experts.

- The term "personal computer" as opposed to minicomputer.

- Being part of a whole new generation of computers.

- Being user-friendly.

Apple went after the Low/Right quadrant—an enormous risk at the time. Was there really a market for a toy-like personal computer for the average person? There was. By using imagination in positioning their idea, the founders made billions as they captured the market they saw on the grid.

SUMMARY

The grid helps you navigate the tricky seas of the marketplace. The waters are neither dull nor pretty, but a code that needs interpretation. The grid tells you everything or nothing, depending on how you read it. Make the right soundings, and patterns will emerge like a safe harbor out of the mist.

CHAPTER THIRTEEN

LOTUS BLOSSOM

"The art of war recognizes eight varieties of ground."

SUN TZU

One day the frog poked his head out of the well and boasted to the sea turtle that no creature was happier than he. Why, he could dive up and down in the mud and enjoy a freer range of movement than all those shrimps and tadpoles living around him. He invited the turtle to come down into the well and see for himself. The turtle declined and instead boasted of his perspective outside the well. "A distance of a thousand miles is not sufficient to describe the extent of the ocean, nor can one ever hope to sound its depth," the turtle said. "It's sad to see you peeping at the sky through a tube." The frog was awed when he heard this and realized how living in a well limited his perspective.

In a way, are we not like the frog? All of the elements of an organization are in separate wells, and we see only what is in our particular well. Buyers are in the well of supply, human resources are in the well of personnel, facilities are in the well of facilities, and so on. The whole organization is operating like frogs in the wells. There is no 360-degree perspective.

We need to get an oceanic view of our problems. We need to know the goals, themes, and sub-themes in order to generate meaningful ideas. Yasuo Matsumura of Clover Management Research in Chiba City, Japan, developed Lotus Blossom, a creative-thinking technique that diagrammatically helps us do this.

LOTUS BLOSSOM

You start with a problem or idea and expand that theme into themes until you've created several different entry points. In the Lotus Blossom, the petals, or themes, around the core of the blossom are figuratively peeled back one at a time, revealing a key component or sub-theme. This approach is pursued in ever-widening circles until the theme is comprehensively explored. The cluster of themes and sub-themes that are developed in one way or another provide several different possibilities.

BLUEPRINT

1. *Draw a Lotus Blossom diagram and write the problem or idea in the center of the diagram.*

2. *Write the significant components or themes of your subject in the circles surrounding the center circle, labeled A to H. The optimal number of themes for a manageable diagram is between six and eight. If you have more than eight, make additional diagrams.*

    To help you decide what themes to use, ask questions like: What are my specific objectives? What are the constants in my problem? If my subject were a book, what would the chapter headings be? What are the dimensions of my problem?

3. *Use the ideas written in the circles as the central themes for the surrounding lotus blossom petals or boxes.* Thus, the idea or application you wrote in circle A would become the central theme for the lower middle box A. It now becomes the basis for generating eight new ideas or applications.

4. *Continue the process until the lotus blossom diagram is completed.*

Suppose, for example, you want to create more value for your organization by increasing productivity or decreasing costs. You would write "add value" in the center box. Next, in the circles labeled A to H surrounding your center box, write the eight most significant areas in your organization where you can increase productivity or decrease costs. Also write the same significant areas in the circles with the corresponding letters spread around the diagram.

Each area now represents a main theme that ties together the surrounding boxes. For instance, in the sample diagram, the word "technology" in the circle labeled A, serves as the theme for the lower middle group of boxes.

For each theme, try to think of eight ways to add value. It's helpful to phrase each theme as a question to yourself. For example, ask, "In what ways might we use technology to increase productivity?" and "In what ways might we use technology to decrease expenses?" If you complete the entire diagram, you will have 64 new ideas or ways to increase productivity or decrease expenses.

6	3	7	6	3	7	6	3	7
2	F Suppliers	4	2	C Travel Expenses	4	2	G Partner ships	4
5	1	8	5	1	8	5	1	8
6	3	7	F Suppliers	C Travel Expenses	G Partner ships	6	3	7
2	B Evaluation	4	B Evaluation	Add value	D Delivery Methods	2	D Delivery Methods	4
5	1	8	E Facilities	A Technology	H Personnel	5	1	8
6	3	7	6	3	7	6	3	7
2	E Facilities	4	2	A Technology	4	2	H Personnel	4
5	1	8	5	1	8	5	1	8

In the Lotus Blossom, ideas evolve into other ideas and applications. Because the components of the technique are dynamic, the ideas seem to flow outward with a conceptual momentum all their own. Lotus allows you to track whole systems of interacting elements. Ideas and thoughts are not merely isolated acts and parts floating around in your mind. Unless you look at a whole system and all of its components, you may miss the key relationships and how they interact.

Chris Messina, a board member for a university, wanted to create more value for her university. She selected the themes "suppliers," "travel expenses," "partnerships," "course delivery methods," "personnel," "technology," "facilities," and "evaluation."

For each theme, she came up with eight ideas. For example, in the "delivery methods" box, she listed the idea of using videophones to interact with students at other universities in general-knowledge quizzes. By expanding the box outward, she made "videophones" into still another theme and listed eight more ideas or applications on how to add value through the use of videophones. One of the ideas adopted by the university is to have foreign language classes taught by native speakers in other countries. Another course delivery method being developed by the school is a program for interactive electronic seminars where outside experts are invited and the professor participates more as an equal than an authority.

An important aspect of this technique is that it shifts you from reacting to a static snapshot of the problem and broadens your perspective toward the problem and the relationships and connections between its components. Production managers at Volvo started with "safer automobile" as the central problem. A theme was how to make the front end of the car safer. One of the ideas was to install an ultrasonic speed sensor on the dash with a built in "required stopping distance (about two seconds)." A "heads-up" display alerts the driver if he's is too close to the car in front. This got the Volvo managers thinking about other uses for sensors as safety devices, so they re-engineered the idea to include warning the car following the driver with an LED screen that reads, "You are too close." With this system, there would always be sufficient stopping distance between three cars minimum, even if only one car has the system.

SUMMARY

In the illustration on the next page, you start with the face of a man that gradually changes into the figure of a woman. If you saw just the first and last picture, you would think they were two separate subjects. By seeing the lines change in relationship to each other, a new pattern evolves.

In a similar way, the Lotus Blossom begins with a theme that evolves into other themes and sub-themes that are interconnected, and those evolve into a new pattern.

Generally, higher-level properties are regarded as emergent. For example, a car is an emergent property of the interconnected parts. If a car was disassembled and all the parts were thrown into a heap, the property disappears. If you placed the parts in piles according to function, you begin to see a pattern and make connections between the piles that may inspire you to imagine the emergent property, the car, which you can then build.

CHAPTER FOURTEEN

PHOENIX

"The general who wins a battle
makes many calculations in his temple before
the battle is fought."

SUN TZU

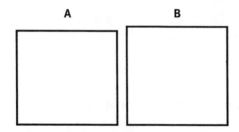

Which figure is a perfect square?

If you chose A, as the majority of people do, you are wrong. B is the perfect square. People tend to overestimate the lengths of vertical lines in comparison to horizontal ones. Consequently, they see the vertical lines of A as the same length as its horizontal lines.

If you had asked yourself the following questions, you would have selected the correct square:

- What is a perfect square?

- How can I determine which figure is a perfect square?

- Can I visually determine which is the perfect square?

- Should I use a measuring device?

Questions help you estimate your challenges; they give conscious direction to your thinking. When you ask yourself a question, you have to think about it. And when you ask yourself the right question, you have to think *up* as well as think *about* something.

Columbo, the famous television detective played by Peter Falk, did not investigate crimes by looking for clues. Instead, he engaged suspects in conversation, seeking, chiefly by questions, to induce them to talk and explain. He claimed no knowledge, except of his own ignorance, and was apparently willing to learn from anyone. The inevitable result of such questioning, however, was that the suspect was reduced to a state of irritation and, finally, a confession of guilt.

Columbo did not solve his crimes with one or two questions but by asking a long series of them. Asking one question would be like hoping to understand the wheel by examining one spoke. It takes many spokes, as well as a hub and a rim, to make the thing called a wheel, and we need to see the whole thing to comprehend it. In the same way, to understand a challenge, you need to ask a series of questions, not just one or two. To do this, use a question checklist.

A checklist of questions helps you make sure that no aspect of a challenge is overlooked. Read the following string of digits at the rate of about one per second then, look away and try to recall the digits in order:

7 9 1 4 0

Now do the same with this string of digits:

2 6 5 8 9 3 1 4 7 0 5 3 9

Most likely, you recalled the first string completely but recalled only part of the second string, perhaps about seven digits. This is because our memory span is usually limited to about seven items, give or take two. Even though you might think you know all the questions you should ask about any situation, you cannot produce them when you have to.

Unless your challenge is extremely easy to solve, you need to know what to ask.

Phoenix is a checklist of questions developed by the Central Intelligence Agency to encourage agents to look at a challenge from many different angles. Using Phoenix is like holding your challenge in your hand. You can turn it, look at it from underneath, see it from one view, hold it up to another position, imagine solutions, and really be in control of it.

Use the Phoenix checklist as a base on which to build your own personal checklist of questions. Note good questions when you hear others ask them, and keep adding them to your own checklist. With the right questions, you can solve a challenge the way Columbo would solve a crime; i.e., ask a number of questions, then suddenly ask the question that turns everything around. When that happens, you might say you "Columboed the challenge."

BLUEPRINT

1. *Write your challenge.* Isolate the challenge you want to think about and commit yourself to *an* answer, if not *the* answer, by a certain date.

2. *Ask questions.* Use the Phoenix checklist to dissect the challenge into as many different ways as you can.

3. *Record your answers.* Information requests, solutions, and ideas for evaluation and analysis.

THE PHOENIX CHECKLIST

THE PROBLEM

- Why is it necessary to solve the problem?

- What benefits will you gain by solving the problem?

- What is the unknown?

- What is it you don't yet understand?

- What is the information you have?

- What isn't the problem?

- Is the information sufficient? Or is it insufficient? Or redundant? Or contradictory?

- Should you draw a diagram of the problem? A figure?

- Where are the boundaries of the problem?

- Can you separate the various parts of the problem? Can you write them down? What are the relationships of the parts of the problem?

- What are the constants (things that can't be changed) of the problem?

- Have you seen this problem before?

- Have you seen this problem in a slightly different form?

- Do you know a related problem?

- Try to think of a familiar problem having the same or a similar unknown.

- Suppose you find a problem related to yours that has already been solved. Can you use it? Can you use its method?

- Can you restate your problem? How many different ways can you restate it? More general? More specific? Can the rules be changed?

- What are the best, worst, and most probable cases you can imagine?

THE PLAN

- Can you solve the whole problem? Part of the problem?

- What would you like the resolution to be? Can you picture it?

- How much of the unknown can you determine?

- Can you derive something useful from the information you have?

- Have you used all the information?

- Have you taken into account all essential notions in the problem?

- Can you separate the steps in the problem-solving process? Can you determine the correctness of each step?

- What creative-thinking techniques can you use to generate ideas? How many different techniques?

- Can you see the result? How many different kinds of results can you see?

- How many different ways have you tried to solve the problem?

- What have others done?

- Can you intuit the solution? Can you check the result?

- What should be done? How should it be done?

- Where should it be done?

- When should it be done?

- Who should do it?

- What do you need to do at this time?

- Who will be responsible for what?

- Can you use this problem to solve some other problem?

- What is the unique set of qualities that makes this problem what it is and none other?

- What milestones can best mark your progress?

- How will you know when you are successful?

Try using the question checklist to solve this difficult problem, known as the Greek Cross. On a table, arrange ten coins to match the following illustration. Move just *two* coins to another position to form two rows, containing *six* coins each when added up either horizontally or vertically.

The solution can be found in this chapter's summary.

Suppose you defined a "rose" as a red, pink, or white flower one gives to a beautiful woman, a pleasant hostess, or a deceased friend. The tagging of a complex flower with the single label (rose) and one description would not inspire your curiosity. However, if you asked a series of questions about roses, you could better describe the flower, how it is grown, its thorns, its blossoms, its fragrance, how others have used it, and how to best package and use it.

Tagging any subject with a single label and description dulls curiosity and limits imagination. Consider the steel industry. Executives tagged a complex process with a single label (big steel) and one description (the integrated process), and suffered for years with an uneconomical industry. Finally, a group of young men asked a series of questions that changed the industry.

The integrated steel process had been uneconomical since it was invented in the 1870s—it involves beginning with iron ore, creating very high temperatures four times only to quench them, and transporting masses of metal over great distances. The only time the industry performed well was in times of war—it was a lump in America's gravy.

A group of new young managers asked aggressive questions about every step of the steel-making process and discovered that the integrated process contradicts basic laws of economics.

What they discovered was that since the early 1970s, the demand for steel had been going up. However, for integrated mills to meet the demand they had to add new units, which required a substantial investment. Since demand rises in small steps, the expansion would not be profitable until the demand reached the mill's new capacity. If a mill chose not to expand, it would lose its customers. In the steel business, if you can't deliver orders on time, customers don't wait. Faced with this choice, companies expanded. Consequently, companies were profitable for only that time when the demand reached the new capacity. When the demand exceeded that capacity, the integrated mills would be forced to expand again. This discovery led to the solution.

The idea: The young questioners proposed a shift from the giant, ever-expanding "integrated" plant to a "mini-mill." The end uses are the same as the integrated mill, only the costs are substantially lower. A mini-mill can be built for one-tenth the cost of an integrated plant, uses heat only once and does not quench it, starts with steel scrap instead of ore, and ends up with one final product (for example, beams, rods, etc.). The mini-mills offer modern technology, low labor costs, and target markets.

An executive stated that if these young men had not asked the right questions, we would still be making steel the old-fashioned way.

A question checklist also helps you increase your observation and association abilities.

A car alarm didn't stop thieves from shattering the window of one entrepreneur's Porsche and stealing his radio. Using the question checklist, he decided that the real challenge was disguising the radio, not finding a failproof alarm system. The question: "Suppose you find a problem related to yours and solved before, can you use its methods?" led him to think of how the military camouflages items it wants to disguise and hide. This association inspired his idea.

The idea: A fake front showing splayed wires and a gashed frame. Attached with Velcro over the real radio, it creates the illusion that the radio has already been stolen.

SUMMARY

The Greek Cross solution:

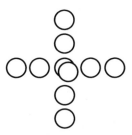

This problem can only be solved by moving one coin from the right arm to the left arm and moving the extra coin at the bottom to a position on top of the center coin.

Most problems like this are solved by sliding coins back and forth, but to solve this one you had to work in three dimensions.

The checklist questions that may have helped were:

- What are the boundaries of the problem? (Nothing prevents you from working in three dimensions.)

- Do you know a related problem? (The Dot Problem in "False Faces," page 44.)

- Can you intuit the result? (After sliding the coins around, you may sense that it can't be solved in two dimensions and that may lead you to thinking about the third.)

- What is the unique set of qualities that makes this problem what it is and none other? (You're working with coins which can be stacked as well as moved.)

Solving a challenge is like walking a tightrope. If the rope is too slack, you will fall; if it is too tight, it has no resiliency, and you will also fall. The rope must be continually adjusted and supported at its weakest point. In the same way, asking questions will constantly adjust and support lines of speculation as you tiptoe toward a solution.

—

CHAPTER FIFTEEN

THE GREAT TRANSPACIFIC AIRLINE AND STORM DOOR COMPANY

> "If the army is confused and suspicious, neighboring rulers will cause trouble. This is what is meant by the saying: 'A confused army leads to another's victory.'"
>
> **SUN TZU**

We do not see the stars in motion, though they move at speeds of more than a million miles per day. We do not see the trees grow or notice ourselves aging each day. We do not even see the hands of a clock in motion. We tend to think statically and are surprised, often uncomfortably and sometimes fatally, by the constant changes in our world. This also applies to the world of business: It is difficult to shake our static notions of business and markets. This is why so many businesses seem to belong to an obsolete yesterday.

Static companies become frustrated and confused about the nature of their business; they often try to become all things to all people. Few things are less effective than those companies, like the apocryphal Great Transpacific Airline and Storm Door Company.

To get effective new ideas for your business, you must know what your business is *and* what it should be. Only by knowing these things can you apprehend the changing business world.

What Is Your Business?

On the face of it, nothing may seem simpler or more obvious than to know what a company's business is. A railroad runs trains, a publisher produces books, an automobile company manufactures cars, and so on. Actually, "What is our business?" is almost always a difficult question, and the right answer is often anything but obvious. Consider Bell Telephone. What could have been more obvious than the telephone business in the late 1800s?

Theodore Vail was fired by Bell Telephone in 1890 when he dared to ask top management "What is our business?" He was called back a decade later, when the consequences of the lack of an answer had become evident—that is, when the Bell System, operating without a clear definition, had drifted into a severe crisis and was being threatened by a government takeover.

Theodore Vail's answer was: "Our business is service, not telephones." That answer brought about radical innovations in Bell Telephone's business policy. It meant employee training and advertising that stressed service. It meant a new financial policy that assumed the company had to give service whenever it was demanded, and it was management's job to find the necessary capital and to earn a return on it.

Waiting until you or your industry is in trouble is like playing Russian roulette. Look at television. Simply put, Ted Turner showed the networks that their days of oligopoly were over. For quite some time, network executives sat around like smug sacred cows feeding each other a steady line of bull, while Turner, a Brown University dropout, parlayed his inheritance into cable television's most successful and influential programming company.

Among its innovations: cable TV's first national superstation; CNN, one of television's most successful networks; and Turner Network Television, an entertainment station with the largest initial viewership ever on cable TV. The major networks forgot to ask what is it that they do, and what it is they should do. Turner didn't. If you don't know what your business is, you may end up on the wrong end of the business food chain.

How Should a Business Define Itself?

Is a company that pays for medical expenses in the insurance business or the health-care business? Are combination gas stations and food stores in the grocery business or the convenience business? Is an NFL football team in the sports business or the entertainment business?

Businesses can define themselves according to products or services, markets, functions, or technologies.

IBM had long defined themselves as a data processing business. When the computer arrived, and with it a new technology that IBM knew nothing about, IBM top management realized that data processing would now have to mean computers, and asked "What should our business be?" They redefined their business from data processing to the new technologies of computer science and got on computers and software like wrinkles on a cheap suit.

On the other hand, life insurance companies have lost considerable ground to mutual funds and pension funds. At one time, they had access to the largest inventory of financial customers in the country and a virtual monopoly on their money. When inflation changed people's attitude toward life insurance and savings, the insurance companies had the resources, marketing, and financial expertise to retain customers. What they lacked was the ability to see the changes in the market.

Look at the illustration in the margin. It appears to be a static design. However, if you move the book in circles, spokes will appear and rotate within the design. If you make a copy of the design and move it in circles near the illustration in the book, spokes will appear and rotate in both.

Once you knew how to look for the motion, you saw it. It is the same with business and markets. They may appear to be static, but changes are inevitably occurring. Once you know to look for the changes, you'll see them.

BLUEPRINT

1. *Ask "What is our business?"* and *"What should our business be?"* These questions focus your attention on where to look for new ideas.

2. *Define and organize your business according to* products or services, markets, functions, and technologies. For instance, the key descriptors for a business book publisher would be:
   Products or services: Books.
   Markets: Books for the business professional.
   Functions: Books that provide business information.
   Technologies: Books based on the latest printing technologies.

3. *Under each variable, list the key words for the business:* Key words describe the products or services, markets, functions, and technologies in your industry.

A key word index for the business book publisher would be:

PRODUCTS	FUNCTIONS	MARKETS
hardback books	information	libraries
softback books	entertainment	bookstores
floppy disks	education	universities
cassettes	training	industry
electronic networks	resource	military

TECHNOLOGIES	SERVICES
print	professional discounts
electronic	book clubs
audio	newsletters
modular	seminars
video	information services

4. *Mix and match* your products, markets, functions, services, and technologies in various ways to explore new ideas.

A business book publisher might connect the following key words to create a new idea: cassettes, training, industry, audio, and seminars.

The idea: Produce audio cassettes about sales training. The cassettes would be based on the publisher's backlist of books on selling and would be sold directly to corporations. The publisher would provide sales training seminars by the authors as part of the package.

Or, connect electronic networks, information, resource, print, and information services to produce another idea.

The idea: An electronic data bank containing all the information from the publisher's backlist business books. The information would be sold as a business resource by way of a computer information network for businesses. Printed reports could also be purchased.

Close your right eye, stare at the X, and move the book back and forth about twelve inches from your eye until you find the point at which the break in the line magically disappears.

You are experiencing how your brain fills in missing information, trying to make some sense out of what it sees. Similarly, when you mix and match the key words for your business, your brain will fill in the missing information and create new ideas.

Consider what happened with the Prudential Home Company. One of the many things that buried savings and loan institutions was mortgage lending. Ten years ago, mortgage lending was dominated by the local savings and loan—a drab brick building on Main Street where an applicant could fill out forms between 9 A.M. and 3 P.M. In 1982, the Prudential Home Company asked the obvious: "What should our business be?" and came up with these key words.

Key Word Index

PRODUCTS	FUNCTIONS	MARKETS
mortgages	assumable	mortgage brokers
	shared appreciation	corporations
	renegotiated rate	real estate agents
	wraparound	other third parties
	bartering	

TECHNOLOGIES	SERVICES
telephone	24-hour
fax	speed
computers	profitability by pricing
electronic mail	control
electronic banking	processing

They mixed and matched the key words and filled in the blanks to arrive at the answer: The mortgage business should be selling convenience, speed, and personal attention, and protecting profitability through pricing.

They created a service that does business only by toll-free telephone lines, fax machines, and modem. They have become famous for speedy delivery, courteous service, and rigorous controls. Dealing exclusively through third parties—corporations, mortgage brokers, and real estate agents—they have created a mortgage company with no offices and whose speed of delivery is legendary.

In 1986, the service's business came almost entirely from corporations helping employees get mortgages. By the end of 1988, more than half of its business came from mortgage brokers who match home buyers with mortgage lenders. When the mortgage business flattens out, Prudential plans to rent its entire processing service—from taking phone calls to closing the loan—to other lenders.

While other companies were devastated by rapid interest rate changes, Prudential thrived and has become the fastest-growing mortgage broker in the United States. They constantly look at the key words in their business: the markets, products, functions, technologies, and services.

As a testament to their success, witness the following story from the chief executive, Marvin Moskowitz: "One of my favorite responses from customers came from an American businessman returning to Chicago from Japan. He said very flattering things about how our courteous service and speedy approval made it the smoothest house closing in his experience. What really impressed him was the fact that he had done the whole thing, application through closing, by telephone from Tokyo."

SUMMARY

An essential step in deciding the nature of your business is a systematic analysis and combination of the key words that describe existing products, services, markets, functions, marketing, and technologies. Are they still viable? Will they remain viable? What can be connected to produce a new idea?

Think of your business as a pot with two handles. One handle represents the nature of your business today, the other represents what your business will be in the future. To hold the pot steady, you have to grasp both handles by asking: "What is the nature of my business?" and "What should my business be?"

FUTURE FRUIT

"In peace prepare for war, in war
prepare for peace."

SUN TZU

One thing is certain: We are all traveling toward the future at sixty minutes per hour, no matter who we are or what we do, and we are all going to arrive there no matter what. The first scratch on a new car is a stinging little reminder of the inevitability of a coming future. What is the future of your business? How can one prepare for it?

All human experience is expansive and omnidirectional, including the future. Because the future is not linear, you cannot prepare for it with one single plan. To harvest profits in the future, you should have several alternative plans based on improbable as well as probable future events. Think of future profit as future fruit. Having only one scenario is planting one strawberry instead of a whole field of possible strawberries. Scenarios, like strawberries, may spoil. If you have only one scenario and it spoils, you have a problem.

In 1973, the world was hit by an oil shortage and a sudden rise in prices. Oil companies were caught with their pants down—except The Royal Dutch Shell company. They had realized that improbable events can take place without warning and that such events demand swift and sure management, ideas, and decisions. They had prepared several different future scenarios, from "boom or bust" to "constrained growth," to address any economic eventuality.

A period of constrained growth did, in fact, follow the oil shortage, and their "constrained growth" scenario positioned The Royal Dutch Shell company to exploit the shortage. The Royal Dutch Shell company grew from number eight to number two during the 1970s by taking quick advantage of unexpected opportunities.

Exxon, by contrast, looked like a horse on ice after the oil spill in Alaska. Exxon, the state of Alaska, and the U.S. Coast Guard had only one scenario for a possible oil spill, and it was totally inadequate. When the Exxon *Valdez* went aground in Prince William Sound in March of 1989, it caused the largest oil spill in U. S. history. Exxon, the state, and the federal government were paralyzed for two days, as oil spilled into the sound from the ruptured hull. Their plan did not consider a spill of that magnitude, the utilization of personnel to handle such a spill, a breakdown in communications between the state and the federal government, or the possibility of not being allowed to use certain chemicals to disperse the oil.

In the end, the Exxon *Valdez* became a tragic symbol of the consequences that are suffered when companies and governments bet on one future scenario and have only one plan. Exxon's strawberry spoiled.

It is one of the strange facts of experience that when we try to think into the future, our thoughts also jump backward. Our mind seems to behave like the white diamonds in the above figure. The white diamonds alternately jump in and out so that either the top right or bottom left can be seen as closer to you.

It may well be that nature has some fundamental law by which opening up the future opens up the past to an equal degree. When you think of your death, for example, you automatically think about how you lived your life.

When you think into the future, your forward-looking and backward-looking thinking combine like two twists of rope, and twine inextricably around each other. Therefore, when you think about the future of your business, you also force yourself to think about what is happening in your business now and what has happened in the past.

BLUEPRINT

The procedures for preparing for the future are:

1. *Identify a particular problem in your business.*

2. *State a particular decision that has to be made.*

3. *Identify the forces (economic, technological, product lines, competition, and so on) that have an impact on the decision.*

4. *Build four or five future scenarios based on the principal forces.* Use all the available information and develop scenarios that will give you as many different and plausible possibilities as a pinball in play.

5. *Develop the scenarios into stories or narratives* by varying the forces that impact the decision. Change the forces (interest rates escalate, a key performer quits, need for your product or service disappears, etc.) and combine them into different patterns to describe the possible consequences of your decision over the next five years.

6. *Search for business opportunities within each scenario.* Then explore the links between opportunities across the range of your scenarios, and actively search for new ideas.

Suppose you are worried about future competitive trends in your business.

1. The problem is "What competitive trends are developing in terms of competitors, technology, and pricing?"

2. A particular decision that has to be made is one of pricing.

3. The forces that have an impact on pricing are profits, return on investment, cash flow, capitalization structure, competition's pricing, and so on.

4. You can now build four or five different, plausible scenarios around the forces you have identified.
   Scenario 1. Nothing changes. Everything remains the way it is today.
   Scenario 2. Your major competitor reduces prices by 25 percent.
   Scenario 3. A major technological breakthrough prices out your major product line.
   Scenario 4. The country is hit by a deep recession and customers postpone purchasing indefinitely.
   Scenario 5. The economy heats up and inflation drives interest rates up to 15 percent.

Each of these scenarios points to different actions you might take and different business opportunities.

What future scenarios might a gasoline-service station owner develop? One might be: A major technological breakthrough makes gasoline obsolete.

Two very real possibilities are methanol and natural gas. Methanol is getting good PR as clean fuel, but its corrosive and toxic qualities require special handling. What if the handling problem is solved and methanol replaces gasoline? Or, consider natural gas which is clean, plentiful, and politically popular and is being used in Holland. So far, compressing natural gas is a cumbersome process, but what if someone solves this problem?

How can you position yourself now to take advantage of new opportunities which alternative fuels will bring? One thing you could do today is install a few methanol pumps for motorists who are willing to handle it and to make more frequent fill-ups.

Methanol will probably require larger automobile gas tanks. Another probable future opportunity will be in the design of the new tanks. Consider getting involved in the design and manufacture of methanol gasoline tanks for automobiles.

Another service station scenario could be predicated upon new technology that makes gasoline more clean-burning and cheap.

The problems with a cheap, clean-burning gasoline become pricing, competition, and service. To position yourself now to exploit future opportunities in this scenario, you could:

- Stress service. Install a car wash and provide free washes with fill-ups. Once they are built, car washes cost operators about 15 cents per car. Experts say washes can pump up gas sales by 25 percent.

- Provide an unusual service, such as haircuts.

- Make your stations into "pit stops." This would appeal to harried commuters. You service the car and bring them their coffee, juice, cigarettes, and morning paper while they wait. You could also have a drive-through window where people who don't need gas can drive up and get coffee, a paper, or whatever.

Creating future scenarios pushes you to think about possible futures which, in turn, pushes you to generate ideas that will work now and give you the edge over your competition. You're thinking about getting into alternative fuels or the automobile design business, adding car washes, barber shops, and pit stops, while your competitor is still pondering whether to use air dryers or paper towels in his washroom.

Observe your reactions as you look at the figure in the margin on the next page.

Most probably, you immediately recognized the global letter (H) and hesitated a fraction of a second before you identified the local letter (S) that makes up the H. This is because processing the global letter interfered with processing the local one. This is the way we normally think. We go from the global to the local, and when we are even slightly surprised, we hesitate.

It is the same with the future. You may have some global notion of what the future may hold, but if you are surprised at what happens at the local level, you may be paralyzed into inaction as you try to process the possibilities. You need specific scenarios which will enable you to deal with the local possibilities immediately. This is why many people who find themselves fired or laid off are unable to cope for a period of months. They were aware of the global possibility of losing a job and yet made no local plans about how to survive.

Henry Ford foresaw the global notion of an America on wheels. Still, the Ford Corporation failed to prepare scenarios for the future consequences, threats, and opportunities of this scenario. Consequently, the Ford Company was paralyzed for a number of years as it tried to process what had happened to its market. What would have happened if Ford had designed fuel-efficient autos or concentrated on quality enhancement before the Japanese and Germans?

In times of good business, scenarios enable you to prepare for the bad; and when business is lean, they help you prepare for the good.

Consider the case of tanning products and booths. Publicity about tanning's negative effects is becoming more and more strident. It's possible that at some point an aggressive Surgeon General may outlaw tanning booths, and people in the tanning business will need something to replace their present products.

One tanning booth manufacturer working with this scenario put all its investment money into developing alternative tanning products. Its research produced a brand-new product. *The idea:* A safe pill that can tan people overnight. People will look tan and healthy without any ill effects. By preparing for the worst, they invented a product that could be a breakthrough for safe tans.

The more possible futures you foresee, the more options you can create; the more options you have, the greater your chances of finding the unexpected opportunity.

SUMMARY

In 1888, Henry Heinz bet everything he had on a single future scenario and bought the entire cucumber crop from a 600-acre farm. A year later, he was bankrupt. "Bankruptcy changes the way a man views the future," he said.

Within a few years, he was back in business. This time Heinz was a full-fledged futurist with "57 Varieties," several different scenarios, and strategies for his products in good times and bad.

Heinz took his "bracketed sets of opportunities" from his future scenarios and became one of the first to endorse the federal Pure Food and Drug Act, an unpopular stance in the food industry at the time. He also developed a model factory in an era when sweatshops were the norm. His workers enjoyed private lockers, a library, piano music, their own swimming pool, free medical care, and free manicures daily. Management from around the world studied his factory, including a delegation from Japan who signed the guest book in 1901.

If you do not plan for the future, you may end up like the farmer who overfarmed his land to the point that he couldn't even raise his voice on it.

Group C

These techniques reorganize information in ways that help you break away from the most obvious and reasonable perspectives. An obvious rearrangement of information is often too closely related to old, familiar patterns to provoke a big idea. The more dramatic your change of perspective, the greater your chance for an original insight or breakthrough idea.

Think about siphoning water from a bucket. You start by doing the unnatural and unexpected—sucking water *upwards* into a tube. Yet, once the water reaches a certain point in the tube, the siphon effect takes over and the water flows naturally out of the bucket. In the same way, a seemingly unnatural use of information can produce a perfectly natural idea.

BRUTETHINK

Technique: Random stimulation.
Profile: Forces a connection between two dissimilar concepts to create a new idea.

HALL OF FAME

Technique: Forced connection.
Profile: Produces ideas and insights by creating a relationship between your challenge and the words and thoughts of the world's great thinkers.

CIRCLE OF OPPORTUNITY

Technique: Forced connection.
Profile: Generates ideas by forcing a connective link between common attributes and your challenge.

IDEATOONS

Technique: Pattern language.
Profile: A way to get ideas by using abstract symbols instead of words.

CLEVER TREVOR

Technique: Talk to a stranger.
Profile: How to get ideas by increasing the number and kind of people you talk to about your challenges.

CHAPTER SEVENTEEN

BRUTETHINK

"To foresee a victory which the ordinary man
can foresee is not the acme of skill."

SUN TZU

The pattern below appears to be a grid, but it is not. None of the lines touch each other, yet we see the empty spaces as circles or squares hiding the grid intersections. We connect the illusory figures to create a street-like effect out of empty spaces.

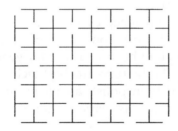

In order to get original ideas, you will always need a way to create new sets of patterns in your mind. One way to do this is to force yourself to see relationships between dissimilar things. When you can do this, you will see ideas where none existed before.

We all see relationships between those objects that we've been taught are related, such as chair and table, ham and eggs, bread and butter, brother and sister, teacher and student, work and money, and so on. In traditional thinking, we put things together because there is a reason to put them together.

In the world of art, however, it is common to put things together which have no obvious connection; the random juxtaposition of unrelated objects provokes new ideas. For example, a modern painting might portray a garbage truck with a sunset painted on it. From the juxtaposition come ideas of function, durability, and mundaneness contrasting with beauty and nature. One observer might feel the need to reexamine routine objects in his life for beauty, while another might look for more function in nature. It is not uncommon for an artist to come up with a unique pattern which scientists later find in nature.

Brutethink lets you learn from relationships that might not occur spontaneously by pairing two things that have nothing in common and seeing what emerges. Trying to define the process is a little difficult, somewhat like trying to bite your own teeth. What would happen, for example, if you paired rectangular black-and-white tiles with parallel lines?

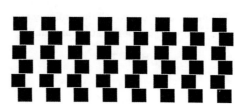

Combining these two elements creates the famous "café wall" illusion. The tiles seem to be wedge-shaped, but the lines are in fact parallel, and the tiles are perfectly rectangular.

One breakthrough idea reached by this method is distortion-free glass.

Alastair Pilkington, production chief of the glassmaking firm of Pilkington Brothers, Ltd., had been working for years on developing a way to rid glass of distortion. At the time, the best technique was to pass molten glass through rollers and then polish away the imperfections, which was costly and not very effective. Glass experts thought the solution lay in developing superior grinders and polishers.

One foggy October evening, Pilkington was washing dishes in his home in northwest England. His mind clear and free, he daydreamed as he watched a bar of Ivory soap float in the greasy water. He visualized glass floating like a bar of soap, and suddenly conceived of an idea that revolutionized the five-thousand-year-old glass industry.

He made a connection between two dissimilar concepts—floating soap and distortions in glass—and invented float glass. In this process, the glass is made in an oven floating in a tub of molten tin. The glass cools and hardens before the tin; it is then rolled into a special annealing chamber without any damage to its finish. No grinding or polishing is needed. Distortion-free glass is now produced cheaply and efficiently, because one individual washing dishes saw a connection between a bar of soap and a whole industry.

Forcing connections opens your mind as wide as a village priest's Bible. You will find that as you develop this thinking tool you will become more open to outside influences. Indeed, you will seek out such influences.

One workshop had the challenge of reducing the very high turnover rate for telephone operators on a toll-free 800 line. They selected a word at random—"prison"—and searched for similarities, connections, and associations between "prisons" and "turnover of telephone operators." After generating many novel ideas, the one they adopted and implemented was to use prisoners to handle their 800 calls.

The idea: They test minimum-security and outside trustee inmates, and offer a two-day training course to the best qualified. Graduates can handle responses from TV, radio, catalogs, dealer referrals, and magazine subscriptions on a toll-free line. Thirty percent of their operators are now prisoners, and the results have been spectacular.

The inmates can earn up to $6 an hour, substantially more than prison pay. They are allowed to keep a portion of their earnings for personal use, a portion goes to a victims' restitution program, and the rest is held in a fund until they are released. In addition, they are considered for full-time employment upon release from prison.

A company spokesman says that they would never have come up with this idea without Brutethink.

WHY BRUTETHINK WORKS

In tetherball, a ball is fastened to a slender cord suspended from the top of a pole. Players bat the ball around the pole, attempting to wind its cord around the pole above a certain point. Obviously, a tethered ball on a long string is able to move in many different directions, but it cannot get away from the pole. If you whack at it long enough, eventually you will wind the cord around the pole. This is a closed system. Like tetherball, human thought tends toward a closed system.

The human brain cannot deliberately concentrate on two separate objects or ideas without eventually forming a connection between them. No two inputs can remain separate in your mind no matter how remote they are from each other. Eventually, like the tetherball, you will wind one around the other. The trick is to hold both of them in your attention and to *look* for relationships and connections between the two. Your attention is the restraint that helps make this a closed system. Once you become aware, you will routinely see connections between dissimilar things.

Many of these connections will be less than complete. The figures below are easily perceived as a triangle, a face, and a circle, even though none of the figures is complete. The brain tends to fill in the gaps in order to perceive complete forms, and to fill in the missing information to make a relationship whole.

The connections will provide you with new information about your challenge: a different perspective about the problem or perhaps an analogy that has its own line of development.

Imagine your challenge is: "In what ways might I improve my relationship with my manager?" You randomly select the word "pencil." You might think the relationships and connections between your challenge and a pencil are:

1. *Eraser.* We both keep bringing up past failures. We need to erase them.

2. *Shaft.* He gives me too much to handle. I'm getting the shaft in my territory because of office work. I need help.

3. *Yellow.* I don't have the courage to confront him and have a heart-to-heart conversation about my career. Perhaps I could do it informally after work?

4. *Lead.* Get the lead out. His support and follow-up are always late and this is hurting me financially. Can I get support from other areas?

5. *Gold circle.* He doesn't think I'm going after the lucrative accounts. How can I demonstrate my commitment?

6. *Cheap.* Our commission plan is not equal to others in the industry. Should I propose a new plan?

7. *Six sides to a pencil.* The six most important things to work on are: improve communications, have a heart-to-heart about my career, propose new commission plan, prioritize accounts, improve time management, and create new ways to follow-up on accounts.

You can now identify many issues and many ways to respond to the challenge of trying to improve your relationship. A chain of ideas stretches out from the random word to link up with the challenge. Some of the links may be helpful, others not. The purpose of using a random word is to generate a large number of different ideas in a short period of time.

The random word "pencil" is used to get things going, to get your creative juices flowing. The key is to do *something*. Nothing happens until you start thinking. You know that empty feeling that comes from stating a challenge and not being able to produce a single idea. You feel like a dead atheist all dressed up in your best suit with no place to go.

BLUEPRINT

1. *When you are looking for a fresh approach to a challenge, bring in a random word.* The word you bring in must be truly random and not selected for any relevance to the stated challenge. Random words will spark a fresh association of ideas in your mind. Like pebbles dropped in a pond, they stimulate other associations, some of which may help you to a breakthrough idea.

   Random words from unrelated contexts are a rich source of connection-making material. There are several ways to select a random word. Among them are:

   • *Soap, Soup, and Sand.* At the end of this chapter is a list of random words—close your eyes and point to one of them with a pencil. Do *not* read the list and select the most likely word for your purposes.

   • Retrieve a random word from a dictionary by opening it, by chance, to any page. Make a point of using only one word per challenge per day. Just knowing that you are going to use another word can defeat the effectiveness of this Thinkertoy.

   • Use a table of random numbers to select a page in the dictionary, and perhaps the word on the page as well. You can also just take the page and word numbers up off the top of your head.

   • You can use any other method so long as you do not deliberately select a word.

   The best words are simple and familiar, words you know well enough that it is easy to visualize the objects they represent. *Soap, Soup, and Sand* is an excellent collection, because the words are:

Simple: You have used these words repeatedly through-out most of your life.

Visual: They easily evoke images.

Connection-rich: Each word will trigger other words and images. For example, "soap" might make you think of baths, showers, sinks, public restrooms, bubbles, lard and other ingredients that make up soap, laundry, soap commercials, slipping on a bar of soap, other products that soap manufac-turers make, and so on.

2. *Think of a variety of things that are associated with your cho-sen word.* Suppose you randomly select "bottle." What are the characteristics of a bottle? What does a bottle do? It contains. What can you do with a bottle? Cork it. Fill it. Empty it. Bottles have labels. Bottles are transparent. Bot-tles are made of glass and plastic. Bottles bring refunds. Bottles are functional and sometimes are aesthetic as well. Beer bottles are packaged in six-packs. You can buy single bottles, packs of bottles, or cartons of bottles.

3. *Force connections.* Make a forced connection between your random word and the challenge you are working on. Suppose your challenge is:

"In what ways might I increase sales this month?"

You select "bottle" as your random word. Draw a picture of a bottle and think about the similarities, con-nections, and associations between "bottles" and "increasing sales."

- Bottles can be filled up. How much are we listening to the customers? Should we devise a program or programs that would allow customers to fill us up with their true needs and desires?

- Six-packs. Can we repackage our goods and services in a new and novel way to differentiate ourselves from all others? Can we make the package part of the product's form?

- Point of purchase. Beverages can be bought singly, in packs, or in cartons. Should we offer different pack-ages for different customer needs?

- Bottles bring refunds. Should we develop a creative financing program that gives rebates for repeat purchases? Should we give rebates when we replace goods or services with newer ones?

- Empty bottles make noise. How much of my work is useful and profit-oriented? Can I develop an index to rate my activities in terms of profit and potential and then discontinue the empty activities?

- Bottles have labels. Should I look for ways to label our goods in such a way that we are easily differentiated from competitors? Labels list ingredients and expiration dates. Should we price our goods and services with a certain time frame to encourage early purchases?

- Empty bottles are sometimes used for holding flowers, or as aesthetic fixtures. Can we develop other uses for our packaging that would add value to our goods? Can the package be made functional? Can we find other uses and markets for our used goods and services?

- Bottles come in various shapes and sizes. Should we develop a greater array of options? Low-end and high-end markets? Different prices for different packages based on customer needs? How many different ways can we reshape our goods and services?

- Bottles are useless when empty. Salespeople continue to work, even when drained of techniques, energy, and ideas. Perhaps some kind of peer jury should examine salespeople once a month to keep them motivated and fresh.

- Bottles break. When a bottle slips from your hand it falls to the floor and breaks. How can we prevent the factory from slipping up on orders and causing lost sales?

4. *List your ideas.* Otherwise, you won't remember them. Not recording your ideas is like sitting in a shower of gold with nothing but a pitchfork.

Allow yourself five minutes for this exercise; this should be ample time. You will find that connections and ideas are still occurring long after your five minutes are up. A good way to practice this technique is to use a random word on some problem for five minutes every day.

Imagine that the CEO of a company is reluctant to make decisions. Other people often cannot act until he makes a decision, yet he delays and waffles for days about even minor matters. The challenge is: "In what ways might we get the CEO to make decisions?"

I randomly select the word "rotating spit." I draw a picture of a rotating spit and think of links, relationships, and associations between "spits" and "indecisive CEOs."

The attributes of a rotating spit could be:

1. Active way to cook.

2. Self-basting.

3. Expensive current.

4. Cooks all the time with constant turning.

5. Put items on in a certain order and take them off in a certain order.

6. Cooks different objects.

7. Heat source, timer, and control are all on same unit.

8. Objects being cooked appear and then disappear from sight.

What connections can you make between the challenge and the attributes listed above? What solution would you propose to the challenge of the reluctant CEO?

My proposed solution would incorporate ideas generated by attributes 1, 4, 5, 6, and 8. Proposal: Consider forming two or three panels that represent different areas, such as manufacturing, marketing, and accounting (cooks different objects). The panels would be comprised of people the CEO respects.

The CEO makes a fast initial decision and gives it to the appropriate panel for review. The panel gives their opinion and sends it back to the CEO who finalizes it or changes it (active way to cook; cooks all the time with constant turning; cooks different objects; items put on in a certain order and taken off in a certain order; objects being cooked appear and then disappear from sight).

This encourages fast initial decisions because the panel review minimizes risk to the CEO, encourages fast analysis because people on the panel need a decision in order to act, and engenders fast final decisions because the panel shares the risk.

In the end, the final idea of having different panels assist the CEO is much like putting the decision on a rotating spit:

1. Active way to make decisions.

2. Decisions being made all the time with constant turning of topics.

3. Decisions are put on in a certain order and taken off in a certain order.

4. Decisions are made on different topics.

5. Topics being decided appear and then disappear from sight.

Ultimately, you will not use most of the connections you come up with, but you can't prejudge which lines of thought will be fruitful—let alone which lines of thought will lead to a big idea, like a wondrously painted Easter egg waiting for someone to part the grass and find it.

Recently, I purchased a stale candy bar from a vending machine. Obviously, people were not patronizing the machine. I selected as my challenge: "In what ways might I improve business for vending machines?"

I randomly selected the word "casino." Among the things the word made me think about were gambling and roulette wheels. These two thoughts merged with my challenge to create a new idea for vending machines.

The idea: A vending machine that would tempt passersby with a roulette-style game. You insert your coin, make your selection, and a roulette wheel starts spinning; if it stops on the lucky number you get your selection free.

Sometimes searching for ideas is like being a mosquito in a nudist colony. You know what you want to do but don't know where to begin. Forcing connections between random words gives you one starting point, but there are some other useful ways to stimulate the random juxtaposition of ideas.

VERBS AND NOUNS

Play with noun and verb relationships to think up new and useful ideas, goods, and services. For instance, take the sales problem for which we randomly chose the word "bottle." Consider the words bottle and sales as both nouns and verbs: "bottling sales" and "selling bottles." Bottling sales suggests looking for ways to close sales; selling bottles suggests looking at ways beverages are sold and distributed.

PACK RAT

Collect and store ideas like a pack rat. Keep a container (coffee can, shoe box, desk drawer, file folder, or the like) of ideas and idea starters. Collect interesting advertisements, quotes, designs, ideas, questions, cartoons, pictures, doodles, words, and other intriguing items that might trigger additional ideas by association.

When you are looking for a new idea, shake up the container and pick one at random, then see what intriguing connections you can discover between the item and your challenge. You may find a diamond shining in the trash.

MAGAZINES

Randomly pick up a magazine and read one article, no matter how remote its subject is to your challenge. Then contemplate the connections between the article and your challenge; try to generate some new ideas. Any such exercise is extremely valuable in helping you set up and cultivate habits that encourage random input.

SHAPES

Select a shape, such as a circle, and focus on that shape for a day. When you enter a room, pay attention only to objects that are circular, and try to make connections between those objects and your challenge.

Here is another way this can work: Assume I want to open an unusual restaurant. I select the circle as my shape and decide to focus on three circular things: oysters, the shape your mouth makes when you say "Owww," and Dante's circles of Hell.

The idea: A restaurant called "The Cruel Grill." The restaurant could feature a grill where patrons could watch the food being prepared. The menu would feature items such as oysters, which could be placed on a grill while still alive. As they fry, their shells would open and shut, making sounds. Shrimp, lobster, and other shellfish could be broiled alive. You could advertise it as the restaurant that serves cuisine from Hell. Such restaurants are already quite popular in Japan.

SUMMARY

Looking for ideas using Brutethink is like sleeping under a too-short blanket. You pull it up, and your toes rebel; you yank it down, and your shoulders shiver; but cheerful folks always manage to yank and pull until they get it just right and sleep in comfort. *Your* comfort results from yanking and pulling on dissimilar objects until you come up with new ideas.

SOAP, SOUP, AND SAND

The words that follow are simple, visual, and connection-rich. They are designed to be used with this Thinkertoy for solving challenges.

bench envelope broom radio landlord cashier toast soup soap beer shoe egg
meat cup umbrella hook door window roof lake violin candy gutter
computer paint man glue water bottle neon light shaft prison bag chain
torpedo ladle insect rose fly fossil butter nut twig bird sword motor
monster dog field gun acid stamp beetle sun summer ice dust Bible drum
fog football bridge rope pulley toe woman plow mattress sunset gate clock
rash car road zoo museum painting sand menu index book ashtray lighter
hip mouse poster aisle milk horse tide knot seed weed bruise toilet closet
shirt pocket pipe rubber cancer plane pill ticket tool hammer circle needle
rag smoke referee sky ocean pepper valve triangle thermostat tube octopus
hook magnet spaghetti disco thumbtack tie sink bifocals television
Jell-O eye pot wedding ring wine taxes pig hoe mouse wok gondola
coconut telephone sleet toll notebook dictionary file lobby clouds volcano
suitcase fish lamp library university fulcrum barbecue canister chimney
rotating spit toxic waste coffee groundhog ribcage parking lot lungs speech
math war brunch sailboat mirrors burdock sludge wastebasket watch flag
helmet eye cactus cowboy tavern butterfly cube X-ray money magazine
screwdriver VCR stereo ink ditches razor tea eyedropper actor homeless
queen artist storm Indian snake fox lobster Satan balloon sauce acne crystal
shrimp army beet brick prostitute catsup explosives diamond camel leaf train
lunch meat liquor pilot lipstick caviar perfume gum cheese flame fruit ham
highway lingerie jellybean bubble choirboy penis pet hair dye eraser bikini
canyon cards button riot jacket film runway flamingo police White House
lava rainforest island sunrise plastic Hindu clay gourmet roast heat limo
campfire fireworks tomato tongue fracture watermelon Christmas politician
quail handball AK-47 donut madman peanut dance song congress arrow
honey bath igloo tub ruler nomad subway mass missing link vein truck
monk dinner label laboratory sandpaper wedge sundial squirrel mustache
organ molar ghetto bag lady ghost athlete herd flute rod constitution
handkerchief key trophy zodiac turkey surf refrigerator dragon turtle seaweed
goulash mud ostrich vine worm planet opera chameleon wart olive map
coupon foam nosebleed mushroom gasoline music recess rain hockey eel
rocket barge trash pyramid dome chapel thunder caterpillars jaguar firefly
wasp moon moss panda stomach brush gland intestine roach exhibition
holocaust ax lamb doorbell marble knot pump umpire shark onion garage
rum attic fireplace deli knapsack circus ant clamp wrench bum software star
crown curb fingerprint guerilla iodine jam silver microscope nail piston
priest doctor salt mouth horizon griddle candle banjo anteater tent funeral
gear carpet windsurfer champagne salmon underwear diaper lug nut microphone

paperweight griddle rifle paperclip EKG copier desk vibrator earrings shower podium Scotch hat jet soda stoplight confession roulette spaceship judge explorer dice electrical outlet nose drain bookmark torch tomb can gold spear beans sparkplug bat lawnmower pothole bookends fly cufflinks belt tile piano skyline creek snow biology cow cowboy bandage calendar calculator cake fence toothbrush rainbow apartment wagon magnifying glass wire dock rock top cursor tire drawer sock taxi zebra elevator stairs brunch ladder bus toy hair rubber band pond dream pencil steak template compass tattoo insulation wheat legs bread paper soda insurance pennant chess stew waiter goose sandwich sneakers chair gutters zipper want ads vest crab lottery rake soldier disk necklace flashlight monument dam teacher bank China fan steering wheel silk earthquake supermarket leash teabag noodles theater mast cabin bone buffalo kite hoop archer hunter ballet shotgun dirt cream skin spoon swing skates curtain wax hose golf fortun cookie change atlas phonebook cuffs vacuum courthouse chips blindfold teeth flowers whale chocolate mantle ball bearings lock terrorist dishwasher laundry toolbox chopsticks bathrobe conscience chalk pool table jar bracelet satellite boot helicopter fishing pole rice puddle wind comic roller mat Volkswagen safari lightning sculpture board keyboard fig pole oceanfront townhouse angel drill orange tobacco myth journey child eagle costume Heaven brain minnow society examination Genesis sin shadow cells fetus hand sex fire poem blood castle psychology Grail symbol globe mow cross intersection parent blueprint forest wigwam iceberg snail jungle syrup parachute pudding parsley ape sidewalk vodka suicide maid comb picture frame jeep Rolex mailbox shampoo pendant rail megaphone skyscraper skyline hubcap carton sugar match deadbolt steam saucer remote control boxing glove noose jeans aerial crayons pipe cleaner ribbon pencil sharpener battery wheel baton orchestra suspenders brassiere tractor candlestick newspaper secretary salesman wallpaper tower kitchen magnifier garden general eyebrow chapter catalog bonnet butcher dinette bed locker professor cereal cotton brochure mime elbow medal fountain fingernail beard student thumb basket purse arch cloak jazz block screen vase basement logo torso pickle pigeon whip lint meatball tape coffin meadow cyclone lips watermelon knee swamp furnace bingo weeds paper studio patch bleach cord pliers magician faucet mason jewels lap sweater band frost girdle stove hotel nipple telescope RV grandfather clock cruise ship stage binoculars audience fur juice buffet husband bacteria spirit sauna Monopoly mold teenager handcuffs Tinkertoys chess scaffold easel flood cockroach frying pan crewcut Hell miracle palm tree choir frankfurter trivia crust oasis stream hostage dandruff rib popovers dope frog pilot milkshake wheelbarrow level aunt pimple pizzeria balcony Communist hedge thesaurus workshop cheesecake gang shelf celebrity rectum leather snowflake salad senator bomb airport cornmeal cornstalks manure cur trumpet cone temperature sauna howitzer rally merchant box willow stick canteen gourd polyester Stetson minute IRA office wand graph amplifier line bagel beef floor barn dolphin aircraft carrier submarine reef casino revolution bow kneecap borscht raincoat dawn steam engine cliff seam tumor zone office psychology Easter scar dancer hero fear hamburger welfare Vaseline media laughter principal script contract forecast grid herring warrior occult putter bush tugboat bonds glove compartment wig deodorizer news display interest leopard team staple hearing aid expressway breeze postcard beets photograph scalp cremation network scripture anchor cauliflower pack rat cult dime robotics engineer tar maple classroom Pope statistician bomber textbook border sagebrush aluminum shutter safety pin cargo lemon garter mustard seed symbol logo United Nations grammar fertilizer feast cigar ornament disease poppy horseradish group strip spinach dividend hospital tank sonar sardine binding scab detective England dumpling prune poker gravy mulch poetry nude trial traveler fraction sausage headhunter matchsticks fat rabbit duck words cartridge dwarf mat shuttle DC-10 bulletin plum check checkers FAA wildfires bluebells vinyl brakes cavity pornography landfill wages vacation dial CIA mosquito cherry rattlesnake saxophone auditorium timer dill cork condom microwave rhinoceros marshmallow scarecrow beam scallop pumpkin plumber lizard lounge official eggshell Peace Corps fugitive gully Hawaii lantern sulfur alligator cobra cattails giraffe ranch vampire emerald confederacy cradle alphabet lettuce reindeer paintbrush dynamite beam supertanker Astrodome cheetah Olympics trout scissors dune forehead Jerusalem muffler résumé chuckhole jellyfish liver shield fuel Japan lacrosse parakeet hock excrement vines

HALL OF FAME

"And therefore only the enlightened sovereign
and the worthy general who are able to use
the most intelligent people as agents are
certain to achieve great things."

SUN TZU

Imagine a man jumping from one boat to another. At the outset, the boats are more or less parallel to one another. As the man jumps from the stern of one boat, it turns and whirls in reaction to his motion. When he lands in the stern of the other boat, it whirls toward the first boat. Rather than going in opposite directions, the boats run into each other.

This is the way your mind works; for every action there is a reaction. When looking for ideas, picture yourself jumping from your challenge to a quotation or great thought. The quotation, like the boat, will turn and crash into your challenge, sparking a new idea.

Hall of Fame helps you gain new insight into your challenges by consulting the world's great minds, both real and fictional. Quotations contain seeds and principles of ideas that can be applied to a variety of challenges, and when you find the seed of one idea you find many ideas.

RESOURCES

To use this Thinkertoy, you'll need quotations. Some suggestions:

- Two of the best reference books are *Bartlett's Familiar Quotations* and Edward's *Dictionary of Thoughts,* but there are countless other reference books containing quotations and thoughts from the world's great thinkers.

- Collect your own quotations and thoughts from books, biographies, the Bible, the Talmud, newspapers, magazines, cartoons, movies, and television. Record and collect any quotation that appeals to you. You can categorize them according to subject, or randomly. Some of my favorites come from the Talmud:

    "He who walks with butter on his head should not walk in the sun."

    "Don't hitch a horse and an ox to the same wagon."

    "One coin in a bottle rattles; the bottle filled with coins makes no noise."

    "Woe to him who makes a door before he has a house or builds a gate and has no yard."

    "If two logs are dry and one is wet, the kindling of the two will kindle the wet one, too."

    "Just as wheat is not without straw, so no dream is without some nonsense."

- Some of my other favorite quotations:

    "Ruling a big country is like cooking small fish."—Lao Tzu

    "Where the telescope ends, the microscope begins. Which of the two has the grander view?"—Victor Hugo

    "There are two ways to spread the light, to be the candle or the mirror that reflects it."—Edith Wharton

    "God is a geometrician."—Plato

    "Handle your tools without mittens; remember that the cat in gloves catches no mice."—Ben Franklin

    "The perfection of art is to conceal art."—Quintilian

"Not only strike while the iron is hot, but make it hot by striking."—Oliver Cromwell

"And I must find every changing shape, to find expression." —T. S. Eliot

"When you eliminated the impossible, whatever remains, however improbable, must be the truth."—Arthur Conan Doyle

"Form ever follows function."—Louis Henri Sullivan

BLUEPRINT

1. *Create your personal Hall of Fame.* Select those people, living or dead, real or fictional, who appeal to you for one reason or another. Following are some of the members of my personal Hall of Fame:

Ben Franklin	Sherlock Holmes	Jesus Christ
Bill Moyers	Diogenes	Julius Caesar
Mark Twain	Ralph Waldo Emerson	Plato
Clarence Darrow	Andrew Jackson	William Shakespeare
Rupert Murdock	Sigmund Freud	Aristotle
George Patton	Peter the Great	Robert Frost
John F. Kennedy	Leonardo da Vinci	Eugene O'Neill
Dorothy Parker	Pearl Buck	Aldous Huxley
W. Somerset	Adlai Stevenson	Sun Tzu
Maugham	Albert Schweitzer	Thomas Jefferson
Winston Churchill		

2. *When you have a challenge, consult your Hall of Fame.* Select an adviser and choose a favorite quotation.

3. *Ponder the quotation.* Write down your thoughts, regardless of appropriateness to the challenge. If you think it, write it, and try to use these thoughts to generate more relevant thoughts. The basic rules are:

> Strive for quantity.
> Defer judgment.
> Freewheel.
> Seek to combine and improve your thoughts.

4. *Choose the thought or combination of thoughts that holds the most promise.* Then restate it.

5. *Allow yourself five to ten minutes to come up with new ideas.* If you produce nothing significant, select another quote or go to another adviser. Keep consulting your Hall of Fame until a quote or passage provokes a train of usable ideas.

Suppose my challenge is: "In what ways might I increase my repeat sales?"

I raid my personal Hall of Fame and select Robert Frost to act as my working consultant on the challenge. I look up Robert Frost in *Bartlett's Familiar Quotations* and review various passages, finally selecting:

"The woods are lovely, dark and deep.
But I have promises to keep,
And miles to go before I sleep."

You can review all of Frost and then select one passage, or pick one at random. I chose this one because there seemed to be some link between this passage and my challenge of improving repeat sales.

I record the thoughts and ideas that the quote elicits from me, without censoring. There are no wrong answers. I write whatever comes to mind, and end up with:

- What does the customer see as important? How can I deliver?

- Can I go the extra mile for the customer? Will it make a difference? Will they become loyal purchasers? What can we do?

- Woods are full of trees. Trees are customers. How are trees tended? Cared for? Harvested? What similarities are there between trees and customers? Can I nourish customers daily? Weekly?

- What are the customer's deep and dark desires? Can I discover them?

- Should I work harder? Longer?

- Should I make company promises in writing?

- Should we rewrite our guarantees?

- What can I do so the customer perceives me as honest and hard-working?

- Wood comes from trees. Wood builds. In what ways can I build better relationships with customers? More establishment? More service? Problem solving? Provide information?

- Robert Frost made personal appearances. Should we have executives make personal calls? Seminars?

- Trees are pruned. Do I have too many customers? Should I prune the unprofitable accounts so I can devote more time to our profitable ones?

The thought that seems to hold the most promise for me is the insight into building better relationships with customers. I restate it as: "How can I build profitable relationships with customers?"

The resulting ideas for building better customer relationships are:

- Analyze the customer's problems and provide the best and most current product information possible to help them address their problems.

- Entertain customers more with the idea of finding out what's important and what is not to the customer.

- Ask key customers to work for me as consultants.

- Help the customer do more business by supporting their endeavors more. Suggest and initiate marketing programs for key customers.

- Inform them about what their competition is doing. Become a clearinghouse of information about the customer's competition.

- Make sure salespeople are compatible with their accounts; if not, switch accounts to ensure compatibility between salespeople and customers.

- Give loyal customers preferential treatment. Larger discounts, a special service line, guaranteed response time, better credit terms, and so on.

Ideas that come from the words and thoughts of others often come through a new route in the imagination by a new and express train of associations.

For years, I was bothered by the ugly speakers that came with my stereo. Finally, I decided to do something about it. I formulated my challenge: "In what ways might I improve the appearance of my speakers?"

I selected Henry David Thoreau for my advisor, looked up Thoreau in *Bartlett's*, and randomly selected:

> "I am a parcel of vain strivings tied
> by a chance band together."

I free-associated from this thought, writing down everything that came to mind. Two of the ideas were significant:

- "Band together"—combine speakers with some other item or items.

- "Vain striving"—make speakers something aesthetic.

I restated the challenge to: "In what ways might I combine my speakers with an aesthetic object?"

I hired a designer to disguise my speakers as ceramic vases. She was so intrigued with my idea that she started a new business that disguises speakers in a variety of aesthetic objects.

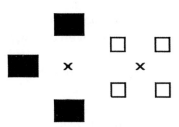

Quotations will give you a new perspective on your challenge. For a graphic demonstration of the difference perspective can make, cover the white squares above and focus on the X next to the black rectangle for thirty seconds. Then, look at the X in the center of the white squares. The vertical distance between the left-hand pair of squares will now appear greater than that between the right-hand pair.

By concentrating on the black, you changed your perspective and created movement of the left-hand pair of squares. When you concentrate on a quotation, your perspective on your challenge will be changed, which will move your imagination to think of new things.

An inventor read about an elderly woman who was so desperate to take her arthritis medicine that, unable to get the child-resistant cap off, she chewed through the bottom of the plastic bottle. He formulated the challenge: "In what ways might I make drug caps more accessible to older people?"

He reached into his box of quotations for something to stir his imagination and pulled out:

"It is always good when a man has two irons in the fire."—Francis Beaumont

His significant thought centered on "two irons." A drug bottle has two tops, the safety cap and the regular cap. The number "two" also provoked him to look for solutions that were not part of the bottle. The bottle + a tool = a solution.

The idea: He developed a pliers-like tool that can cut through or pull off the safety cap mechanism, leaving only the regular cap underneath.

A dead coal can be rekindled when a live coal is placed next to it. When your creative fire has gone out, place a quotation or great thought in your mind to rekindle it. For variety, you may wish to try another way of consulting advisors: Create your own personal, imaginary Board of Directors.

BOARD OF DIRECTORS

The Board of Directors is a fantasy board of powerhouse business leaders and innovators who will assist you in overcoming your business challenges. Imagine having at your disposal the experience, wisdom, and know-how of Thomas Edison, Douglas MacArthur, Alfred Sloan Jr., Lee Iacocca, Thomas Watson, John D. Rockefeller, Bernard Baruch, Sam Walton, Andrew Carnegie, J. P. Morgan, Henry Ford, Donald Trump, Ted Turner, or whomever you admire most, living or dead.

BLUEPRINT

1. *Select the three to five business movers and shakers, living or dead, whom you admire most.*

2. *Get photographs of your Board (these could be photocopied from magazines),* and pin them on your wall in a prominent spot. These photographs will constantly remind you of the talent at your disposal.

3. *Research your heroes:* Hit the library, read their biographies and autobiographies, read what their critics say about them; in short, read everything about your heroes that you can get your hands on.

4. *Take notes on your favorite passages,* perhaps about obstacles and how they overcame them, or anything that strikes you as relevant and interesting. Pay particular attention to the creative techniques they employed to solve problems, their secrets, what made them stand out, what made them extraordinary, and so on. Keep a separate file on each hero.

5. *When you have a challenge, consult the members of your board and imagine how they would solve it.* How would Henry Ford resolve a labor problem? Can you think of the ways Thomas Edison would suggest to look for new products or services? How could you use Thomas Watson's sales techniques?

CONSULTING THE BOARD

The sales manager of a tire company was concerned about flat sales. His challenge was: "In what ways might we improve tire sales?" He consulted his file on super salesman Thomas Watson. Watson's history inspired him to consider ideas about better motivating *all* employees to sell, not just salespeople. Watson's question became this: "How can I get the people to put their heart into the business and the business into their heart?" Turning to his next adviser, David Packard, he noted the quote "by having overall objectives that are clearly stated and agreed to." He also became intrigued by the entrepreneurial atmosphere Packard created at Hewlitt-Packard. Now, in addition to motivation, he considered the entrepreneurial spirit and agreed-to objectives.

His challenge became: "In what ways might we clearly state objectives that everyone agrees to; objectives that will foster an entrepreneurial attitude and will motivate all employees to participate in selling tires?"

The idea: The objective everyone agreed to was for all employees to participate in selling tires. Our sales manager asked each employee to chip in one dollar a week to finance promoting the tires with shopping mall displays and cards left on windshields. This small contribution gave employees a sense of ownership (entrepreneurial attitude). To get the employees excited and give them a new sense of purpose (motivation), he exhorted them with speeches, songs, and slogans (such as "We make them, we can sell them"). He asked all employees to sponsor and participate in a tire-selling campaign.

SUMMARY

> "As is your sort of mind,
> So is your sort of search; you'll find
> What you desire."
> Robert Browning

Have someone hold up a newspaper just far enough away that you cannot read the headline. Ask the person to tell you what the headline says. As soon as they do, you will actually be able to read it. This is known as the newspaper headline illusion, and it is based on expectation. You read the headline because you *think* you can read the headline because you *expect* to read it.

If you expect to find ideas in the thoughts and words of others, you will believe you can, and you will.

—

CHAPTER NINETEEN

CIRCLE OF OPPORTUNITY

"The flavors are only five in number
but their blends are so various that
one cannot taste them all."

SUN TZU

179

Landing a plane is a delicate, dangerous operation requiring exact timing, so air traffic controllers land only one or two airplanes at a time. If traffic is heavy, inbound flights "stack up" above the airport, waiting for clearance. Getting ideas can be delicate as well. Circle of Opportunity randomly isolates one or two attributes of your challenge for comprehensive consideration—all the other attributes stay "stacked up," allowing you to comprehend or "land" a new idea.

If you concentrate long enough on the figure, the circles will begin to appear hexagonal. Prolonged viewing also causes triangular, hexagonal, and rhomboid groupings of the circles to emerge.

By using selective concentration, you allow your brain to process the circles into a variety of new and different shapes, assigning them new meanings.

Concentrated study of one or two randomly selected attributes will allow your brain to process existing information into new relationships and meanings, which leads to original ideas and insights.

BLUEPRINT

To play Circle of Opportunity, you need a pair of dice.

1. *State the challenge you want to solve.*

2. *Draw a circle and number it like a clock (1 through 12).*

3. *Select any twelve common attributes,* or choose twelve attributes specific to your challenge. (Think of attributes as the various aspects of a subject.) Write the attributes next to the numbers on your circle.

Common attributes include substance, structure, color, shape, texture, sound, taste, odor, space, and density; marketing, selling, manufacturing, function, and time; responsibilities, politics, and taboos.

4. *Throw one die to choose the first attribute to focus on.*

5. *Throw both dice to choose the second attribute.*

6. *Consider the attributes both separately and combined.* Free-associate about the individual attributes and the combination.

Free-associating is a great way to release creative energy. Start with your first idea about the attribute and keep making connections until you trigger an idea or the beginning of a line of speculation. Free-associating should feel like driving a car around a long, gentle curve until you arrive at something worthwhile. In the figure below, the attribute "yellow" spreads into a number of associations.

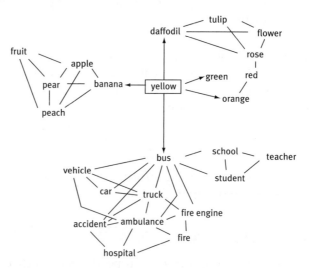

The spread of association resembles what happens when you drop a stone into a pool of still water. The magnitude of the disturbance depends upon the size of the stone and the amount of time elapsed since the rock entered the water. The spread of associations depends upon the strength of the initial attribute and the amount of time that has passed since you did the exercise. When the links are strong, the associations will spread far and fast; when the links are weak, the spread will be slow and restricted.

Write down the associations as they occur to you.

7. *Search for a link between your associations and your challenge.* Ask yourself:

- What associations can I make?

- What do the associations remind me of?

- What analogies can I make from the associations?

- What are the relationships between the associations and the challenge?

- Any new insights?

An advertising agency wanted to create a novel promotional campaign for an airline. They drew up this Circle of Opportunity:

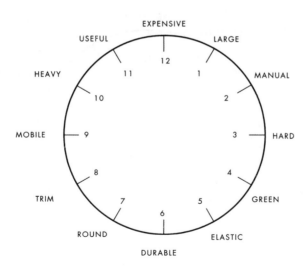

The creative director threw the dice and got 4 (green) for the first attribute and 9 (mobile) for the second.

She free-associated the following thoughts: green lawns, green eyes, green emeralds, travel, tourists, in transit, green "flash" at sunset in the Florida Keys, peas, green islands in the sun, money, green apples, and several others.

She combined green eyes, travel, and tourists to produce the idea for the campaign.

The idea: People with green eyes get 50 percent off their fare on vacation flights to the Caribbean. The airline, hoping there aren't that many green-eyed people, offers the eye-catching promotion for one year.

When you find an idea using the circle, it's like finding one of those tiny, exclusive French restaurants that have no sign. You find it almost by instinct.

A retailer looking for new ways to make money at his airport gift shop tried the Circle and rolled "round" and "elastic." He free-associated and originated a novel way to make money. He developed a simulated golf game in which players hit golf balls into an elastic net as a diversion for travelers who are delayed or stuck.

Let's construct another Circle of Opportunity with a different set of common attributes. Imagine that we are trying to come up with a new package design for a product. Instead of randomly selecting attributes, this time we'll use attributes that pertain to packaging: inexpensive, loud, rectangle, light, selling, exotic, blue, strong, words, porous, sharp, and conservative. Our circle would look like this.

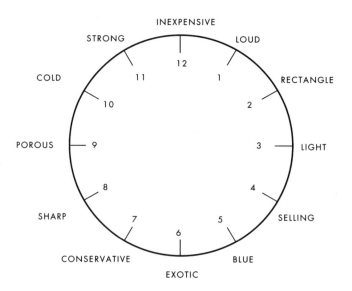

I toss the dice and get 6 (exotic) for the first attribute and 4 (selling) for the second. When I consider "exotic" and "selling" separately and combined, the associations I call up are tropical shirts, tropical islands, exotic music, quality photos of exotic locations, selling exotic things, selling my product, selling the package to the company, selling the package, selling packaging, selling exotic packaging, selling something exotically packaged, and so on. I take the material that I conjured up and, in spite of its seeming irrelevance to my stated challenge, look for ideas.

Trying several different ideas, I settle on selling packages. At first I thought of selling my idea for packaging a product to the manufacturer. Then I thought about selling exotic packaging services. And then it occurred to me: Packaging is a statement, so why not make it your own? Why not just sell packaging?

The idea: Many people tape music for their friends. Produce an audio cassette cover kit so people can package the audio tapes as gifts. The kit would contain everything to customize tapes, such as high-quality photos of exotic places with adhesive backing, a mailing envelope for sending it to a friend, and press-on lettering.

SUMMARY

The Circle leads you to explore associations and links that would not ordinarily be brought to bear on your challenge. It increases your probability of perceiving the challenge in a new way. Like mangrove trees that make their own soil, you make new ideas from within a closed circle of common attributes.

CHAPTER TWENTY

IDEATOONS

"Therefore, when I have won a victory I do not
repeat my tactics but rearrange them to
circumstances in an infinite variety of ways."

SUN TZU

Although written language evolved from pictures and symbols, it is not necessarily more advanced—after all, a great advance in computer technology was the graphic symbol. Many professions rely on graphic languages: Physicists draw diagrams, executives use charts, football coaches draw X's and O's, and corporations are known by their trademarks.

Visual and verbal thinking complement one another. As you focus on the figure below, you will notice lines A and B interchanging places. First, A will be in front, then B. Then A will be in front again, and so on.

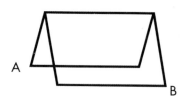

This is how visual and verbal thinking work. What we call verbal thinking is always on the outside. But the visual thinking is always there, on the inside, and when we turn our thinking inside-out, we call that thinking, too.

Consider a rubber glove with a red exterior and green interior. When the red side is out, it fits your left hand. Strip it off, turning it inside out, and it fits the right hand. First the red was visible and the green was invisible, then vice versa.

There is no right or wrong way to wear this glove; both the red and the green are equally functional. In the same way, verbal and visual thinking coexist in your mind. There is no reason to believe that one is better than the other, but we tend to rely too heavily on the verbal. Ideatoons show you how to liberalize your thinking by turning it inside out.

Visual thinking helped physicist Niels Bohr, who found language simply inadequate to describe what goes on inside the atom. Bohr reported that he originally worked out his complex atomic models not with classical mechanical notation but with pictures. Later, he translated the visual to the verbal.

Pattern language is a visual thinking technique. It was originally invented by architects Christopher Alexander, Sara Ishikawa, and Murray Silverstein to help create new building designs. The visual, flexible nature of pattern language makes it a useful creative device for seeing new and different relationships between attributes.

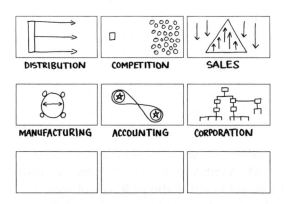

This language consists of a number of abstract visual symbols that you create to substitute for words. Do not dwell on drawing expert symbols; your drawing skills are not relevant. Remember that one blade of grass of your own raising is worth more than a wheelbarrow of roses from your neighbor's garden. The only consideration is what the graphic representations mean to you.

Some business symbols I have used are illustrated above.

BLUEPRINT

1. *Divide your challenge into attributes.*

2. *Describe each attribute by drawing an abstract graphic symbol.* Each drawing should represent a specific attribute and be on its own index card. Draw whatever feels right

for you. Allow the image of the attribute to emerge in its own way—to state what it wants to say. On the back of the card, write the attribute.

You can make pattern language as simple or as complex as you wish. One possible technique is to use a different color for each parameter of the challenge in addition to the graphic symbols that describe the attributes. For instance, in marketing a product you might have four parameters: packaging, distribution, promotion, and selling. You could draw the appropriate graphics on red cards for packaging, yellow for distribution, blue for marketing, and white for selling.

3. *Place all of the file cards on a table with the graphic symbols facing up.* Group and regroup the symbols randomly into various relationships. Try letting the cards arrange themselves without conscious direction, as if they were telling you where they wanted to be. Mix and match the symbols to provoke ideas.

4. *Look for ideas and thoughts that you can link to your challenge.* Try to force relationships. Try free-associating. Record the most idea-provoking arrangements.

5. *When stalemated, you may want to add other Ideatoons* or even start an entirely new set. A New Hampshire banker who wanted to solve the problem of stolen checks used several different sets of Ideatoons to search for a solution. Finally, the act of using pictures *itself* prompted him to think of the answer.

The idea: He invented a system that lets banks print customer's pictures on their checks.

Many people are trying to save money these days by selling their own homes. Some of their problems are:

- Not being home to show the house to a serious prospect.

- Identifying serious buyers.

- Getting key information about the house to serious prospects.

Let's work on the challenge: "In what ways might we provide a product or service to assist homeowners in getting key information to serious buyers?"

I take the whole, "the process of selling houses," divide it into attributes, and describe each attribute with a symbol.

Grouping, shuffling, and regrouping the cards, I link mailbox (from the one in front of the house), house data (taxes, selling price, points, etc.), commission (which reminded me of coins to use in vending machines), and contract (which reminded me of a roll of paper). This new set of images—a mailbox, things that dispense, house data, and rolls of paper—inspires an idea.

The idea: The "house data box," a box shaped like a mailbox that could be placed in front of the house for sale. In the box would be a roll of tear-off sheets listing information about the house such as asking price, various taxes, how long owned, points, special features, etc. The prospect would drive up, pull out an information sheet, and drive away. The serious ones would call back for an appointment. This should considerably reduce the number of missed prospects and save homeowners from wasting time saying the same thing over and over. The house data box could be manufactured and sold or rented to homeowners.

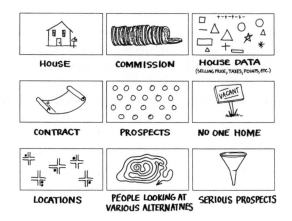

HOUSE	COMMISSION	HOUSE DATA (SELLING PRICE, TAXES, POINTS, ETC.)
CONTRACT	PROSPECTS	NO ONE HOME
LOCATIONS	PEOPLE LOOKING AT VARIOUS ALTERNATIVES	SERIOUS PROSPECTS

Physically rearranging our cards will invent new relationships and provoke new ideas. Try turning your symbols upside down and sideways to generate new patterns. Juggle the symbols and test the limits of your imagination.

An advertising executive who specialized in small billboard-type ads on buses framed the challenge: "In what ways might I create ads that once seen are never forgotten?"

He separated his challenge into several attributes. Among them were: billboards, high traffic, buses, unique, media, and memory. Using pattern language, he drew the symbols below.

His abstract symbol of a bus reminded him of a cow. Shuffling the cards again and again, he came up with the idea of billboard advertising on cows. He located farms near high-traffic areas, such as airports, and convinced the farmers to rent him space on their cows for two-by-three-foot pieces of oil-cloth carrying advertising messages. For an extra fee he offered his customers a rented cowbell to attract attention. Also, if the cow gives birth while carrying a customer's sign, that customer gets a sign on the calf for free. Billboards who have babies. What a value. Ads are commonplace, but people who see a billboard on a cow will remember it for the rest of their lives.

| BILLBOARD | HIGH TRAFFIC | UNIQUE |
| MEDIA | MEMORY | BUS |

Ideatoons is a device that allows you to express, see, and think about your business challenge in a different and unique way by seasoning your challenge with the sauce of pictures.

A travel agent looking for ways to increase business drew Ideatoons to represent practically everything he could think of that is a component of travel. He drew symbols representing airplanes, travel agencies, travel books, globes, boats, travel videos, travel audio cassettes, desks, chairs, airport lounges, and so on. He grouped and regrouped his cards. Finally, the idea bounced up and hit him.

The idea: He created a new design concept for travel agencies: A travel center with lounges for viewing travel videos, private suites for discussions, and a gift shop selling books, cassettes, and globes. His concept won a design award.

SUMMARY

Creative businesspeople have begun using pattern language to increase their capacity to divide wholes into parts and regroup the parts into a variety of new patterns. Symbols also help you develop a deeper insight into any situation. One major advertising agency in New York tests pattern language abilities in job applicants with the following exercise:

> A delegation of Martians has just landed in Central Park. They do not understand any Earth languages—only graphic symbols. Prepare a short speech composed of graphic symbols to welcome them and tell them just what kind of a place Central Park is.

Take a few minutes to compose such a graphic speech for the fun of it. How did you do?

Sometimes when your imagination has been warmed by verbal techniques—many times, too many times—it ends up like coffee that has been microwaved too often. You need to change your techniques and alter the way you use them to keep your imagination fresh-perked. Pictures permit you to look at challenges with a pair of fresh eyes. With fresh eyes, you may see the idea bouncing around on your desk like a chicken trying to avoid becoming Sunday dinner.

CHAPTER TWENTY-ONE

CLEVER TREVOR

"He who exercises no forethought but
makes light of his opponents is sure
to be captured by them."

SUN TZU

My friend Clever Trevor once said: "When a distinguished and successful expert states something is possible, he is almost certainly right. When he states something is impossible, he is very probably wrong." Some famous experts and their opinions:

Charles Duell, director of the U.S. Patent Office, in 1899: "Everything that can be invented has been invented."

Grover Cleveland in 1905: "Sensible and responsible women do not want to vote."

Robert Millikan, Nobel prizewinner in physics, in 1923: "There is no likelihood man can ever tap the power of the atom."

Lord Kelvin, president of Royal Society, in 1895: "Heavier-than-air flying machines are impossible."

The King of Prussia who predicted the failure of railroads because: "No one will pay good money to get from Berlin to Potsdam in one hour when he can ride his horse in one day for free."

Sometimes it seems that the test of a truly brilliant idea is whether or not the "experts" discount it. Often these are the ideas that later seem obvious—even to the experts.

There are as many stories about experts failing to understand new ideas as there are keys on a piano. In 1861, Philip Reis, a German inventor, built an instrument that could transmit music and was very close to transmitting speech. Experts told him there was no need for such an instrument, as "the telegraph is good enough." He discontinued his work, and it was not until fifteen years later that Alexander Graham Bell patented the telephone.

Some social scientists believe that the more expert you become in your field, the more difficult it is to create innovative ideas—or even obvious ones. This is because becoming an expert means you tend to specialize your thinking. Specializing is like brushing one tooth. You get to know that one tooth extremely well, but you lose the rest of them in the process.

When experts specialize their thinking, they put borders around subjects and search for ideas only within the borders of their expertise. This can be illustrated by the following figure of two gray squares. The square on the right of the shaded border appears brighter than the one on the left.

However, if you cover the border between the two squares with a pencil, you will discover that there is no difference; the illusion of brightness is created by the border itself.

This is what happens when experts think. They put borders around subjects and events, creating the illusion of right and wrong classifications where none, in fact, exist. Consequently, they dramatically limit their possibilities by failing to investigate the whole.

Nonexperts do not have enough expertise to draw borders. As a result, they look everywhere for ideas. This is why breakthrough ideas are usually found by nonexperts.

This is the principle that prevented the "experts" at Univac from seeing the huge business market for computers. The computer, they said, was designed for science, not business. The same thinking, in 1905, led the German manufacturer of Novocain to wage a furious national campaign to prevent dentists from using it because their company "experts" developed the drug for doctors, not dentists. And the same borders explain why virtually every "delivery expert," including the U.S. Postal Service, unanimously declared Fred Smith's concept for Federal Express unworkable, as people would not pay a fancy price for speed and reliability.

Very much aware of how experts think, Sir Clive Sinclair, the British inventor of the pocket calculator and the flat-screen television, has said that when he enters a new field, he reads "just enough to get a base, just enough to get the idiom" of the field. Anything more and he would start drawing borders.

Clever Trevor's all-time favorite story about experts is about Xerox. Chester Carlson invented xerography in 1938, but more than twenty major U.S. corporations, including IBM and Kodak, showed an "enthusiastic lack of interest" in his system, as Carlson put it. No major corporation or office-supply expert saw a market for xerography. After all, who would buy a copy machine when carbon paper was so cheap and plentiful?

To get ideas, talk to people (nonexperts) outside your field.

BLUEPRINT

1. *Talk to someone who is outside your field and from an entirely different background.* The more casual the relationship, the more likely he or she will give you a unique perspective. If you're looking for ways to increase sales, ask a priest, teacher, doctor, bartender, or Girl Scout for ideas.

   Frank Perdue (the "it takes a tough man to make a tender chicken" man) was told by the chicken experts that a chicken is a chicken is a chicken—consumers bought by price and price alone. Purdue went to work as a clerk in a supermarket and talked to housewives about chicken. He discovered what the experts and their market research did not—that the color of a chicken and unplucked feathers were more important than price.

   A gynecologist developed a new birth control device. He perfected the new design in a casual discussion before a dental exam. The dentist came up with the new shape and form almost immediately after the gynecologist described his challenge.

2. *Seek out idea-oriented people.* Surround yourself with people who love ideas and use them in their businesses and lives. They will fire up your imagination. Who is the idea person in the figure on the next page?

   Surround yourself with people:

- Who are creatively alert—people who are always offering alternatives, ideas, and suggestions about anything and everything.

- Who have a keen interest in life and are excited about being alive.

- Who are naïve about your business but not stupid or ignorant.

- Who have a great wit and see the absurdity in things.

- Who have different value systems than yours.

- Who travel and pay attention to what they observe.

- Who are voracious readers.

Make a list of friends, neighbors, and relatives who stimulate your creativity and arrange to spend more time with them. Discuss your challenges and ask them for their ideas.

A steel company executive was finding it harder and harder to locate people to work in his plant. He discussed the challenge with his minister, who suggested recruiting at local churches. They formed a network of three local churches to search for qualified parishioners, and the executive has hired every candidate the ministers have sent his way. He's thrilled with the results. "The ministers sift out the best candidates," he observes. "They don't send loafers or drifters, just solid citizens with strong families and work ethic."

3. *Draw out the creativity in strangers you meet casually.* Everyone has at least one idea that might be useful to you. H. J. Lawson got his revolutionary idea for using a chain to power the bicycle from a waiter at his favorite restaurant.

   An executive of a major motel chain was conversing casually with his garbage man about the motel business when the garbage man said, "If I were you, I'd sell pizza in my motels. You can't believe the number of pizza boxes we pick up in the trash at motels and hotels." The executive installed pizza ovens in his chain with great results. Once the garbage man said "pizza," the executive realized that he was missing out on a big market.

4. *Listen.* Joseph Kennedy withdrew his money from the stock market before the 1929 crash after listening to numerous strangers (including his bootblack) on the street warn about stock speculation. At the same time, the experts, including leading Yale economist Irving Fisher, were saying that stocks had hit a "permanently high plateau."

   Frieda Caplan listens. She is the chairperson and founder of Frieda's Finest, a thriving specialty produce company. In a field dominated by generic products and devoid of new ideas, she's created a brand identity and persuaded millions of Americans to buy fruits and vegetables they never heard of. How? By listening. Her cardinal rule: "Always have an open door; always listen to what anyone has to offer."

She listened one day when a stranger asked if she had ever heard of a fruit called the Chinese gooseberry. She had never seen one but promised to keep an eye out. Six months later, by sheer coincidence, a broker stopped by and offered a load of Chinese gooseberries. The gooseberries were fuzzy, green, wholly unappealing little fruit.

What the fruit needed was some good PR. Frieda gave the fruit a new name, one suggested by another stranger: Kiwifruit, derived from the kiwi bird of New Zealand. She convinced local restaurants to serve kiwi desserts and developed posters that explained to shoppers what a kiwi was and how it could be used.

By listening to a stranger, Frieda changed American cuisine.

LISTEN UP

Here are two simple tests that allow you to rate yourself as a listener. There are no correct or incorrect answers.

1. Circle the term that best describes you as a listener.

    Superior   Excellent   Above Average   Average

    Below Average   Poor   Terrible

    On a scale of 0–100 (100 = highest), how would you rate yourself as a listener?_____

2. On a scale of 0–100, how do you think the following people would rate you as a listener?

    Your best friend _____

    Your boss _____

Business colleague _____

A job subordinate _____

Your spouse _____

Eighty-five percent of all people rate themselves as average or less. Fewer than five percent rate themselves as superior or excellent. On the 0–100 scale, the average rating is 55.

When comparing the listening self-ratings and projected ratings of others, most respondents believe that their best friend would rate them highest as a listener—and that rating would be higher than the one they gave themselves.

People usually think their bosses would also rate them higher than they rated themselves. We tend to listen to our bosses better . . . whether it's out of respect or fear doesn't matter.

The grades for colleague and job subordinates are just about the same as the listeners rate themselves . . . around 55. But when you get to "spouse," something really dramatic happens. The score here is significantly lower than the 55 average. And what's interesting is that the figure goes steadily downhill. Newlyweds tend to rate their spouse at the same high level as their best friend. As the marriage goes on, the ratings fall. So in a household where the couple has been married fifty years, there could be a lot of talk. But maybe nobody is listening.

Following are ten keys to developing better listening habits that could last a lifetime.

TEN KEYS

1. *Find areas of interest.* Ask "what's in it for me?"

2. *Judge content, not delivery.* Skip over a speaker's errors.

3. *Hold your fire.* Don't judge until you've heard everything.

4. *Listen for ideas.* Try to discern the central themes.

5. *Be flexible.* Use four or five different systems to help you remember the content.

6. *Work at listening.* Work hard, keep your body alert.

7. *Resist distractions.* Fight or avoid distractions; tolerate bad habits and know how to concentrate.

8. *Exercise your mind.* Use difficult expository material to keep your brain working.

9. *Keep your mind open.* Interpret color words; do not get hung up on them.

10. *Capitalize on the fact that thought is faster than speech.* Challenge, anticipate, mentally summarize, weigh the evidence, and listen between the lines to tone of voice.

Most people are inefficient listeners. Tests have shown that immediately after listening to a ten-minute oral presentation, the average listener has heard, understood, properly evaluated, and retained approximately half of what was said. Within forty-eight hours, that drops off another 50 percent to a final 25 percent level of effectiveness. In other words, unless you work hard at listening, you will probably retain only one-quarter of what you hear.

SUMMARY

Multiply your ideas by multiplying the number and kind of people you talk to about your challenge.

How would you describe the following figure?

There are so many things in our world that we take for granted, noticing them only when they are brought to our attention. Why, for example, do we only see the figure as three groups of two lines each, rather than six single lines? It is because we have become experts at perceiving nearby elements as a group instead of as a row. We only realize this when it is pointed out that the lines can also be perceived as six single lines in a row.

In much the same way, we take so many things for granted in our fields that we can only notice this state of affairs when it is brought to our attention by someone outside our field.

A salesman for Panasonic hosted a birthday party for his son at which the children all played with sample camcorders. The salesman discussed the merits of the camcorders with some of his son's friends and asked for their suggestions as to how they could be improved. One of his son's friends said: "The camcorders are great, but where can I get one for left handers?" An obvious question, but apparently no one had marketed a camcorder with a viewfinder that swivels to accommodate both right-handed and left-handed people. Panasonic does now. It immediately came out with a camcorder called "The Switch-hitter."

By talking to strangers outside your field, you'll get the kind of creative fiber you can't get from your breakfast cereal.

CLEVER TREVOR

PART TWO

INTUITIVE
THINKERTOYS

Intuitive Thinkertoys allow you to tap into your unconsciousness and find the ideas that you already have.

Tilt the book slightly, and examine the figure on the previous page under a moderate light. Many people are able to see impressions of light pastel shades of colors, organized in small hexagonal cells at right angles to the diagonal lines. This is called the Luckiesh-Moss figure and was first introduced in 1933. You see the colors. Yes, no matter how hard or long you study it, you just can't explain how it works. No one has been able to explain why the colors appear in this figure.

In the same way that the mysterious colors are contained within the black lines, the answers to all our challenges are within our unconsciousness. We need only to know how to see them.

A person is sitting around minding his own business, and suddenly—flash!—he understands something he didn't understand before. As Einstein put it:

> The supreme task . . . is to arrive at those universal elementary laws from which the cosmos can be built up by pure deduction. There is no logical path to these laws; only intuition resting on sympathetic understanding.

To solve a problem, you have to believe that you already have the answer in your unconscious. It is as if you misplaced your watch somewhere in your house; if you keep searching, you will eventually find it. This is a different perspective from, "Is there a watch anywhere in this house?" The knowledge that the watch is there will lead you in your search to find it. The theory behind intuitive techniques is that at some level you already know the answer to your challenge. Once you make this assumption, you need only know how and where to look for it. This is a different perspective from, "Is there a solution?"

Increasingly, companies and universities are probing for ways to cultivate intuitive skills. In our era of rapid change, intuitive skills are more important than ever. The International Institute for Management in Lausanne, Switzerland, recently studied top managers from the United States, Europe, Japan, and Brazil. According to their findings, successful managers claim to use intuition in most major business decisions. They describe intuition as a flash of brilliance coming from an unknown source.

This section contains intuitive techniques that show you how to take advantage of your right-brain capability to perceive insights and "whole" solutions, all at once, from your unconscious. You should eventually learn to use all the intuitive techniques described in this section. Favoring only one or two techniques is like trying to learn the rules of chess by observing moves made in one small corner of the board.

Profiles

CHILLING OUT

Technique: Relaxation.
Profile: Relaxation techniques designed to clear your mind.

BLUE ROSES

Technique: Intuition.
Profile: Ways to use intuition, and how to develop it.

THE THREE B'S

Technique: Incubation.
Profile: Describes incubation and demonstrates how to use it.

RATTLESNAKES AND ROSES

Technique: Analogies.
Profile: How to use personal, direct, symbolic, and fantasy analogies to originate ideas.

STONE SOUP

Technique: Fantasy questions.
Profile: Coaches you to direct your imagination with fantasy questions and how to use the fantasies to generate ideas.

COLOR BATH

Technique: Creative visualization.
Profile: How to use colors, money, and other objects to invoke desired qualities and energies.

DREAMSCAPE

Technique: Dreams.
Profile: How to capture the ideas in your dreams.

DA VINCI'S TECHNIQUE

Technique: Drawing.
Profile: How to use freehand scribbling, doodling, and drawing to inspire ideas.

DALI'S TECHNIQUE

Technique: Hypnogogic imagery.
Profile: How to originate surrealistic imagery, and how to find the associative link between the images and your challenge.

NOT KANSAS

Technique: Imagery.
Profile: How to direct your imagination with guided imagery scenarios to find ideas in unlikely places.

THE SHADOW

Technique: Psychosynthesis.
Profile: How to create your own spiritual adviser to help you solve your challenges.

THE BOOK OF THE DEAD

Technique: Hieroglyphics.
Profile: How to find ideas in the hieroglyphics from the Egyptian Book of the Dead.

CHAPTER TWENTY-TWO

CHILLING OUT

"He who is prudent and lies in wait for an
enemy who is not will be victorious."

SUN TZU

Stars cannot be seen during the day, because their faint points of light are overwhelmed by the sun. In a similar way, some ideas cannot be discovered, because their faint points of light are overwhelmed by your brain's active beta waves, which are as noisy as a goose eating dominoes.

In the illustration, the problem is to get the beetle inside the box. Resolution seems impossible. However, if you relax, clear your mind, and stare passively at the box for a minute or two, something strange will happen: The problem will solve itself. It sort of turns inside out, and you'll see the beetle inside on the checked floor of the box. You become the medium through which the problem solves itself.

You can become the medium through which *any* problem solves itself by using relaxation and meditation. These techniques produce alpha brain waves that are slower and deeper than beta waves. Alpha waves quiet your mind so you can see the solutions that are already there.

One champion of alpha waves is financier Wayne Silby, founder of the Calvert Group, which today manages billions of dollars in assets. Silby, whose business card reads "Chief Daydreamer," occasionally retreats for inspiration to a sensory deprivation tank where he floats in warm water, sealed off from light and sound. "I went into the tank during a time when government was changing money-market deposit regulations, and I needed to think how to compete with the banks. Floating in the tank, I got the idea of joining them instead. We wound up creating an $800 million program. Often we already have the answers to our problems, but we don't quiet ourselves enough to see the solutions bubbling just below the surface."

Alpha waves are promoted by four simple things:

1. *A quiet environment.* A quiet room or a pleasant, quiet place outdoors.

2. *A specific mental technique.* If you already have a favorite technique for relaxing deeply or entering into a meditative state, practice it and use it frequently. Otherwise, use one of the techniques described in this chapter.

3. *A passive attitude.* Empty your mind. Do not dwell on thoughts as they pass through your consciousness.

4. *A comfortable position.* Select a position that will allow you to remain still for at least fifteen minutes without falling asleep.

RELAXATION TECHNIQUES
TRIPPING IN THE PAST

Recall the time when you were most relaxed and at peace with yourself and the world, in as much detail as possible. For instance, it might be a past vacation where you remember relaxing in the sun. Feel the sun and the sand. Experience the warm breezes. The seagulls. The boats. The more incidental details you remember, the deeper your relaxation will be. The experience might be a tranquil scene in the mountains, a drowsy afternoon in front of the fireplace, a crisp fall evening, or a Key West sunset. The more you practice conjuring up your most pleasant past experience, the more you will strengthen the link between the image and total relaxation.

Affirm the pleasantness you feel every time you conjure up your images. Say, "This, or something better, now manifests for me in totally satisfying and harmonious ways for my good and the good of all concerned." Trip in the past only so long as you find it enjoyable. It could be three minutes or thirty minutes. Repeat it every day, or as often as you can. The more you trip, the more you will imprint the pleasant relaxing experience upon your mind; the stronger the imprint, the more relaxing the trip becomes. With practice, this technique will help you become as cool as the other side of a pillow.

THE JELL-O SYNDROME

This is a deep-muscle relaxation technique.

Get comfortable. The basic technique is to relax your body by relaxing each muscle in turn, from your toes to your scalp. Imagine that as each muscle relaxes the tension flows out of your body. Try to relax each muscle group sequentially without exerting too much conscious effort. Let go a little at a time, stop frowning, let your arms, hands, shoulders, and jaw go. By systematically relaxing your muscle groups you can achieve a state of deep relaxation in which the conscious is subdued and quieted, and that still, small voice from the unconscious can come through.

If you have trouble relaxing your muscles in sequence, imagine that your body is a series of inflated rubber balloons. Two valves open in your feet, and your legs begin to collapse until they are two deflated rubber tires lying flat. Next the valve in your chest is opened, the air escapes, and your entire trunk goes limp. Continue with your arms, neck, and head.

When your body is totally limp, breath deeply and slowly from your stomach. Fill your lungs with air. Breath in, whisper "re-e-e-e" (pause), then exhale whispering "la-a-a-a-ax." Do this until you feel totally free and relaxed.

A slightly different way to achieve the Jell-O Syndrome begins with lying down, as comfortable as possible. Then, systematically tense each muscle group. (The groups are listed in the exercise below.) Focus on the tension in the specific muscle group, then relax. Focus on the experience of feeling the tension leave the muscle group.

Tape the following script so you can listen to it as you perform the exercise. Give yourself plenty of reminders to focus on the feelings of tension and letting go. Remember, you tense, pause, and let go.

Close your eyes. Think of deeply relaxing all of your muscles . . . now clench your fists . . . relax them . . . flex your hands toward your shoulders . . . relax them . . . place your hands on your shoulders . . . flex your biceps . . . now relax your arms by your sides . . . shrug your shoulders . . . frown . . . relax your face . . . close your eyes tightly . . . relax them . . . push your tongue against the roof of your mouth . . . relax . . . press your lips together . . . relax . . . push your head back . . . push your head forward . . . relax your neck . . . arch your back . . . relax . . . suck your stomach in, tensing the muscles . . . relax . . . tense your buttocks . . . relax them . . . flex your feet . . . relax them . . . curl your toes . . . relax them . . .

Now repeat this exercise, letting go of even more tension in each muscle group. Remember, the key to the Jell-O Syndrome is to concentrate on the tension in the muscle group and then to experience the tension leaving your body.

When your muscles are deeply relaxed, breathe from your center. Breathe through your nose, and become aware of your breathing. As you breathe in, whisper the syllable "re." Pause. Breathe out, whispering the syllable "lax." Let the air flow slowly and naturally: r-e-e-e (pause) l-a-a-a-x. Continue for ten to twenty minutes.

When you are totally relaxed, you will sense yourself drifting deeper into another level of peacefulness and spaciousness. Do not worry about whether you are successful in achieving a deep level of relaxation. Be passive and allow relaxation to occur at its own pace. Soon you'll be lying there without a care in the world like a shivering tub of Jell-O.

TRUMAN'S FOXHOLE

President Truman bore up under the stress and strain of being a wartime president better than any previous office-holder. Despite a multitude of problems, the office of the presidency did not age him or exhaust his vitality. When a reporter asked how he managed, Truman answered, "I have a foxhole in my mind." He explained that, just as a soldier has a foxhole for protection, he would retreat to his own mental foxhole, where he allowed nothing to bother him.

You can create your own inner sanctuary, and you can create it any way you want.

Close your eyes and relax as deeply as you can. Visualize yourself in an ideal environment, any place that appeals to you, such as a forest, by the sea, on a mountain, in a meadow, a cave, a foxhole, a desert, or wherever. Create a vivid mental picture of your sanctuary. It might have a house with a fireplace, a grass shack by the ocean, a spaceship orbiting Earth, or just a peaceful place surrounded by a soft light.

This is now your special place, where you can go just by closing your eyes and wishing to be there. Retreat to your own inner sanctuary whenever you wish peace and tranquility.

Denise Parker, one of the top archers in the world, creates what she calls her "happiness room," a place to which she withdraws to visualize an upcoming match. She described it this way in a *New York Times* article:

> There's stairs leading up to it and these big doors you go through. It has brown wall-to-wall carpeting, a king-sized waterbed, stack stereo, a big-screen TV and a VCR, posters of Tom Cruise and Kirk Cameron on the wall, and a fireplace that's always blazing. That's where I go when a meet's coming up. I drive up to it in a Porsche, go inside, lie down on the waterbed, and watch a tape of myself

shooting perfect arrows. Later, when I get to the tournament, everything seems familiar. Even at the Olympics, I was calm as I began to
shoot.

HOT-AIR BALLOON

Close your eyes and breathe deeply and slowly as you count backwards
from ten to one. Gradually allow yourself to feel deeply relaxed.

Imagine a giant blue hot-air balloon moored in the middle of a lush
meadow. Picture it as vividly as you can. Now, picture yourself placing all
your worries in the basket. When the compartment is fully loaded, imagine
the hot-air balloon being released from its mooring and floating away from
you. There is nothing more you need to do as the balloon carries your mental baggage into the distance.

LETTING GO

You can catch a monkey by burying a narrow-mouthed jar of nuts in the
ground. A monkey comes along, puts his paw into the jar, and grabs a handful of nuts. But the mouth of the jar is too narrow to let him withdraw his
clenched fist. The monkey is unwilling to let go of the nuts and so is trapped.
You too can be trapped by not letting go—of your beliefs, opinions, worries,
and anxieties.

If you are experiencing a mental block of some kind, try this exercise.
Imagine that your mental block is physically represented by something you
are wearing, such as a ring. Then take off the ring, and you will feel tremen-
dously relieved and relaxed.

WARM STONES

Autogenic training teaches you to move through a series of bodily states that
correspond to shifting states of consciousness. For instance, many people
find it difficult to think of an abstract notion such as relaxation; they find it
easier to think about warmth and heaviness. By thinking of making your
hands warm and your limbs heavy, you can induce a state of self-hypnosis
that enables you to relax.

Picture yourself lying stretched out on your bed. See yourself lying there
with heavy stone legs and arms. See how the mattress sinks down under
your heavy, inert weight and the pressure you are exerting on it. The mattress sags close to the floor from the weight. Close your eyes, breathe deeply,
and relax for a few minutes, then repeat silently: "My hands are warm, my
legs and arms are feeling heavy like stone." Feel the warmth creep into your
hands. Feel your arms and legs grow heavier. And heavier. And heavier.

The brain, by nature, is constantly chattering. When you are striving to become deeply relaxed, stray thoughts may arise to distract you. To quiet the ongoing chatter of consciousness, some Eastern mystics focus on a specific *Mantra,* a special sound or word repeated over and over to clear the mind.

"AUM" is a popular mantra that represents to our ears the sound of the energy of the universe, which is manifested in all things. You start in the back of your mouth "ahhhh," and then "oo," you fill the mouth, and "mm" closes the mouth. All vowel sounds are included in the pronunciation. Consonants are regarded as interruptions of the essential vowel sound. All words are fragments of "AUM." AUM is a symbolic sound that puts you in touch with the universe; the AUM of being in the world. It is called the four-element syllable. A-U-M—the fourth syllable is the silence out of which AUM arises. One need only hear Tibetan monks chanting AUM to appreciate the meaning of this word.

A Harvard study found that mantras were very useful for reducing hypertension in patients. (They used one-syllable words like "one," "me," "yam," and "oh" to avoid the religious connotations of a traditional mantra.)

An anonymous Catholic monk wrote in the fourteenth century:

> Choose one word of one syllable such as "God" or "Love": Choose whichever one you prefer, or if you like, choose another that suits your tastes, provided it is one syllable. And clasp this word tightly in your heart so that it never leaves it no matter what may happen. This word shall be your shield and your spear whether you ride in peace or war. With this word you shall beat upon the cloud and the darkness, which are above you. With this word you shall strike down thoughts of every kind and drive them beneath the cloud of forgetting.

SLEIGHT OF HEAD

Describe the figure in the margin.

If you see an old woman in full profile looking down, a slight change in focus will allow you to see a young woman looking away. (You can see the tip of the old woman's nose as the young woman's chin.) If you first saw the young woman, with a slight change in focus you can see the old one.

With a slight change in focus, you cleared your head of your initial inferences about the figure and changed the nature of the illustration. In the same way, you can clear your head of inferences about a challenge by changing your focus of attention. When you clear your head of inferences, you allow yourself to think in a more free and relaxed way. You do this by pretending to walk away from the problem.

Great ideas sometimes come when you pretend to walk away from your challenge. This technique is called "sleight of head," and it is a favorite of creative consultants for getting a group to clear their minds. While working on a particular problem, the consultant will ask clients to pretend to work on something else.

One consultant took her shoe company clients on a "pretend" excursion—a conscious walk away from the problem. One manager imagined he was on a tropical island walking on the sand in his bare feet. One of the marketing people became intrigued, and the group focused on what people enjoy about walking around without shoes. They decided it was lightness and the ability to pivot. These two attributes led to the design of a highly successful new shoe with an innovative two-piece sole that makes it easier to pivot.

In another group, engineers were wrestling with the challenge of identifying uses for a new semiconducting polymer. The consultant took the engineers on a "pretend" excursion into their favorite hobbies and sports. One of the engineers recounted a tennis game that was decided by a dubious out-of-bounds call. The engineers focused on the problems of making in-bound calls for tennis matches and suddenly came up with an imaginative new use for the polymer.

The idea: A touch-sensitive boundary for tennis courts. They created a wafer-thin material out of the polymer to ring tennis courts. The material records precisely where a ball lands, making it difficult to dispute calls.

SUMMARY

Learning how to chill out takes time. If you're uptight six days a week and you really try to relax on the seventh, then maybe the next six days aren't going to be quite as stressful. These exercises will, with practice, relax you and clear your mind. When that happens, you will begin to think the way a child skips rope, the way a mouse waltzes.

BLUE ROSES

> "It is according to the shapes that
> I lay plans for victory, but the multitude
> does not comprehend this."
>
> **SUN TZU**

In ancient times, an emperor declared that his daughter would marry the first suitor who brought her a blue rose. The emperor's daughter was as wise as she was beautiful and various suitors tried to win her, one with a sapphire rose, another with a dyed rose, and a third with a porcelain teacup on which a blue rose was painted. One evening, she met a minstrel outside the palace and fell in love. When he returned the next day, he brought a common white rose. The emperor's daughter declared that it was, indeed, a blue rose, and the wedding took place.

The emperor's daughter made her choice by relying upon her intuition. Using intuition means paying attention to your feelings and knowing their accuracy, and how well you apply them. An important assumption when using intuition is that you already know the answer.

George Washington solved his most difficult problems during the Revolutionary War with intuition. He would instruct his orderlies not to let anyone disturb him while he relaxed and intuited decisions. In fact, the founding fathers thought intuition was so important that they tried to remind us of its power on the back of the dollar bill. There is a picture of an unfinished pyramid with an eye above it. The pyramid is not complete until the seeing eye is settled in the capstone position. Or, until the intuitive component of the mind plays a major role in developing ideas or making decisions.

A number popped into Conrad Hilton's head when he was bidding for the Stevens Hotel in Chicago. He offered the number and won the world's largest hotel by $200. A number popped into Henry Heinz's head and that number, "57," became one of the most successful trademarks of that time, despite the fact that Heinz had many more than 57 fine food products. George Eastman, founder of Eastman Kodak, said that the legendary Kodak trademark "K" came to him out of the blue.

Successful managers have more than a sardine of intuition. Present an intuitive manager with a company's financial report and he or she will make an accurate assessment of the firm's strengths, weaknesses, and future. Present the same manager with a personnel problem and he or she will assess the problem and intuit the solution and/or possible courses of action. Present the same problems to managers with no intuitive skills, and you will most likely get answers scraped out of the dog dishes of business textbooks.

FIVE WAYS MANAGERS USE INTUITION

Harvard business professor Daniel Isenberg studied sixteen senior managers in major corporations. He spent days observing them as they worked, interviewing them, and having them perform various exercises designed to figure out what made them successful.

Isenberg identified five different ways successful managers use intuition:

1. To help them sense when a problem exists.

2. To rapidly perform well-learned behavior patterns.

3. To synthesize isolated bits of data and experience into an integrated picture.

4. To check on the results of rational analysis. They search until they match their "gut" feeling and their intellect.

5. To bypass in-depth analysis and come up with a quick solution. Charles Merrill of Merrill Lynch once said that if he made decisions fast, he was right 60 percent of the time. If he took time, analyzed a situation and made a decision carefully, he would be right 70 percent of the time. However, the extra 10 percent was seldom worth the time.

One manager at a film company sensed that productivity was down because of low office morale. His gut feeling led him to initiate a sports betting pool. The pool had a tremendous unifying effect on the office workers, bringing everyone from librarians to executives together. They now publish a humorous weekly update on the results, hold an end-of-the-season party, and winners routinely buy colleagues a drink. Morale and work performance have soared. The manager was able to *sense* the problem and to *feel* what would unify the office.

Intuitive people develop superior insight that enables them to perceive whole situations in sudden leaps of logic. John Mihalasky and E. Douglas Dean at the New Jersey Institute of Technology discovered that 80 percent of the CEOs whose profits doubled over a five-year period had above-average intuitive powers.

Consider George Foerstner, founder of Amana Refrigeration, Inc., and the marketing of the microwave. We had the microwave technology from the early 1940s, and many people were aware that it could be used for cooking. Yet, they believed that the consumer market didn't understand or care about microwave cooking. Foerstner didn't give a damn what the experts thought. His gut told him that it could be produced and consumers could be convinced that they need microwaves.

Foerstner demanded a microwave oven shaped like a box with a $500 price ceiling, and he persuaded consumers that they needed it. His intuitive decisions on design, price, and marketing made the microwave oven a household reality.

Look at the lines above. All of them originate at a point off the page on your lower right. Turn the book clockwise so that this point is directly in front of you. Tilt the book slightly away from you and close one eye. The lines will magically "pop" straight up from the paper.

Once you know how, you can make the lines pop up from any position. In much the same way, once you know how to use your intuition, answers and insights will pop up in your mind.

BLUEPRINT

The two basic principles of intuition are: It must be *developed*, and it should be incorporated with reason.

1. *It must be developed.* You cannot fly like an eagle with the wings of a wren. Strive to be aware of your intuition on a daily basis. How do your intuitive impulses feel? When do they occur? Practice your intuitive skills by making guesses before a situation is fully analyzed.

   To condition your intuitive mind, try asking yourself some "yes" and "no" questions to which you already know the answers. For instance: birthdates, the name of the company where you work, the names of brothers and sisters, and so on. Observe how you get the answers. You may hear a yes or no in your mind, you may *see* a yes or no, or you may see flashes of color (green for yes, and red for no). However your answer comes, concentrate on getting future answers in the same way.

   Do the same with choices. Start by thinking about a choice you have already made, and imagine the options you had when you made the choice. As you think of the choice you have already made, observe the word, phrase, image, or symbol that represents that choice. Concentrate on how you got the answer, and focus on getting future answers in the same way. Continue to remake choices you have already made, and continue to concentrate on how the response appears. Try making a few simple choices you *haven't* made before.

2. *Combine intuition with reason.* Jonas Salk, the scientist who discovered the polio vaccine, said in an interview:

   "I'm saying we should trust our intuition. I believe that the principles of the universe are revealed to us through intuition. And I think that if we combine our intuition with our reason, we can respond in an evolutionary sound way to our problems. Effective creative conceptualization requires that one incorporate reason and logic, as well as intuition and feeling."

Like a marriage counselor bringing a separated husband and wife back together, these exercises on the following pages will reintroduce you to your intuitive senses.

Telephone Calls

When the phone rings, before you answer it, ask yourself the following questions:

1. Is the call for you or someone else?

2. Is it a male or female?

3. Is it a routine call? Or is it from someone you haven't heard from in quite a while?

4. Is it long distance or local?

After the call, intuit the answers for the next call and write down the answers by the phone.

Work

If you're in sales, think about the following before you go out on calls:

1. How many sales will I close today? This week? This month?

2. Select one customer and decide what color he or she will be wearing. Solid or print? Dark or light? What mood will the person be in? Happy or depressed? Will they buy now? Later?

3. Where will you park? Near the business? What street? What is the location in relation to the office?

4. What objections do you feel the customer will raise during your presentation?

5. What will customers buy and what won't they buy?

Mail

Before the mail arrives, ask yourself:

1. How many pieces of mail will there be? How many bills? How many pieces of junk mail? Personal letters? If personal, happy news or sad? Business mail?

2. Will there be any extraordinary mail such as an announcement that you won a prize?

MEETINGS

Before a meeting, try to predict the mood of other people who will be there. Will they be happy or depressed? How will they be dressed; i.e., what colors, formal or informal, etc.? Who will be positive? Who will be negative? Who will be the best prepared? Intuit the positions of each participant on issues before issues are raised, and the results of the meeting.

Sam Walton, the founder of Wal-Mart, understood how to combine intuition with reason. Sam felt in his gut that one could build a retailing empire by ignoring major cities and offering cut-rate prices to the heartland of America. His intuition told him to bring a down-home spirit to retailing, call his employees associates, treat them like team members, and lead the cheerleading. There isn't a single graduate school of business that teaches this.

Starting with one store in 1962, Wal-Mart is now one of the largest retail empires in the world.

PROBLEM SOLVING

Professor George Turin, of the University of California at Berkeley, states that the components of solving problems with intuition are:

1. The ability to know how to attack a problem without knowing how you know.

2. The ability to relate a problem in one field to seemingly different problems in unrelated fields. The ability to see links, connections, and relationships between ideas and objects.

3. The ability to recognize the crux of a problem.

4. The ability to see in advance a general solution to the problem.

5. The ability to recognize solutions because they feel right. The ability to focus on what *may be* rather than what is.

People who are expert at the intuitive problem-solving approach can rarely provide an accurate account of how they obtained their answers and may be unclear on just what aspect of the problem they focused on.

Consider the illustration on the following page. See if you can determine the system being used to place either inside or outside the circle all the letters of the alphabet. A goes inside, B goes outside, C goes outside, D goes outside, E goes inside the circle. Where do the rest of the letters go? Can you determine the system?

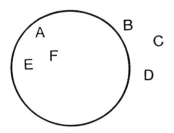

Did you solve it? If you assumed there was some complex intellectual system involved, you probably failed. The solution is in the simple shape of the letters themselves. Letters with curved lines go outside the circle, letters with only straight lines go inside. If you have strong intuitive skills, you probably saw the shape of the answer immediately.

The owner of a travel agency funded a complex and costly advertising and marketing program to bolster his struggling business. The program failed and he sold his business. One cold snowy day in January, the new owner's intuition told her that the way to sell travel was to be where the people had to go in bad as well as good weather—the grocery store. She immediately approached a supermarket chain and opened fifty-three travel centers throughout the chain. Sales went through the roof. Once she saw the shape of the problem, she intuited a simple solution.

BRAINWRITING

Brainwriting is a way to solve problems using intuition. Find a quiet spot and get relaxed. Write out your particular challenge and concentrate on it for a few minutes.

Write down some pertinent questions about your challenge: What is in my best interest? What should I do? What are other alternatives? What alternative is preferred? And so on. Then wait for the answer. It may come as a voice in your mind, or it may seem that you are communicating with someone else. Write down your answers as they come. Don't analyze or think. Write whatever occurs to you. Keep asking questions, and keep writing the responses until the responses stop. Finally, read and review what you have written. The answer to your challenge may be there.

The owner of a diet center framed the challenge: "In what ways might I develop a new diet product?" She tried brainwriting. Two of her responses were:

- People drink a lot of water when they diet.

- People exercise with weights as they diet.

These two thoughts sparked an idea. *The idea:* One-pound water-weights that carry liquid in plastic bottles for exercise now and refreshment later.

Summary

In intelligence work, agents often lack the time to make a detailed analysis of a dangerous situation; they must make fast decisions and accept the consequences. One agent makes decisions by flipping a coin: heads is yes and tails is no. If he feels comfortable with the result, that is his decision; however, if he feels uncomfortable with the result he will make the opposite decision. This is not a waste of time. However the coin falls, the decision is ultimately made by his intuition. This agent also told me: "When your life is on the line, about the only thing you trust is your gut instinct."

—

CHAPTER TWENTY-FOUR

THE THREE B'S

"To wait at ease while the enemy
is toiling and struggling, to be well fed
while the enemy is famished—
this is the art of husbanding one's strength."

SUN TZU

A well-known physicist once said that all the great discoveries in science were made in one of the three B's—bus, bed, and bath. Many successful people report that their best ideas come when they are not thinking about solving problems. This is because of the principle of incubation.

The most famous example of this principle involves Archimedes, the Greek mathematician. A king, suspecting that a golden crown contained more silver than gold, asked Archimedes to devise a method for determining the metal's purity. Archimedes wrestled with the problem for many days. Finally, he decided to put it out of his mind and relax in a hot bath. While sitting in the bathtub, he noted that the bathwater was overflowing—and suddenly an ingenious solution occurred to him. He realized that a pure gold crown would displace a different amount of water than one made of alloy. According to legend, Archimedes was so excited by his discovery that he rushed naked into the streets of Syracuse shouting, "Eureka!" (I've found it!).

Incubation works because your subconscious mind is continually processing information. It usually involves setting your problem aside for a few hours, days, or weeks and moving on to other projects. This allows your subconscious to continue working on the original challenge. The more interested you are in solving a challenge, the more likely it is that your subconscious will generate ideas.

As Bertrand Russell wrote in *The Conquest of Happiness:*

I have found, for example, that if I have to write upon some rather difficult topic, the best plan is to think about it with very great intensity—the greatest intensity with which I am capable—for a few hours or days, and at the end of that time give orders, so to speak, that the work is to proceed underground. After some months, I return consciously to the topic and find the work has been done. Before I discovered this technique, I used to spend time worrying because I was making no progress; I arrived at the solution none the faster for this worry and the worrying time was wasted.

Note that shadowy gray spots mysteriously appear at the intersections in this grid. However, when you concentrate on any specific intersection, the spot disappears.

Sometimes ideas, like the gray spots, mysteriously appear only when you are not concentrating on them. Modern science recognizes this phenomenon yet cannot explain why it occurs.

William Carrier, a twenty-five-year-old Cornell University engineering graduate, was waiting on a foggy railway platform in Pittsburgh. He had been working on the problem of regulating humidity for a printing company and had decided to give up for a while and take a vacation. Carrier gazed absentmindedly at the mist surrounding the station and tracks, wondering how late his train was going to be. Suddenly, the answer to one of the most vexing problems of his time appeared to him out of the fog.

The answer was air-conditioning, which was the result of marrying two technologies, refrigeration and electricity. His idea was to blow air through a fine mist that would act like a condenser, drying out the air. Since air's moisture content varies with temperature—cold air is drier than warm—changing the temperature of the mist would also alter the humidity. His invention fathered an industry that brought prosperity and growth to the hot, muggy areas of the world.

By taking a vacation from his problem, he removed the artificial limitation of a deadline and solved his problem. Incubation will help you break the artificial limitations that you impose on yourself. Your mind will become less frantic and better able to deal with concepts, patterns, even the ridiculous combinations of thoughts that are such great aids to creativity. It's like the breaking up of a long, hard winter.

BLUEPRINT

1. *Identify.* Identify a challenge worth working on and think of the consequences of solving it. If you can envision a world in which your challenge is solved, you will be pulled subconsciously toward a constructive, creative answer.

2. *Prepare.* Collect and gather all available information and literature about your challenge. Read, talk to others, ask questions, and do as much research as you can. Consciously work on the challenge as intensely as you can, until you are satisfied that you have prepared as thoroughly as possible.

3. *Instruct.* Instruct your brain to find the solution to the problem. Close by saying: "Okay, find the solution to this problem. I'll be back in two days for the answer" or "Let me know the minute you work it out."

4. *Incubate.* Let go of the problem. Don't work on it. Forget it for a while. This period may be long or short. Take a walk or a shower, go to a movie, or sleep on it. Incubation has to occur and it will.

5. *Eureka!* It may take five minutes, five hours, five days, five weeks, five months, or whatever, but insight will occur.

Thunder is impressive, but it is the lightning that does the work. Long after the thunder of conscious thinking has faded from your mind, insight and creative ideas will arrive like flashes of lightning.

A stockbroker searched for months for a new business opportunity. He collected information and did considerable research about financial services. He then forgot about his challenge. A week later, while shopping for shoes, his idea suddenly arrived.

The idea: He created a one-stop IRA store in a high-traffic location. He saves consumers the trouble of shopping for an IRA and choosing among the many complex programs. He can charge a reasonable fee and make a commission from the IRA sellers as well. He opened branches in office buildings and other malls.

BENEFITS OF INCUBATION

Incubation helps you put the challenge in perspective. Edna Ferber wrote, "A story must simmer in its own juices for months or even years before it is ready to serve."

An architect was uncertain where to place sidewalks between buildings in an office complex. He did nothing for a period of time, letting the problem "simmer." One day, he noticed that people walking on the grass had left pathways between the buildings—paths that were perfectly sized for traffic flow. He paved the pathways, which directly met user needs in an aesthetic fashion.

You put your subconscious to work on the challenge. As a simple experiment, write the alphabet vertically on a piece of paper. Now write a sentence vertically next to the alphabet, stopping with whatever letter parallels Z. Now you have a row of initials. Think of as many famous people as you can (real or fictional) for each set of initials in ten minutes. If you couldn't come up with some names but then suddenly thought of them while you were working on other initials, you experienced your subconscious mind at work.

When you leave a problem and come back to it fresh, you will likely develop a different perspective on it. A volunteer in upstate New York faced the challenge of raising money for a certain charity. He considered the usual fund-raising methods and then let go of the problem for some weeks. One day while he was fishing on the Genesee River, he remembered the challenge and wondered about ways of combining raising money with sport. This inspired the latest craze in fund-raising.

The idea: A plastic duck race. Three-inch-long plastic ducks are numbered and then tossed toward a finish line a mile down the river. Spectators pay $5 to bet on the ducks, and the first-place winner receives a prize. Volunteers follow the plastic ducks in rowboats, scooping up strays in handheld nets. In addition, nets are strung across the river at the finish line so that the ducks do not contribute to pollution.

Incubation can help you realize your personal goals. Write down a goal that is important to you. It could be a short- or long-range goal. Then, write out the ideal situation exactly as you would like it to be when your goal is realized. Describe it in the present tense, as if it had already happened, in as much detail as possible.

When you have finished, write at the bottom of the page: "This or something better is now manifesting for me and will be manifested for me in a totally satisfying way." Then sit quietly, visualize the realization of your goal, put the paper away, and forget about it. Months or years later, when you find and read it, you may be surprised to find that the goal has somehow come into being in your life.

SUMMARY

One prominent French scientist observed that practically all of his good ideas came to him when he was not working on a problem or even thinking about a problem, and that most of his contemporaries made their discoveries in the same way. When Einstein was troubled by a problem, he would lie down and take a long nap.

When you have a case of the dooms about a challenge, incubate it. Then, when you least expect it, in perfect silence, the answer will come like a flock of birds breaking out of a tree, but you will feel as if the tree itself is breaking up, sending particles of ideas into the air.

CHAPTER TWENTY-FIVE

RATTLESNAKES
AND ROSES

"Now the shuai-jan is a snake found in the
Ch'ang mountains. Strike at its head, and you
will be attacked by its tail; strike at its tail,
and you will be attacked by its head;
strike at its middle, and you will be attacked
by head and tail both."

SUN TZU

Sun Tzu drew an analogy between the behavior of the shuai-jan and that of soldiers in battle. To succeed in war, he observed, men must have tenacity and unity of purpose and, above all, a spirit of sympathetic cooperation.

Analogies are comparisons of the similar features of two things—they are also mental telescopes through which you can spy ideas. For instance, consider the following inventions and their counterparts in nature:

Helicopters: The hummingbird can also hover and fly backwards.

Hypodermic needles: The scorpion uses the pointed tip of its tail to inject poison.

Sonar: Bats used sonar long before man. They emit sounds inaudible to the human ear that bounce off objects in their way.

Anesthesia: Many snakes use venom to paralyze and desensitize their prey before eating it.

Snowshoes: The caribou's feet are designed to skim over snow.

Tanks: The turtle is a virtually impregnable mobile unit.

Airplanes: Planes brake with flaps just as birds brake with tailfeathers.

Are there similarities between a telephone network and the human body? Bell developed a new self-healing communication system based on an analogy with the human circulation system. When important telephone arteries are damaged or cut, the system pumps phone service through new channels, keeping communications alive.

A bird's special gift is flight, ours is the imagination to make connections between two dissimilar areas of experience. For example, take the two non-sense words "maluma" and "tuckatee" and match them to the figures, A and B.

A   B

Gestalt psychologist Wolfgang Kohler used the above exercise to demonstrate that humans somehow make universal metamorphical-analogical connections. Kohler's patients would unerringly match "maluma" to A and "tuckatee" to B. Did you?

Suppose my challenge is to improve the common flashlight. I draw the following analogy between two dissimilar areas of experience:

"Improving a flashlight is like attending medical school to learn surgery."

Next, I'll describe what's involved in learning surgery:

1. I'll need textbooks and manuals.

2. I'll need to attend class and talk with professors.

3. I'll have to learn how to administer anesthesia.

4. I'll have to insulate myself from social demands while in school.

5. I'll practice surgery on cadavers.

I examine each item and see what ideas it might stimulate.

1. Package first-aid pamphlets with flashlights (from "textbooks and manuals").

2. Incorporate a radio transmitter and radio receiver (from "talk with professors").

3. Include a mace-spraying device for protection (from "administering anesthesia").

4. Insulate flashlights to protect batteries from extreme temperatures (from "insulating from social demands").

5. Include a miniature tool kit (from "practicing on cadavers").

By making analogical connections between flashlights and learning surgery, I quickly came up with a number of unconventional ideas for improving the common flashlight.

When you use analogies to generate ideas, you'll find that analogies grow like plants, like trees, like children, like love. They go through a series of stages, finally maturing into something rich with ideas.

MAKING THE FAMILIAR STRANGE

Most of us are threatened by the strange and unfamiliar and have a need to understand it. When confronted with something unfamiliar, we tend to break it down and analyze the different parts to see if this will allow us to understand it or make it familiar. We also generalize by analogy, asking "What's this like?" Our minds compare the unfamiliar object with things that *are* familiar, and this process can convert the strange into the familiar.

Look at the collage of shadows in the above illustration.

Notice how your mind first perceives the shadows as strange, then searches for meaning. The search continues until your mind is satisfied that it represents the image of a bearded man in a white robe standing against a background of brush. Your mind searches for meaning until it makes the strange shadows into something familiar.

This tendency explains why *making the familiar strange* is a key to creative thinking. When you reverse the usual process, you push your mind to search for new connections and ideas.

Venturing into strange areas which seem totally unrelated to your challenge will increase your chances of seeing the challenge in a new context. You do this by using analogies.

The stranger the analogy (the greater the distance between challenge and example), the greater your chance of generating a unique idea. For instance, if your challenge is to improve the stamina of rose bushes, you are more likely to see the challenge from a unique viewpoint if you look at stamina in rattlesnakes instead of in other flowers or plants.

A new nightclub was having its grand opening, and the owners wanted to send out clever and amusing invitations. They worked with the following analogy: "An invitation is like an aspirin." In other words, they made the familiar strange. How can an invitation be like an aspirin?

This analogy forced them to search for connections and similarities between the two items. The search resulted in one of the year's most unusual invitations.

The idea: Make the invitation pill-like. The club sent out a blue pill nestled in a black velvet ring box. Instructions on the box read "Drop into warm water, stir, and let dissolve." When immersed, the capsule dissolved and a piece of cellophane with the time, date, and place floated to the top. The invitations cost $1.10 each, and the opening was a smash.

Using analogies allows one to dismiss all unrelated thoughts, as though parting the grass to find the path leading to a new idea.

The owner of a jewelry store needed to sell more high-end items; customers balked at high prices and had doubts about how the jewelry would look with their wardrobes. He made an analogical connection between high-end jewelry and paper dolls. With paper dolls, children cut out and play with paper wardrobes and jewelry. This stimulated his idea.

The idea: Paper cutouts of jewelry. He created punch-out paper representations of expensive jewelry, and sent the paper copies to prospective customers so they could try out the jewelry at home with various outfits. Once people modeled the paper cutouts, their doubts disappeared, and they came in and purchased his jewelry.

To satisfy hunger, you must take some kind of action. You cannot just sit there and expect your hunger to disappear—you have to make something to eat or go to a restaurant. Similarly, you cannot just wish to have an idea. You have to act. One action you can take is to make the familiar strange with one of the four kinds of analogy: personal analogy, direct analogy, symbolic analogy, or fantasy analogy.

Of these four, the *direct analogy* is the most productive idea-getter and the only one that requires a detailed blueprint. The others are described in enough detail that you don't need a blueprint to understand and use them.

PERSONAL ANALOGY

This analogy involves identifying with some part of your problem and trying to see the challenge from its perspective. Imagine that you are trying to design a new clock. Ask yourself what it would be like to be the hands of a clock.

The personal analogy demands that you lose yourself in the object of the challenge. Wear the problems' clothes, talk its language, eat its food, sing its songs, recite its slogan and mottos. Become a kind of blood-hyphen with the object.

Look at this man.

Can you imagine him merging with a rat? This figure can be seen as either a man or a rat: The man's glasses are also the rat's ears, the man's nose is the rat's head, and his chin is the rat's tail. You should merge as completely as this with your problem.

The basic questions to ask yourself are: "How would I feel if I were . . . ?" or "What would it say to me if our positions were reversed?" or "What would it say to me if it could think and talk the way I can?"

T. A. Rich, a famous inventor at GE, describes how he comes up with his new ideas this way: "I put myself in the middle of a problem; try to think like an electron whose course is being plotted or imagine myself as a light beam whose refraction is being measured." Einstein imagined he was a beam of light hurtling through space, which led him to the theory of relativity.

A tiny company that markets wall coverings had the challenge of competing with enormous conglomerates. Fortunately for this tiny company, innovation is one of the few precious resources that can't be bought; the best ideas have always been simple enough to scribble on the back of a cocktail napkin, and the CEO knew this.

This CEO kept asking himself, "What would wall coverings say to me if they could talk?" "What would their concerns be?" "What would they worry about?" "How would I feel if I were a wall covering?" He asked himself these questions every day and was finally able to imagine himself as a wall covering.

One concern he imagined wall coverings would have is the fear of fire. Wall coverings are often made of vinyl, polypropylene, and other fabrics that are highly toxic when burned. The giant wall covering companies were all selling these potentially dangerous products.

The tiny company developed its own nontoxic, fire-resistant fiberglass material. This company then sent flyers to distributors, architects, and others who choose or buy wall coverings. The flyers detailed the high toxicity of the giants' vinyl and polypropylene wall coverings and emphasized the danger of litigation. In the event of fire, the victims or their estate could file a class action suit naming the property owner, the architect or engineer who specified the dangerous wall covering, the distributor, and the maker.

Suddenly the tiny company was getting orders from nursing homes, hotels, casinos, prisons, hospitals, schools, and major hotel chains. The giant companies were rocked to their heels. The distributors and designers they'd done business with for years were questioning their products and moved their business to the safe little company.

Suppose you own an outdoor advertising business and are looking for creative new ways to advertise. Imagine that you are an outdoor billboard. What would you feel? What would your problems be? How would you advertise your products?

If I was a billboard, I would like to talk to the passing motorists about my products; I would like a chance to sell them my products in person. This prompts an idea.

The idea: Display a provocative back view of a male or female model with a phone number to call. Callers would find themselves listening to real or taped sales presentations from the sexy models, extolling the virtues of the product and implying that the model could be found on a certain beach using the product.

DIRECT ANALOGY

The direct analogy is probably the most productive for generating ideas. With direct analogies, you can imagine comparisons and similarities between parallel facts and events in different fields or "parallel worlds." "If X works in a certain desirable way, why can't Y work in a similar manner?"

$$+ \quad \perp \quad X \quad \times$$

Alexander Graham Bell observed the comparison between the inner workings of the ear and the movement of a stout piece of membrane and conceived of the telephone. Edison invented the phonograph one day, after developing an analogy between a toy funnel and the motions of a paper doll and sound vibrations. Underwater construction was made possible when someone observed how shipworms tunnel into timber by first constructing tubes.

Consider the story of George de Mestral, a Swiss inventor who went hunting one day in the late 1940s. He and his dog accidentally brushed up against a bush that left them both covered with burrs. When de Mestral tried to remove the burrs, they clung stubbornly to his clothes. This would be a minor annoyance to most of us, but de Mestral was curious about why the burrs were so hard to remove. After he got home, he studied them under a microscope and discovered that hundreds of tiny hooks on each burr had snagged to the threads of his pants. Burrs, he thought, would make great fasteners.

After several years of work, he finally succeeded. The result: Velcro fasteners, now used on millions of items, from blood pressure cuffs to tennis shoes.

The analogy does not have to be long or complicated. Stamp collecting is a specialized hobby yet its components can be compared to those of many businesses: supply and demand, information requirements, search procedures, rarity of certain items, utility of certain items, classification, marketing, word of mouth, value, value added, and so on.

In the above illustration, one plus one equals four or more. Of the two lines, one crosses the other horizontally in their centers, creating four arms. You can also, with imagination, see four rectangles, four triangles and four squares. By shifting the lines from the centers, you can also create several unequal and unique figures.

In the same way, your subject plus a dissimilar object will produce four or more ideas.

Assume my challenge is "In what ways might I become more creative at work?" I look into an unrelated field—home appliances—and decide that my analogy will be: Being creative at work is like being a toaster. One (being creative at work) + one (toaster) = four or more ideas.

Following are descriptors of a toaster. A toaster:

- is operated by pushing down a lever or bar.
- is plugged into a power source.

- takes bread in completely.

- concentrates its energy on the surfaces of bread.

- accepts different sizes and types of bread.

- may shock you if you tamper with it with a fork or knife.

- produces toast, which is sometimes combined with butter or jam to improve it.

I examine each descriptor and produce the following ideas on how to become more creative at work:

- I should push down negative thoughts about my creative abilities. (From "pushing down" the bar on a toaster.)

- I need to identify the real benefits to me of being creative. (From "power source.")

- I need to accept the challenge of being creative completely. (From "takes in bread completely.")

- I should concentrate my energies on ideas instead of digging for reasons to come up with ideas. (From "concentrates its energy on the surfaces of the bread.")

- I should try different kinds of creative techniques. (From "accepts different sizes and types of bread.")

- I should become a risk taker and try for the dramatic idea. (From "you may get shocked.")

- I should combine creative-thinking techniques. (From "butter and jam.")

With a little imagination, the ordinary household toaster pops up a whole program for improving my creativity at work. One (improve creativity) + one (toaster) = seven ideas.

BLUEPRINT

The basic blueprint for using direct analogies is:

1. *State your challenge.* A lumberyard owner stated: "In what ways might I sell more lumber?"

2. *Choose a key word or phrase in the challenge.* He chose "sell."

3. *Choose a parallel or distant field.* The greater the distance the parallel world is from your challenge, the greater your chance of producing new thoughts and ideas. A business analogy to a business challenge is too close— analogies from television or cookery might be more likely to stimulate creative thought.

    The field selected for the challenge of selling more lumber was "computers."

4. *List the images that you associate with your chosen field, then choose one or more particularly rich ones.* Listing images will allow you to describe the analogy in as much detail as possible. Among the images evoked by the computer field are: science, multiple uses, user-friendly, hardware, software, add-ons, computer-aided design, schools, business uses, and recreational uses.

5. *Look for similarities and connections between the two components of your analogy.* Don't think of looking for connections as something arduous, or feel as though you were forcing yourself to swallow something unpleasant for your own good. Think easy. Let your thoughts come and go as they wish.

    The lumberyard owner looked at a number of connections between the images and his challenge of selling more lumber, ultimately discarding most of them. The final images he focused on were: computer-aided design (CAD), computer add-ons, and recreational uses.

    He combined and connected these three concepts with his challenge of selling lumber, stirring an idea.

    The idea: Use CAD to design backyard decks. Provide a computerized system in the lumberyard with which salespeople can design decks to a customer's specifications. One would set up a user-friendly kiosk with a large video screen and easy-to-use controls for the salesperson. The customer could specify the deck's size and the number of stairways needed, and select railings and spindles. The system would then design the deck from the ground up and calculate the cost. If the cost came out too high, the customer could change the dimensions. Once the price is right, the computer could print out full instructions. This free service would encourage more people to build decks, and the lumberyard will sell more lumber.

The "parallel world" you select must be something you know well, and you should use a specific object, situation, event, or example from that world. For instance: "The NFL Champion San Francisco Forty-niners" will make for a much more fruitful analogy than "football." The more detailed images you can record, the better. If you decide to use "restaurants," choose a specific, familiar restaurant.

Following is a sample list of different worlds, fields, and disciplines which parallel the business world. Use this list to get started, but do develop a unique list of parallel worlds that best suits your particular knowledge. When choosing a parallel world, examine four or five possibilities in order to select the one that best suits the general principles of your challenge.

Parallel Worlds

Accounting	Acupuncture	The animal kingdom
Architecture	Art	Astrology
Astronomy	Ballet	Baseball
Basketball	Biography	Biology
Birds	Cancer	Bowling
Calculus	Cartoons	Cardiology
Caribbean	Chiropractors	Chemistry
China	Composers	The civil rights
Comics	Dentistry	movement
Dance	Economics	The Civil War
Deserts	Entertainment	Computers
England	The fast-food industry	Department stores
Farming	Fishing	Education
Fine cooking	Funeral homes	Evolution
Football	Geology	Finance
Geography	Government	Flying
Golf	Grocery stores	Garbage collecting
The Great Depression	Hunting	Germany
History	The I.R.S.	Great books
India	Inventions	Hawaii
Interior decorating	Jungles	Hypnosis
Journalism	Insects	Japan
Korea	Law	Literature
Mafia	Law enforcement	Math

Medicine	Manufacturing	The military
Mining	Meteorology	Monuments
The moon	Monasteries	Music
Mythology	Movies	Nutrition
Oceans	Nuclear physics	The Olympics
Pharmacology	The old west	Photography
Physical fitness	Philosophy	Physics
Planets	Physical therapy	Political science
Politics	Plumbing	Printing
Psychiatry	Pornography	Publishing
Religion	Psychology	Restaurants
The Revolutionary War	Resorts	Sculpture
Seminars	Sailing	Skiing
Soap operas	Shakespeare's plays	South America
Space	Sociology	Stars
Taverns	Special education	TV news
The steel industry	Television	Talk radio
Tennis	The sun	Television
Transportation	Terrorism	Theater
The U.S.S.R.	The travel industry	Unions
Wall Street	The Vatican	The Vietnam War
World War I	Wholesalers	Wine
World War II	The Yukon	

Examine your parallel world for details and information that you can compare to your challenge. Work the analogy over like a Chinese chef who leaves hardly any part of the duck unserved.

Suppose you have a problem selling copiers. You select "Television," and then decide to focus on television evangelists. Next, you list the characteristics of television evangelists and then compare these characteristics to the principles of selling copiers. Your objective is to draw meaningful relationships which may lead to a productive idea. Take a few minutes and try it.

How did you do?

One could say that evangelists sell a product—their sermons. One could also say they sell hope, which is the product of the sermon. In other words, hope is the "product of the product" of the TV evangelist. What is the "product of the product" in selling copiers? Is it convenience? Service? Efficiency? If you promoted the product of your product, could you sell more copiers?

Now compare selling copiers to a full-service restaurant. You might discover that your menu (product line) is comprehensive but you have too many restrictions, which cloud the customer's mind. For example, your company may have specialized salespeople (waiters). Thus, customers can't order everything from one salesperson (waiter) but need to order beverages from the beverage waiter, salad from the salad waiter, potatoes from the potato waiter, fish from the fish waiter, meat from the meat waiter, and so on. In this case, one solution would be to consider ways of simplifying the product line and ordering procedures.

A friend of mine disliked the standard 20 by 40-foot rectangular swimming pool. He wanted an affordable pool which would allow a variety of water activities—swimming, diving, serious lap swimming, and horsing around—to take place simultaneously.

He decided to design his own swimming pool but needed ideas. He selected the parallel world of golf and began to look for analogies. He considered course layouts, sand traps, fairways, the rough, golf clubs, golf clothing, and golf equipment. He eventually focused on golf equipment; in particular, the clubs.

He drew connections and relationships between the number one wood—the driver—and his challenge of designing a swimming pool.

Above is the pool he designed.

His pool is a modified octagon. Six of its sides are 23 feet long, while one side extends to form a sixty-foot lap area. This allows all water activities to take place simultaneously. In addition, the pool takes up less room and uses one-third less water than conventional designs, which saves on pumping, filtration, and chemicals. Its unusual shape can be adapted to unusual sites and can even be wrapped around a house. It also has a zippered cover, much like a golf club cover.

My friend, who is strictly a meatloaf-and-yams man, explained: "Using the direct analogy with golf clubs I had twenty-four ideas that jumped between my ears. I grabbed the last one and designed my pool."

Symbolic Analogy

A symbolic analogy is a representation of the key elements of a challenge in visual image. This technique works best when you disassociate yourself entirely from labels and words and just make mental pictures of the problem. One of the most famous examples of this technique was Fredrich von Kekule's discovery that benzene and other organic molecules are closed chains or rings—a direct result of a symbolic analogy in which he visualized snakes swallowing their tails.

To try this technique, close your eyes and picture your challenge or problem in your mind. Block out verbal thoughts. (This can be done by repeating a simple word such as *aum*, *one*, *om*, or *so* over and over, until it becomes meaningless.) The resulting visual ideas can be expressed verbally, drawn, or written down at a later time.

A group of engineers used symbolic analogies to invent a compact jacking mechanism that extends some three feet and can support up to five tons. Among the mental images the group produced were:

- The Indian rope trick in which a rope is at first coiled and soft, then becomes hard as it extends.

- The hydraulic principle of the erection of the penis.

- A steel tape measure.

- A bicycle chain with flexible links that stiffen as they are driven out of the jacking mechanism.

These images combined to provide a concept on which the design for the compact jack was ultimately based.

Try it. Imagine that your challenge is to create a unique design for directional signs that will mark major intersections within a housing development. Picture directional signs as your subject. Repeat a simple word, over and over, to block out your verbal thoughts. Write down what you visualized.

What did you get?

Among the images and associations I came up with are:

- *Images of landmarks.* People use landmarks to locate things. Association: Think of a sign as an artistic landmark.

- *Images of hunting dogs.* Dogs assist hunters by pointing to prey. Association: Use an animal cutout as a sign.

- *Colors.* People use colors to denote direction ("Turn right at the red house."). Association: Use different bright colors to denote major and minor intersections.

These images and associations produce a unique design idea: Mark major intersections with giant metal animals (perhaps a horse, steer, and wolf) that function both as art and landmarks. Mark secondary intersections with metal birds (roadrunner, owl, blue jay). Paint the signs with bright colors such as hot pink, yellow, and turquoise. ("Turn left at the blue horse and right at the pink owl.")

A salesperson confronted the challenge of getting druggists to display baby lotion in both the baby department and the adult section. He coaxed out a mental image of a diamond ring hidden behind aspirin bottles and interpreted this image into an effective sales promotion.

The idea: He built an entire campaign around the notion of "hidden profits." He listed all the ways you could make money by placing baby lotion in the adult section, in small print, on a leave-behind card with a little magnifier attached to it. This little gimmick was one of the most successful sales promotions in the company's history.

Think of symbolic analogies as imaginary mushroom clouds (destroying nothing, making nothing) rising from a blinding consciousness. It is your careful interpretation of the clouds that gives them meaning and value.

FANTASY ANALOGY

The fantasy analogy involves using your imagination without reference to objective reality. When faced with a problem, imagine the best possible world—one that would permit the most satisfying solution to the problem. This fantasy analogy will permit you to combine words, concepts, and assumptions with apparently irrelevant objects and events. The result is a rich treasure of associations; an imagination avalanche with whole mountains of ideas crashing down.

An artist can paint the world however he wishes but a businessperson is limited by tradition. Using a fantasy analogy allows you to imagine the best possible solution to a problem because you temporarily suspend all judgment. This allows a businessperson to create ideas like an artist.

Most of the business concepts we work with have been handed down to us by others, but we are expected to adhere to these prepackaged concepts. Creating your own world where these concepts do not hold enables you to think and act with a Maker's responsibility. This attitude modifies your view of the real world and nullifies the effect of traditional beliefs.

As Maker, you can visualize anything, not excluding even the wildest ideas; for example, training insects to perform small business tasks. It's like inventing a sky with new stars in it.

The Navy didn't think of training insects to perform routine tasks, but they did spend a lot of time thinking about training marine life in response to the challenge: "In what ways might we improve our security against saboteurs, reduce cost, and minimize risk to human life?"

Using fantasy analogies to generate ideas, a Navy problem-solving group developed a clandestine program to train and use dolphins to guard the Trident nuclear submarine base in Bangor, Washington. Dolphins are faster than Carl Lewis running the 100-meter dash and have better sonar than anything man has invented. This was the first use of dolphins in domestic surveillance.

Putting aside traditional beliefs allows you to visualize a more coherent hypothesis than you might have thought possible. Push aside the ordinary laws of doing business and take a peek at the other side before the laws snap back into control.

A salesperson confronted the challenge: "In what ways might I discover the prospect's real objections to my product?" She felt that once she determined the real problems, she could overcome them.

Her fantasy analogy was to make her customers into judges who would bang their gavels every time they had an objection. This hatched the idea.

The idea: She began handing each prospect a gavel, saying, "You be the judge; if you have a question or an objection, bang the gavel!" She would then make her presentation on why the prospect should buy her product. She increased her closing ratio by 80 percent. It was a quick attention-getter that the customers enjoyed.

You may get the best ideas by combining types of analogy. Assume you sell law books direct to lawyers and would like more productive sales techniques. Start with a fantasy world, such as the following:

"Imagine a world in which lawyers line up outside your door and plead for your services, and you select which lawyers will have the privilege of buying your books."

You may then find yourself going from the fantasy analogy to the direct and then to the personal. For instance, a direct analogy for the above fantasy might be the medical field where patients come to an office and wait until the doctor has time to see them. A personal analogy would be imagining yourself as the lawyer or patient and empathizing with him.

Possible ideas to implement the fantasy analogy and get lawyers to come to you might be:

- *Selection of customers.* Provide a greater array of services for preferred lawyers. The longer they do business with you, the greater the number of services you provide. For instance, you could team up with a travel agent to offer "preferred lawyer" discount travel arrangements. You could also offer free reservation services for theaters and restaurants to big accounts.

- *Prestige.* Personal recognition is important to most lawyers. Invite lawyers to work with you as book reviewers, authors, coauthors, and marketing consultants.

- *Convenience.* One reason people visit doctors is because of the medical resources concentrated in one office. Concentrate legal resources in your office (i.e., books, videotapes, data banks, online computer services, a legal reference library, legal secretaries, journals, and so on) to motivate lawyers to come to you.

Just as soil needs some elements to fertilize it, just as vitamin-starved sailors call for lemons, so too the imagination needs nourishment. The fantasy analogy feeds your imagination; it allows you to move through space by walking or flying, or stay still and watch the components of your challenge as they fly around you. Becoming an observer will permit you to stand back from your challenge and obtain both physical and psychological distance. How important does any problem seem, for example, when viewed from Mars?

SUMMARY

Consider water. Civilization as we know it is based in part on running water—supplying it, distributing it, and turning it off and on when we need it. That overall system had to be well thought out. A similar sort of planning lets you design a waterworks for the mind.

Rattlesnakes and Roses is a utility, a commodity, a waterworks for your mind, the spigot that dispenses images and experiences when you turn the handle. But the system must be based on the fluidity of your thought. Thoughts, like water, go nowhere when frozen.

CHAPTER TWENTY-SIX

STONE SOUP

> "When campaigning, be swift as the wind; in
> leisurely march, majestic as the forest; in
> raiding and plundering, like fire; in standing
> firm, firm as the mountains. As unfathomable as
> the clouds, move like a thunderbolt."
>
> **SUN TZU**

A lion has to be a lion all its life; a dog has to be a dog. But a human being can play with and bring about one of a huge number of different identities; the one he finally chooses will be determined by neither reason nor common sense, but by imagination.

Consider the role the beggar's imagination plays in the following story, based on an old Eastern European children's fable.

The weather had grown cold and the trees had burst into color, the reds and yellows glowing as though the leaves had gobbled the light of the fall sun and were releasing it slowly. The fields were piled with golden pumpkins and russet squashes and trees with red apples so sweet you could smell the juice.

The barefoot beggar's clothing was torn, his hair tangled. He could smell roasting meat from the villagers' kitchens and his mouth filled with saliva—he had not eaten in two days. Desperate, he built a small fire at the edge of the village, put his pot on the fire, and placed a small stone in the pot. "Just suppose," he thought, "this stone could make a delicious soup." He sat on a box and imagined that he was really making soup.

The curious villagers came out and collected around his crackling fire. They asked him what he was brewing and he told them about the magical stone that made a delectable soup. "Stone soup tastes best when the frost is in," he told them. The villagers were fascinated with this soup and began to comment on its fine aroma. The beggar invited them to join him. The excited villagers said they would bring their own dinners to complement his gourmet soup.

They returned with vegetables, fruits, turkeys, hams, eggs, and sausages. "Now let us pray," the village priest said. The beggar thought, "I pray the food doesn't get cold before he finishes." Then the beggar dug in. He ate everything there was to eat, like there was no tomorrow. He broke apart four fried eggs with the tip of his knife and ate them with whole slices of fried ham. He cut two pieces of turkey, forked the meat into his mouth, and then added some boiled potatoes and beans—and then tore off a hunk of buttered bread and ate that too. He didn't seem to notice that the villagers sipped bowl after bowl of his wonderful soup while he ate everything in sight, including half of a strawberry pie.

When he finished, he sat there for a few moments as if stunned. Finally, he got up, packed his stone and left. He didn't look back.

By directing his imagination, the beggar was able to create the illusion of a wonderful soup. Once the villagers convinced themselves that it was, in fact, a wonderful soup, the beggar was able to feast on their food and thus accomplish his goal of getting a hearty meal. His imagination fed his belly. Your imagination can feed your business belly if you just ask "What if . . . ?" and "Just suppose . . . ?"

E. L. Doctorow told of having a writing block that lasted for three months. He was frantic for ideas. One day, he gazed absentmindedly at the wallpaper and wondered about the age of the paper, and then about the age of the house. He pursued this thought and discovered his house was built in the early 1900s. "Just suppose," he thought, "I could be transported back in time to the date my house was built."

He imagined it. His imagination took him back to the early 1900s and he began the astonishing novel, *Ragtime,* which re-creates with stunning authenticity all the sights, sounds, aromas, and emotions of the time when his house was built. "Just supposing," created a best seller.

Doctorow discovered what Einstein knew, which is that anything goes when you are limited only by your imagination. Einstein developed some of his early theories by speculating. "Just suppose bodies could be in motion and at rest at the same time." He asked, "What would that mean?"

Look at the four black arrowheads.

What if the arrowheads are white and the background is black? When you imagine the white arrowheads, they become as real as the black. Your sense of the arrowheads is now a product of your imagination.

Imagination is everything you have ever experienced. It so permeates the human condition that many people feel they have no imagination. Yet, imagination is the crux of every human perception. Your sense of time, space, and history, of planning for tomorrow, are all products of your imagination. Without it, you would be as oblivious to your surroundings as a fish is to water.

"What-iffing" is a great way to learn to direct your imagination toward a desired goal. This technique lets your ego relax, and the playfulness of the ideas it generates will cause it to relax even more.

What if our attitudes about sex and food were reversed? Would this mean that people would engage in public sex acts in restaurants while fast-sex stores dotted the landscape? People would never eat in public, and children would be told not to say "knife" or "fork." Would all the eating be done behind closed doors, and might there be movie houses featuring "food flicks" for "perverts" who sneak food items into theaters under their raincoats?

Most humor uses imaginative possibilities to create new insights. For instance, take the story about the boastful Texan vacationing in Maine. The Texan, surveying a tiny farm, explains that back home on his ranch, he can get into his car and drive all day without ever crossing his own property line. The Maine farmer pauses for a moment to digest this thought, picks his teeth, and replies, "Ayuh. Had a car like that myself once."

At the point in the story where the two lines of thinking (property and cars) meet, the farmer's imagination creates a whole new perception of events by following the less obvious direction. "What-iffing" pushes you to produce something new. In the joke, we produced something funny. In business, you can produce the profound.

The figure on the next page is known to psychologists as the Penrose triangle. If you follow the white surface, it appears to go from being the outside of a three-dimensional triangle to being the inside. The three-dimensional figure is impossible; it cannot exist.

Like the triangle, individual genius sometimes comes from moments of absolute fiction that provide a ray of insight leading to an innovative solution. To achieve that ray of insight, one must take the imaginative chance, abandon the usual ways of looking at things, transcend the possible, and reach for the impossible.

Following are some examples of general imagination-spurring questions:

- What if you had eyes in back of your head as well as the front?

- What if human beings never died? How would this affect our personal, business, and religious lives?

- What if every five years you experienced a natural sex change (if you're male, you become female; if you're female, you become male)?

- What if trees suddenly started to produce petroleum in great quantities?

- What if people slept twenty-three hours every day and were awake for only one hour?

- What if every worker in the United States had to adopt one homeless person and take care of that person for life?

- What if fashion were done away with and everyone, regardless of station in life or occupation, had to wear the same uniform?

- What if as you aged you became more beautiful and intelligent?

- What if international disputes were resolved by awarding victory to the country that could make the world laugh the hardest?

- What if our genitals were on our foreheads?

- What if you could eat clouds for breakfast?

After you ask the questions, try to answer them. What if a pill was developed that would do away with all prejudice and bigotry in all of its present forms? How would this affect TV talk shows? What would happen to all the political action groups? Would some sort of new hatred replace bigotry; for example, would people become prejudiced against dogs or oak trees? Would our political institutions change? Would the court system improve? Would life be better, and, if so, how? Would global politics become more or less intense?

In trying to answer the questions, you find yourself developing new insights that may lead to new ideas. Suppose our question is: "What if people were like skunks and could repel attackers with odor?" Trying to answer it inspires an idea. Clip a plastic capsule that contains synthetic skunk oil onto one's clothing. If a person is attacked, he or she squeezes the capsule to release an odor so offensive it drives the attacker away. A concentrated deodorizer could be applied to neutralize the odor once the attacker has fled.

Playing "what if" games on a daily basis will free you from boredom and let you connect previously unrelated thoughts and experiences.

"What if you could lose weight by writing down the number of pounds you want to lose?"

The idea: A computer simulation that will motivate dieters by showing them what they will look like after losing ten to twenty-five pounds.

Once you understand how to direct it, your imagination will become a hard and inescapable reality instead of an escape from harsh reality.

BLUEPRINT

The easiest way to begin is by saying: "I need fresh and novel ideas to solve my challenge. I will suspend all judgment and see what free and easy idea I can think up. It doesn't matter how weird or offbeat they are, since no one need know about them." Allow yourself the freedom to conceptualize without judging your ideas in terms of the real world.

1. *Stipulate your challenge.* One environmental dilemma is how to dispose of old porcelain toilets that are being dumped in already overloaded landfills. Our challenge is: "In what other ways might we dispose of toilets?"

2. *List as many "what if" scenarios as you can.* One scenario is: What if we simply threw all the old toilets into the ocean?

3. *Try to answer the questions posed by your scenarios.* Toilets would make ideal reefs for fish. Porcelain fixtures are just as good as rock as far as fish are concerned—they are just funny-shaped devices with lots of spaces for fish to hide. Toilets would make great reefs for the very reason they are terrible in landfills: A toilet lasts virtually forever.

To find radical solutions to old problems, it is essential to take the imaginative leap to produce an image or metaphor that you can grip and mold into a new idea. For instance, imagine you own a company that manufacturers television sets in a country where only the rich can afford to own one. Your sets are outperformed in the city market by every competitor and you lack the resources to advertise nationally. What do you do?

Matsushita faced this problem in the early 1950s. They were outranked and outperformed by just about every competitor, in Japan and elsewhere. The executives knew, as everybody else did, that television was "too expensive for the Japanese." In 1955 the chairman of Toshiba said, "Japan is too poor to afford such a luxury." Toshiba and Hitachi made better sets at the time, but they showed them only on the Ginza in Tokyo and in big-city department stores, making it clear to the average Japanese that this product was beyond their reach.

The national sales manager at Matsushita said, "What if Japanese farmers were rich and could afford television?" and proceeded to devise a sales plan based on this fantasy. His salesmen sold televisions to poor farmers door-to-door, something no one in Japan had ever done with anything more expensive than cloth or aprons. The Japanese farmers could not afford the sets, but they bought them anyway. Those farmers wanted access to the outside world and were willing to make incredible sacrifices to get it.

Directed imagination focuses you on how to solve a problem instead of wondering if the problem can be solved. Once the sales manager imagined the farmers as a market, he set about to make it happen. Today, Matsushita is better known by its brand name—Panasonic. *The lesson:* In a land of withering grapes, imagination can make a raisin a king.

Suppose you own a company and your challenge is: "In what ways might I increase sales?" See how many "what if" scenarios you can create. These are mine:

• What if personal selling were outlawed by the government, and I had to find ways to get customers to come to me and ask to buy?

- What if I were selling a telephone to a Trappist monk? He must observe a strict rule of silence but can nod acceptance at the close. How would I sell it?

- What if I had to get a year's worth of sales in eight hours?

- What if I could read the customer's mind before I entered his or her office?

- What if dogs could be trained to sell my products?

- What if I had to use a set number of words in sales presentations? For instance, no more or less than forty-five words.

- What if all products, goods, and services cost the same amount? A car would cost the same as a pencil, a house the same as a hamburger, and so on.

- What if I couldn't speak? How would I sell?

Let's work with: "What if dogs could be trained to sell my products?" What are the characteristics of dogs and how can they be related to selling?

Characteristics of dogs include: You train dogs by using repetitious techniques with small rewards for good behavior; dogs bark when threatened; they are loyal, territorial, affectionate, and eager to please. Dogs bury bones and chase cats. Some people are afraid of dogs.

What connections can you make between the characteristics of a dog and the characteristics of selling? What ideas does this "what if" question inspire? What would it be like if dogs could sell?

Possible lines of speculation:

- *Dogs are rewarded for good behavior with small rewards.* Create an incentive plan that gives an immediate reward upon the closing of a sale. Pay commissions, or a portion of the commission, immediately.

- *Dogs bark when threatened.* Develop an early warning system to alert us to the defective goods or services that salespeople hear about from customers. Reward salespeople who spot new problems.

- *Dogs are loyal.* Create loyalty among salespeople by publicly petting workers for good and consistent performance. Give tangible symbols of recognition. Reward loyal customers with surprise gifts and/ or discounts.

- *Dogs are territorial.* Redefine company policy to afford more autonomy to salespeople in their territory. The salesperson makes all decisions regarding that territory and runs it as if he or she owned it. Involve the salesperson in every decision that affects the territory.

- *Dogs are affectionate and eager to please.* Develop a customer-oriented campaign. Create a system wherein you periodically call customers after a sale to find out how things are and what more you can do. Send every customer a birthday card with a personal note.

- *Dogs bury bones.* Create an options package for customers with buried benefits that are triggered throughout the year. Consider a sales commission plan that buries a portion of each commission in an investment program that salespeople can draw on at a later date.

- *Dogs chase cats.* Develop a training program that concentrates on identifying and aggressively overcoming objections during the sales presentation. Train yourself and others to enjoy the identification and the handling of objections. Record objections and keep a tally of "caught" objections. Have a contest to see who catches and overcomes the most objections during the week.

- *Some people are afraid of dogs.* This fear diminishes once the person realizes that the dog is friendly. Create a useful premium to give to customers as a gift or a gesture of goodwill when cold-calling. Differentiate yourself from other salespeople by establishing a friendly relationship with the client before you concentrate on the sale. Become a problem-solver for the customer.

Years ago, the president of a Swiss pharmaceutical company wistfully said, "What if our customers were dogs, would we be better off?" Months passed and he noticed that some of the orders for his antibiotics were from veterinarians. After researching the market he discovered that veterinarians had found that some antibiotics developed for humans were effective for animals, but the companies that developed these drugs refused to supply the vets. They disliked having to repackage and reformulate the drugs for animals. In addition, most thought it was a misuse of a noble medicine and were embarrassed by the thought of their drugs being used on animals.

The Swiss company approached the other manufacturers and obtained licenses for veterinary use of their drugs. Human medications have since come under price pressure and regulations, making veterinary medicine the most profitable segment of the pharmaceutical industry. The company that is harvesting the profits is the one that wondered what it would be like if its customers were dogs. Today the Swiss company is the world leader in veterinary medicine, although it never developed a single drug.

Summary

You take imaginative chances by asking imaginative questions. Spencer Silver took an imaginative chance with 3M's Post-it notepads. He discovered the sticky substance that eventually was applied to notepads, and went around 3M for five years saying, "What if we used it for this?" or "What if we used it for that?" He finally caught the attention of the right person, Arthur Fry, and Silver's glue, the glue that no one wanted, caught the attention of the world.

Percy Spencer was another person who could see "what ifs." In 1943, while prowling around Raytheon, he discovered that standing in front of a microwave guide had melted a candy bar in his pocket. Experimenting further, he found that microwaves could pop popcorn. When he was finished, he changed the eating habits of America.

Some people transform the sun into a yellow spot while others, like Silver and Spencer, can look at a mustard stain and see the sun.

—

CHAPTER TWENTY-SEVEN

TRUE AND FALSE

"The sun rises and, on the
same day, it does not rise."

SUN TZU

A man from Crete said all Cretans are liars. Did he tell the truth or lie? If he told the truth, then he would have to be a liar, making his statement false, meaning that Cretans are truth-tellers. But if he lied and all Cretans are actually truth-tellers, then his statement would be true, meaning that they are really liars. In other words, if he told the truth, then he lied, and if he lied, he told the truth. The statement is paradoxically both true and false.

This paradox makes us feel ambivalent and uncertain because we're taught to keep things separated and to think in terms of cause and effect. As I'm writing this, I'm looking at a wreath of flowers. In a wreath, no flower is the "cause" of any other, yet together, they are the wreath. What is the cause of the growth of the acorn? The oak that is to come? Is what is occurring now causing what is to happen in the future? And, at the same time, is what occurred in the past the cause of what is happening now? If so, then a great number of roundabout things are causing what is happening now. Everything then, all the time, is causing everything else in a dynamic and circular, rather than a static and linear, way.

Thinking in terms of contradictions and paradoxes are hallmarks of creative thinking. In medicine, Louis Pasteur discovered the principle of immunology by discovering that some infected chickens survived a cholera bacillus. When the infected chickens and the uninfected chickens were inoculated with a new virulent culture, the uninfected chickens died and the infected chickens survived. The surviving chickens were simultaneously diseased and not diseased. The discovery that disease could paradoxically function to prevent disease has saved millions of lives over the years.

On the following page is an illustration of a penguin. It's also an illustration of a rabbit. How can one image be of two animals? It is contradictory.

The penguin faces right and the rabbit faces left. You can, with a little practice, paradoxically see both images separately and also simultaneously.

The image of a penguin and a rabbit existing in the same space is a visual contradiction.

Imagining two opposites or contradictory ideas, concepts, or images existing simultaneously is beyond logic. It is a type of conceptualizing in which the thinking processes transcend ordinary logical thinking. If you hold two opposites together, your mind moves to a new level. The suspension of logic allows an intelligence beyond thought to act and create a new form. The swirling of opposites creates the conditions for a new point of view to bubble free from your mind.

The resulting conditions of ambivalence and incongruity are tolerated by creative people. For instance, imagine being a success and a failure simultaneously. Ambivalence changes the way we feel and see and makes a different thought process possible. The paradox of success and failure can inspire the idea of learning to fail your way to success. An example is Thomas Edison. Edison's assistant asked him why he persisted in trying to perfect the light bulb filament after having failed five thousand times. Edison said he didn't understand the word *failure*. "I've discovered five thousand things that don't work," he said.

To think in terms of simultaneous opposites, convert your subject into a paradox and then find a useful analogy. Suppose you wanted to make a lot of money. The opposite of this might be that you lack ambition. The paradox is you want to make money, but you're too lazy to do much to make it. Next, you find an analogy that contains the essence of the paradox, for example, "I want light but without using electrical energy." The solution to the analogy is using natural energy from the sun. Finally, apply this principle to your original problem "how to make money when you're too lazy to work." One solution is to take a vacation to the South Sea Islands and write a travel book.

Einstein's Paradox

Albert Einstein's theory of special relativity proposed that time and space are not absolute. He wanted to "generalize" his theory to include Newton's theory on gravitation.

Problem. The key idea of general relativity is that gravity pulling in one direction is completely equivalent to acceleration in the opposite direction. An elevator accelerating upwards feels just like gravity pushing you into the floor.

Paradox. The contradiction was, how can an object be in motion and at rest at the same time?

Essence. Moving while resting

Analogy. To better understand the nature of the paradox, Einstein constructed an analogy that reflected the essence of the paradox. An observer, Einstein posited, who jumps off a house roof and releases any object at the same time, will discover that the object will remain, relative to the observer, in a state of rest. Einstein realized that an observer who jumps off a house roof will not, in his or her immediate vicinity, find any evidence of a gravitational field. This apparent absence arises even though gravitation causes the observer's accelerating plunge.

Unique Feature. The unique feature of this analogy was that the apparent absence of a gravitational field arises even though gravitation causes the observer's accelerating plunge. This was the analogy that Einstein said was his happiest thought in life, because it pertains to the larger principle of general relativity.

Equivalent. This analogy and its unique feature inspired the equivalent insight that gravity, as well as motion, can affect the intervals of time and of space.

New Idea. This inspired Einstein's general theory of relativity.

This kind of paradoxical thinking is sometimes called Janusian thinking, named after Janus, the two-faced Roman god. It involves creating a paradox or contradiction by conceiving of two opposing ideas as being currently true. Here are some business examples:

- Lead by following.

- Win by losing.

- Take risks, but be conservative.

- Seek diversity, but build a shared vision.

- Encourage creativity, but be practical.

- Build a cohesive team, but welcome conflict.

- Set realistic yet challenging goals.

- Reward team effort, but create a high-performance climate for individuals.

Consider the paradox that might be stated as "the best control comes from not controlling." The legendary founder of Wal-Mart, Sam Walton, was a living demonstration of this contradiction. Walton was normally in his office only from Friday and Saturday to noon, yet Wal-Mart was considered one of the more tightly managed organizations in the retail industry.

Someone once asked Walton how he could possibly run Wal-Mart when he was out of the office much of the time. He responded by saying, simply, that this was the only way to run a customer-focused organization. He spent Monday through Thursday in the field interacting directly with customers and employees and seeing what the competition was up to. In fact, while Walton was alive, Wal-Mart stores were built without an office for the store manager for the same reason. The manager's job was to be out with the customers and employees.

BLUEPRINT

1. *Problem.* A CEO noted that when his high-tech company was small, people would often meet spontaneously and informally. Out of these meetings came their best ideas. With the company's rapid growth, these informal meetings (and the number of good ideas) declined. He tried the usual ways to stimulate creativity (meetings, dinners, parties, roundtables, etc.), but they did not generate novel ideas. He wanted to re-create the spontaneous creative environment.

2. *Paradox.* Convert the problem into a paradox. One of the things that distinguishes creative people from ordinary people is their tolerance of opposites. Physicist Niels Bohr, for example, was delighted when he discovered the paradox that light is both a particle and a wave. This contradiction led to the principle of complementarity, which won him the Nobel prize. The question to ask is: What is the opposite or contradiction of the problem? Then, imagine both existing at the same time.

Example: The paradox of the company's situation was that unless the gatherings were spontaneous and unorganized they wouldn't produce novel ideas.

3. *Essence.* What is the essence of the problem? Summarize the essence in a book title that captures the essence and contradiction of the problem. Reducing the paradox to a book title makes it easier to work with and comprehend, such as:

- Sales target: *Focused Desire*

- Different level employees: *Balanced Confusion*

- Seasonal sales cycles: *Connected Pauses*

- Birth control: *Dependable Intermittency*

- Nature: *Rational Impetuousness*

   Example: In our example, the CEO summarized his paradox into the book title *Unorganized Gatherings.*

4. *Analogy.* Find an analogy that reflects the essence of the paradox. Think of as many analogies as you can and select the most suitable.
   Example: Our CEO found a suitable analogy in nature. He thought of herring gulls, which are very unorganized scavengers but effective survivors.

5. *Unique Feature.* What is the unique feature or activity of this analogy? Creative ideas often involve taking unique features from one subject and applying them to another.
   Example: In our example, the CEO determined that the unique feature of his analogy is *scavenging.* The gulls gather for an easy meal when fishermen throw unwanted fish and fish parts back into the sea.

6. *Equivalent.* Use an equivalent of this unique feature to trigger new insights.
   Example: The equivalent of this unique feature might be to have people come together for convenient meals at attractive prices.

7. *New Idea.* The company will serve inexpensive gourmet food in the company cafeteria. By subsidizing the cost of the gourmet food, the CEO encourages employees to

gather there (much like the herring gulls drawn to the fishermen's free food) to meet informally, mingle, and exchange ideas.

W. J. J. Gordon used this strategy to develop Pringles potato chips. Pringles was a matter of designing a new potato chip and package that would allow for more efficient packaging of chips without the need to fill the bag with more air than chips. The paradox was a compact chip that would not destruct. The "book title" that captured the essence of the paradox was *Compact Indestructibility.*

The analogy they worked with was bagging leaves in the fall. When you try to shove dry leaves into a plastic bag, you have a difficult time. But when the leaves are wet (the unique feature), they are soft and formable. A wet leaf conforms to the shape of its neighbor with little air between them. By wetting and forming dried potato flour, the packaging problem was solved and Pringles got its start.

Years back, I held a workshop with a group of engineers that worked in a foundry that cleaned forged metal parts by sandblasting them. They used sand to clean the parts, but the sand gets into the cavities, which are time-consuming and expensive to clean. The paradox is that the particles must be *hard* in order to clean the parts and at the same time *not hard* in order to be removed easily. The "book title" they used to describe the essence of the problem was *Disappearing Hardness.* This led them to think of *ice* as an analogy. The unique feature of ice was that it *melts.* The solution to the problem was to make the particles out of dry ice. The hard particles will clean the parts and later turn into gas and evaporate.

Paradoxical thinking is a raw thinking process that ignores the common rules of ordinary logical thinking. It is like light, in which wave and particle natures are two sides of one thing whose nature cannot be logically expressed. Light seems to be both continuous and discontinuous, and experiments show that it is neither continuous nor discontinuous. But, at a level beyond logic, we know that there is a unity to which opposites apply— a "both/and" instead of an "either/or."

SOCIAL ENTREPRENEURSHIP

Think of two antagonistic concepts: one is making money, the other doing social good. Instead of "either/or," use "both/and" to create a new business concept.

Problem: How to integrate business with social activism.

Paradox: The business and social activist sectors of society are separate and have different goals. The business sector seeks profits. The social activist seeks social good.

Essence: Social Entrepreneurship

Analogy: The Catholic order of Jesuit priests, the only truly effective global service organization

Unique Feature: Jesuits have a hybrid value chain where they integrate work for the church with work for the people. When they find an innovative solution for a problem in one part of the world they apply it to problems in another.

Equivalent: The equivalent of this unique feature might integrate social activism and business. Business would be the "church," and social activism would be the "work for the people"—in effect, a hybrid value change in global partnerships between social entrepreneurs and business.

New Idea: Create an organization to link together similar innovations to amplify their impact, and package ideas in ways that take them from the local to global level.

An example is Cemex, the big Mexican cement producer. They invented a plan that encourages families in urban slums to save for cement to build home additions, then provides them with discounted engineering services. Community activists love the program, since it promises to alleviate family abuse sparked by overcrowding. And it's great in principle for Cemex, since it creates a new market for their product.

Cemex partnered with AIDS activists who had created a Mary Kay–like network to provide sex education and AIDS prevention training throughout Mexico. Their strategy involved using the AIDS activists' existing distribution system, paying commissions to safe-sex educators for referring cement customers. The partnership allows the activists to improve the quality of life for many people while creating new alternatives to generate money for projects.

Cemex plans to team up with similar social activist networks to distribute cement across Mexico and elsewhere, while the AIDS activists plan to use their network to help promote other products that improve quality of life and generate income for their cause.

DAR UM JEITO

Dar um jeito is an expression in Brazil that, loosely translated, means "no problem is unsolvable and no barrier too great to cross." This is the attitude that Dr. Randas Batista of Curtiba, Brazil, adopted when he had many patients dying of congestive heart failure. When the heart is weakened by heart failure, it tries to compensate by stretching its muscles to help it beat, thus enlarging it. But as the heart's muscular left ventricle enlarges, it becomes less efficient at pumping blood through the body.

Dr. Batista lacked the resources necessary for the standard American treatments for the disease—drug therapy and heart transplant—so he came up with a radical solution. His solution was to cut off pieces of the heart to make it smaller. Dr. Batista described the solution as paradoxical, because you cut away part of the heart to make it stronger. Surgeons around the world are learning new lessons from Dr. Batista's procedure.

SUMMARY

Consider the contradiction of the mirror: Why does a mirror seem to invert left and right but not top and bottom? That is, why are the letters of a book backward but not upside down, and why is your left hand the double's right and your right the double's left? When we look into a mirror we imagine ourselves turned left to right, as if we walked around a pane of glass to look the other way. This conventional perspective is why we cannot explain what is happening with a mirror.

To understand a mirror's image, you have to psychologically reverse the way you perceive your image. Imagine your nose and the back of your head reversed: If your nose points north, your double's nose points south. The problem is on the axis running through the mirror. You have to imagine yourself reversed or "squashed" back to front. Stand in front of the mirror with one hand pointing east and the other west. Wave the east hand. The mirror image waves its east hand. Its west hand lies to the west. Its head is up and its feet are down. Once you look at a mirror with this paradoxical perspective, you gain an understanding about the axis of the mirror.

Psychologically reversing the way we perceive our image helps us understand a mirror. In the same way, thinking paradoxically may lead to a different insight or a breakthrough idea.

CHAPTER TWENTY-EIGHT

DREAMSCAPE

"Supreme excellence consists in breaking the
enemy's resistance without fighting."

SUN TZU

Dreams are a rich source of ideas, as they often contain combinations and rearrangements of objects, challenges, and events that would be almost impossible to come up with while awake. Ideas twinkle in dreams like bicycle lights in a mist.

Many dreams are so bewildering, so crowded with bizarre details, that they seem to defy interpretation. Others work almost like poems, providing uncanny distillations of a situation.

On November 10, 1619, during a freezing winter in Germany, a young aristocrat dreamed throughout the night. When he awoke, he recorded his dreams in a now-famous dream diary, which detailed a new system of thought. His dreams that night changed the course of science and Western civilization. Much of the contemporary scientific method is based on the dream journals of that young aristocrat, René Descartes.

Robert Louis Stevenson dreamed his novels before he wrote them. Physicist Niels Bohr conceived of a model of the atom in a dream. James Watt revolutionized the ammunition industry with his dreams of falling lead. Dmitri Mendeleyev dreamed the solution for the arrangement of the elements. Samuel Taylor Coleridge dreamed the poem "Kubla Khan" before he wrote it.

Sleep psychologists claim that we have approximately six dreams each night, but we tend to forget most of them. You can learn to initiate a productive dream state, choose the subjects of your dreams, and remember them clearly.

1. *Formulate a question about your challenge.* Write the question several times and then, before you drift off to sleep, repeat it to yourself several more times. If necessary, do this several evenings in a row. The mind must work consciously on a challenge before the subconscious becomes employed.

2. *If you don't remember your dreams, wake up thirty minutes earlier.* This increases your chance of waking during a dreaming period rather than after one. When you awake, lie still. Prolong the quiet as long as possible as you reflect on the dream. Do not allow daytime interests to interrupt your ruminations. Dreams vanish like boats sailing into a fog bank, so record the dream after you've thought it over.

3. *Record the dream in a dream journal.* Keep the journal next to your bed, and record as many details as you remember. Sketch the vivid portions of the dream. If you can't remember a dream, record whatever is on your mind—these thoughts often come from the dream and provide a first clue to retrieving it.

4. *After the dream is recorded, ask yourself the following questions:*

    • How were the people, places, and events in the dream related to my question?

    • Who were the key players in the dream?

    • How does this relate to my question?

    • Does the dream change the nature of the question?

    • What elements in this dream can help solve my problem?

    • What associations does the dream conjure up that might help with my problem?

    • What is the answer from the dream?

5. *Take one or two dream images or ideas and free-associate from them.* Write down whatever comes to mind, and do it day

after day. Soon the next dream will come along and your interpretation will go further.

6. *Keep the diary current.* Record your dreams daily. After you begin recording dreams you will remember more dreams, in greater detail. You will begin to see patterns and themes unfolding and repeating; your dreams will become richer and richer with metaphorical meanings.

You will find that your dreams are based on a body of experiences, both past and present, that have some influence on you and your challenge. In the figure below, the black and white shapes are intermixed to form something. Can you determine what it is?

Most people cannot identify the figure without prolonged study. But once you know that it is the head of a cow, you can no longer see it as confusing. The cow's head is on the left side of the illustration; the dark area near the bottom is its mouth. If you still have trouble seeing it, try viewing the picture from a distance.

Ideas in dreams are like the cow in the picture—that elusive and that real.

The owner of a hobby store was making a reasonable profit but wanted to do even better. His challenge was to improve his financial well-being. Trying creative dreaming, he had a recurrent dream of himself alone on a rock by a stormy sea. The wind was always blowing, and all the gold he sought was locked away below him in the rock. Then lightning would hit and split the rock, and golden disks would float out and circle in the sky. When they descended, they stacked themselves on top of the rock.

His interpretation of this dream was that he wasn't in business alone—there were other hobby and do-it-yourself stores in various locations around the city. The gold locked in the rock represented a potential profit for all of them. When the golden disks are freed by the lightning, they layer themselves on top of the rock, concentrated and available. Finally, this interpretation led to an idea.

The idea: A theme building. He bought a seven-story building and made it into a gigantic do-it-yourself hobby and toy center. He then convinced the other stores to lease space from him. His building is a concentration of hundreds of thousands of items that appeal to do-it-yourselfers. In addition, it offers ongoing classes in fields such as painting, bookbinding, stained-glass making, ceramics, household repairs, plumbing, and remodeling. It is *the* place to go for hobbies, toys, household repairs, or any do-it-yourself project.

Sometimes it seems like the ideas that are most deeply rooted in our minds, the most private and singular ones, came as spores on the prevailing night dreams, looking for any likely place to land, any welcome.

Frustrated by his inability to come up with a new idea for a seminar topic, a psychologist dedicated himself to creative dreaming to find one. He dreamed of a man who carried his genitals in a little box on his back and could send his penis off on adventures of its own. The man lay down to take a nap by a little stream and found a beautiful woman on the other side. After the penis finished its business, it returned to the box. The man woke up and continued on his way.

The psychologist pondered this dream and designed a seminar based on the question: "Is your sexuality something for which you are responsible or not?"

With creative dreaming, the "right" interpretation is the one that works for you. The unanticipated images from your dreams are starting points on which to hang your own personal meaning. Dreams weave together current experiences with ones from the past to create a unique narrative. Sometimes dreams remind you of what once was, like an Indian head nickel in a handful of new coins.

A retired dentist dreamed of a giant tooth with hair. When he awoke, he mused about the tooth walking into an old-fashioned barbershop for a haircut, and then, suddenly, he sat up straight. He had an idea for a new business venture.

The idea: Walk-in teeth cleaning services. Offer busy dental patients the same convenience they've come to expect when they want their hair trimmed. Get your teeth cleaned and polished in just thirty minutes, without an appointment, for $20. The business would be staffed by two dental hygienists working three cleaning stations. If any kind of dental problem is found, the patient would be referred back to their own dentist.

An apparently trivial dream may be very important in discovering what the dreamer's immediate difficulty actually is. Sometimes the same dream will give a clue to the solution.

Sports Illustrated reported that Nate Newton, a 320-pound Dallas Cowboy guard, was trying to use dreams to lose weight. "Every night I tell myself, 'I'm going to dream about my girl.' But it's always ham hocks."

My nephew Karl tried creative dreaming to address the challenge of deciding on a college. He dreamed he was at the family's summer cottage. The tide was rising and gigantic, crashing waves had reached the cottage. Boats were disappearing beneath the sea. Then he saw a long object floating in the distance. A voice told him that the object was the only thing that could rescue him, that he had nothing to fear if he could reach it. He looked closely at the object and saw it was a baseball bat.

Most of the dream could be interpreted as symbolizing the feelings of any person who is about to begin some sort of independent life, but the bat was a purely personal reference. Karl associated the cottage with carefree summer life and a complete lack of responsibility, and also with financial security.

When I asked him what his association was with the bat, he said, "I have that baseball bat in my room." When I asked why, of all the objects in his room, his dream should choose this particular one, he was puzzled. Then he suddenly realized that the bat was the only thing in his life that he had bought with his own money.

The dream provided advice: "It seems I should select a college where I can try to pay at least part of my own way." He added, "It's kind of like the things you can trust most are the things that really belong to you."

SUMMARY

Dreams reveal things you did not know you knew. Elias Howe, struggling with his design for a sewing machine, reportedly dreamed he was captured by savages carrying spears with holes in their tips. Upon awakening, Howe realized he should put the hole for the thread at the end of the needle, not the top or middle. This minor modification made the sewing machine a reality.

It may be that our earliest mode of thinking was symbolic imagery—one reason, perhaps, that poetry can stir us as it does. Some dreams can haunt us with a power more pervasive even than that of poetry, shimmering in the mind like some lost city.

CHAPTER TWENTY-NINE

DA VINCI'S TECHNIQUE

"The book of Military Administration says:
'As the voice cannot be heard in battle, drums and
bells are used. As troops cannot see each other clearly
in battle, flags and banners are used.'"

SUN TZU

Imagine a rectangular tray containing a rubber bag partially filled with oil. A steel marble dropped onto the bag's surface gradually sinks to the bottom, pushing the surface of the rubber bag before it. When the marble comes to rest, it is in the center of a depression. Drop a second marble and it will roll down the contour and come to rest against the first one. The second marble is *active;* it does not stay where it has been put down, but follows the slope created by the first one. All subsequent marbles will roll toward the first marble, forming a cluster.

In the same way, an active mind allows incoming information to organize itself into a new cluster, giving rise to new perspectives and new ideas.

One good way to originate new clusters of information is through pictures. In the beginning, humans communicated with pictures. The alphabet evolved from the various pictographic techniques; however, this does not mean that verbal thinking is more advanced.

Albert Einstein observed that:

The words of the language, as they are written or spoken, do not seem to play any role in my mechanism of thought. The physical entities which seem to serve as elements in thought are certain signs and more or less clear images which can be voluntarily reproduced and combined.

Leonardo da Vinci's technique for getting ideas was to close his eyes, relax totally, and cover a sheet of paper with random lines and scribbles. He would then open his eyes and look for images and patterns, objects, faces, or events in the scribble. Many of his inventions came forth unbeckoned from this random scribbling.

Scribbling allows you to put your abstract ideas into a tangible form. Imagine yourself flying over your challenge in an airplane to get a clear overview. While in the air, sketch what you see below you. Sketch as many alternative concepts as you think you see. You are your own audience; therefore, you can draw or sketch freely without worrying about what anyone will think. Sketching is a way of talking to yourself. Thomas Edison made hundreds of sketches and doodles before beginning to formulate an idea. GE has a collection of his doodles about the light bulb, most of which are indecipherable to anyone but Edison.

Graphic ideation (sketching, doodling, or drawing) is complementary to verbal ideation and can help you muster up new ideas.

BLUEPRINT

1. *Review a challenge you are working on.* In your mind's eye, scan its various aspects. Write the challenge on paper and reflect on it for a few minutes: What doesn't fit? What are the major obstacles? The unknown? What do I want to understand? At this point, the way I see it is . . . What's bothering me most is . . .

2. *Relax.* When relaxed, you will find your intuitive consciousness uses images and symbols more freely. (You will find a good relaxation technique in chapter 22, under "The Jell-O Syndrome.")

3. *Allow your intuition to offer images, scenes, and symbols that represent your situation.* You need not know what the drawing will look like before you draw it.

4. *Provide a format for the challenge by drawing a boundary.* This can be any size and shape you wish, and can be carefully or roughly drawn. The purpose is to separate the challenge from its surroundings and allow you to focus on it.

   A boundary also gives your drawing its own atmosphere or depth and helps establish a wholeness which in itself is meaningful and gives meaning to your drawing.

5. *Draw as your mind wants to draw.* Practice drawing without conscious direction. (Some people use their opposite hand to get less conscious control of the images.) Pretend the lines and scribbles are dictating how to draw and place them. Do not censor what you draw—the drawing is private and need not be shown to anyone. Let the drawing flow from you onto the paper.

    Chance, or randomness, gives depth to your scribbling. It points to an unknown but active principle of order and meaning that can be thought of as a secret message from your unconscious.

6. *If one drawing does not seem enough, take another piece of paper and do another one, and another—as many as you need.*

7. *Examine your drawing.* The drawing is a message from your subconscious. Look at the image as a whole and then at the separate parts. These are visual representations of your thoughts. Search the symbols and scribbles for unexpected signs and new information.

8. *Write down the first word that comes to mind for each image, symbol, scribble, line, or structure.*

9. *Combine all the words and write a paragraph.* Free-associate, writing whatever thoughts come to mind. Compare the paragraph with your drawing. If you feel the need, revise your paragraph until you are comfortable that the drawing and the words represent the same thoughts in two different languages: verbal and graphic.

10. *Consider how what you wrote relates to your challenge.* Has your viewpoint changed? Do you have new ideas? New insights? Surprises from your subconscious? What parts puzzle you? What's out of place?

    Be especially attentive to questions that pop up in your mind such as: What is that? How come? Where is that? What could that mean? If you feel it's important to find the answer to a particular question, you are on the way to a breakthrough solution.

Think of every drawing as an artichoke in which not only the heart and leaves but the spiny choke as well are edible.

One accountant drew his images on the back of scrolls of adding machine paper. He started asking himself questions about the paper he was using. He knew some of his colleagues felt so passionately about the bottom line that they rewound adding machine paper to use the other side. He designed a gadget to do the job for them: Instead of feeding onto the desk, the paper rewinds onto a roll on the back of the adding machine. It pays for itself after twenty rolls. His invention was the direct result of asking questions about *every* aspect of his drawing.

If you are unable to provoke new ideas with this technique or have failed to gain a deeper insight, keep repeating the technique each day. After you're relaxed, ask yourself, "Well now, what is the status of my challenge today?" and repeat the exercise.

University textbooks are normally sold through university bookstores. Many times, these textbooks are packaged with study guides, learning notes, course readers, and other auxiliary items. The bookstores resist stocking these extra items, pleading lack of space and low profits. Many textbook publishers had to rely on inserts and advertising to sell the auxiliary items, with minimal success. The major obstacle to overcome is reliance on the bookstore.

The challenge is: "In what ways might I create new channels of distribution for auxiliary items that accompany university textbooks?"

After contemplating this challenge for a few days, I begin to draw whatever images came to mind. I drew without conscious direction and tried to draw and place the images as if they were dictating to me where to place them. I made several drawings before one galvanized my imagination. My final drawing looked like this:

I studied the drawing, writing down the first word that came to mind for each image, combined the words, looked for and forced connections between the images and my challenge, and paid attention to every question that popped into my mind. Some of my thoughts were:

- Different channels.

- Computer programs.

- Computer floppy disk.

- Stack of coins.

- People lined up in front of a machine.

- People all converging on one spot.

- Tombstone.

- Slot for coins.

- Six round heads and one square one.

My intuitive interpretation of the images suggested an idea for a new and different channel of distribution.

The idea: Set up a system of software dispensing machines on campuses. Students can purchase a "disk" or bring one of their own, and load it, for a fee, with one of the following:

- Study guides for various textbooks.

- Lecture notes for various classes.

- Sample test questions for various classes.

- Math learning programs.

- Course readers.

- Bibliographies.

- Campus phone book.

- Games.

The software dispensing machines publish "on demand," obviating the need for the traditional marketing channel, the bookstore. The machines would be compatible with both IBM and Apple.

Once your subconscious thoughts are expressed in pictures you can hang conscious ideas, analogies, and metaphors on them. This lets you organize disparate thoughts and begin to imagine new possibilities and solutions.

Sometimes a question comes up that you can't answer but that seems very important to the solution. (For instance, "I wonder what that figure means, it seems very significant.") When this happens, your mind will not rest until an answer is found; it will search for the primal meaning slumbering beneath the world of appearances. It may take time, but eventually your mind will find the answer.

NATURE'S HANDWRITING

Leonardo da Vinci taught himself to read nature's handwriting, which can be seen everywhere: in wings, eggshells, clouds, snow, ice, crystals, and other chance conjunctions. He used these insights in his quest for new ideas and solutions to problems. Leonardo could have coaxed ideas out of a salesman's shoe. Robert McKim's *Experiences in Visual Thinking* provides this illustrative excerpt from Leonardo's notebooks:

> I cannot forbear to mention . . . a new device for study which although it may seem trivial and almost ludicrous, is nevertheless extremely useful in arousing the mind to various inventions. And that is, when you look at a wall spotted with stains . . . you may discover a resemblance to various landscapes, beautiful with mountains, rivers, rocks, trees. Or again, you may see battles and figures in action, or strange faces and costumes, and an endless variety of objects which you could reduce to complete and well-drawn forms.

Leonardo also wrote an essay agreeing with Botticelli that you can throw a paint-soaked sponge at a wall and see a host of different images in the splashes. These images are starting points for ideas; your mind superimposes the possibility of meaning onto them.

The pattern in the margin was created by splashing some ink on paper. Study the pattern. Can you free-associate from the pattern to an idea for a new product, service, or process?

A friend studied the pattern and saw:

- String.
- A spider's web.
- Coffee spill on a rug.
- McDonald's logo.

These images clustered into a new idea. He thought of fast food, liquids that spill, containers for liquids, and webbed objects. Then, bingo, he came up with an idea to replace cardboard trays at concession stands and fast-food outlets.

The idea: A cup carrier made out of plastic loops that hang from a web of strings and can tote four cups at once.

The design eliminates spilling—lids aren't even necessary. The carrier costs less and takes up less space than most paper trays.

SUMMARY

Understanding your drawings is like untying a knot. When a knot is untied, the string must be drawn back the way it traveled when the knot was tied. When you search your drawings for ideas, you are drawn back to your unconscious, which is where the drawing came from in the first place.

The ideas do not rise up from your drawing but from the deepest part of your unconscious, the secret archive stored in the soul at birth, enhanced by every waking moment of life, which has the power and the vision to let you create something never before heard or seen.

CHAPTER THIRTY

DALI'S TECHNIQUE

"When the strike of a hawk breaks the body of
its prey, it is because of timing."

SUN TZU

You can reach the center of a circle from any point on the compass. Similarly, you can reach into your unconscious from a variety of different starting points.

One starting point is *hypnogogic imagery.* This technique produces autonomous inner imagery that can be captured just before you fall asleep. It's a somewhat difficult technique to master, but when mastered it can provide strong images.

Can you identify the figure in the margin?

It is the letter E. It is difficult to see because it is such a strong and deep E. If you have difficulty seeing it, try looking at it from a distance. Once you understand what it is, it becomes impossible *not* to see the E. The images produced by hypnogogic imagery are like this—somehow deeper and stronger than those produced by other techniques.

This imagery can be either visual or auditory—it cannot be controlled or directed. Some people are even able to envision fantastic surreal imagery in colors that appear deeper and plusher than seemingly possible.

Salvador Dali used this technique to conjure up the extraordinary images in his paintings. He would put a tin plate on the floor and then sit by a chair beside it, holding a spoon over the plate. He would then totally relax his body; sometimes he would begin to fall asleep. The moment that he began to doze the spoon would slip from his fingers and clang on the plate, immediately waking him to capture the surreal images.

Hypnogogic images seem to appear from nowhere, but there is a logic. The unconscious is a living, moving stream of energy from which thoughts gradually rise to the conscious level and take on a definite form.

Your unconscious is like a hydrant in the yard while your consciousness is like a faucet upstairs in the house. Once you know how to turn on the hydrant, a constant supply of images can flow freely from the faucet.

These forms give rise to new thoughts as you interpret the strange conjunctions and chance combinations.

BLUEPRINT

1. *Think about your challenge.* Consider your progress, your obstacles, your alternatives, and so on. Then push it away and relax.

2. *Totally relax your body.* Try to achieve the deepest muscle relaxation you can. You may wish to use the technique described in chapter 22, under "The Jell-O Syndrome."

3. *Quiet your mind.* Do not think of what went on during the day or your challenges and problems. Clear your mind of chatter.

4. *Quiet your eyes.* You cannot look for these images. Be passive. You need to achieve a total absence of any kind of voluntary attention. Become helpless and involuntary and directionless. If you fall asleep easily, hold a spoon loosely in one of your hands. You can enter the hypnogogic state this way, and, should you begin to fall asleep, you will drop the spoon and awaken in time to capture the images.

5. *Record your experiences immediately after they occur.* The images will be mixed and unexpected and will recede rapidly. They could be patterns, clouds of colors, or objects.

6. *Look for the associative link.* Write down the first things that occur to you after your experience. Look for links and connections to your challenge. Ask questions such as:

   • What puzzles me?

   • Is there any relationship to the challenge?

   • Any new insights?

   • What's out of place?

- What disturbs me?

- What do the images remind me of?

- What are the similarities?

- What analogies can I make?

- What associations can I make?

- What do the images resemble?

A restaurant owner used hypnogogic imagery to inspire new promotion ideas. He kept seeing giant neon images of different foods: neon ice cream, neon pickles, neon chips, neon coffee, and so on. The associative link he saw between the various foods and his challenge was to somehow use the food itself as a promotion.

The idea: He offers various free food items according to the day of week, the time of day, and the season. For instance, he might offer free pickles on Monday, free ice cream between 2 and 4 P.M., free coffee on Wednesday nights, free sweet rolls in the spring, and so on. He advertises the free food items with neon signs, but you never know what food items are being offered free until you go there. The sheer variety of free items and the intriguing way in which they are offered has made his restaurant a popular place to eat.

Another promotion he created as a result of seeing images of different foods is a frequent eater-program. Anyone who hosts five meals in a calendar month gets $50 worth of free meals. The minimum bill is $20 but he says the average is $30 a head. These two promotions have made him a success.

The images you summon up with this technique have an individual structure that may indicate an underlying idea or theme. Your unconscious mind is trying to communicate something specific to you, though it may not be immediately comprehensible. The images can be used as armatures on which to hang new relationships and associations.

A college professor who taught a mixed-media art class was bored with the traditional first assignment of painting a self-portrait. He wanted an exercise that would explore space and perception. Using hypnogogic imagery for inspiration, he saw Technicolor trees dressed up like human beings walking around and talking. He thought about this image for days, and then the idea for a new assignment struck.

The idea: He had his students personalize a two-by-four board and carry it around with them everywhere. The students shaped and designed their boards to express their experiences, personalities, and interests. The board served as a yardstick for students to relate to their environment and forced them to work with materials they wouldn't normally use.

One student made an environmental statement by painting her board blue and black, attaching tree branches and press clippings about forest fires, and scorching parts of it. Another student made his board an extension of his Mexican heritage. He decorated it like Mexican folk art, with carvings of an eagle, snake, and cactus. He depicted his family tree and attached cloth poinsettias, a rosary, and even a piñata.

SUMMARY

Treat the images as fact, but make no assumptions about them except that you experienced them, and that somehow they must make sense. One workshop contemplated ways to clean up the environment. One of the participants reported that she got the following image using this technique.

What is your interpretation? What is the associative link between the image and the challenge? Can you use the image to produce an idea to clean up the environment?

The workshop made the following associations:

- A dead bird found on a polluted beach.

- The hand that polluted the beaches killed the bird.

- The same hand tenderly holds the bird.

- The hand did not intend to kill the bird.

- The hand is a corporate hand.

These associations led to the idea of asking oil and chemical companies for a hand in cleaning up the environment. They approached Exxon Chemical and asked them to convert collected trash into plastic, barnacle-proof beach benches.

You will not always be able to convert the images into meaningful ideas. At times, the message may be too complex and difficult to link with your present situation. When that happens, certain images' meanings may remain forever out of reach like delicate balloons bouncing along the ceiling.

—

CHAPTER THIRTY-ONE

NOT KANSAS

"Toto, something tells me we're not
in Kansas anymore."

DOROTHY IN *THE WIZARD OF OZ*
(MGM, 1939)

It may well be that modern man's only true remaining adventure lies in the inner realm of the unconscious self. Not Kansas is a technique for using the imagination, under the guidance of the intellect and will, to take you on such an adventure. It will help you coax out messages from your unconscious.

This Thinkertoy has to be experienced before its power becomes evident. I'm always anxious when others first try it. I feel as if I am watching one of those old war movies in which a nurse is removing the last foot of white bandages from a soldier's eyes. Will he see?

BLUEPRINT

1. *Relax.* You may wish to use the technique described in chapter 22, under "The Jell-O Syndrome."

2. *Ask your unconscious for an answer to your challenge.* Write out the challenge and ask your unconscious to give you a symbol or image of how to solve your challenge.

3. *Take a guided imagery journey.* There are two model journeys described in this section: The Dakotas and Storm.

4. *Accept whatever messages emerge.* Don't censor anything. Trust your messages. The more you trust, the freer the images become, and the more truth you will find inherent in the images.

5. *Use your imagination to make the images as clear and vivid as you can.* Record or draw them immediately.

6. *If confusing images occur, conjure up others.* Become a Sam Spade of images, tracking down the ones you can use to solve your challenge.

7. *Look for qualities, patterns, relationships, and clues.* Use the messages, images, and symbols as a departure point for free association.

After reading the following example of a guided imagery journey, close your eyes and take a few minutes to visualize the scene it describes. Then, try using it to solve one of your challenges. It's a bit like sex—you can't realize what it's really like by just reading about it. You have to do it.

THE DAKOTAS

Think of a challenge you are currently working on. Write the challenge on a piece of paper as objectively as possible, as if you were a reporter writing a brief description of the challenge for the paper. Contemplate the challenge for a few minutes after you write it. Ask for an answer.

Close your eyes and relax deeply for five to ten minutes. Clear your mind. Try going to your private, inner sanctuary to breathe deeply and relax.

When you are deeply relaxed, imagine you are camping in the deep Dakotas next to a deserted mine shaft. It's late afternoon and getting cool. As the sun sets, the buttes and coulees, the cliffs and sculptured hills and ravines have lost their burned afternoon look and are glowing with yellow and rich browns and a hundred variations of red and silver gray with streaks of coal black. You go to a thicket of dwarfed and wind-warped cedars and junipers, and once there are stopped, surprised by the color and clarity of light.

Against the descending sun, the rocks are dark and clean-lined, while to the east, the landscape shouts with color. The night, closing around you, is lovely beyond thought, for the stars are so close that, although there is no moon, the starlight makes a silvery glow in the sky.

The air cuts your nostrils—the wind is blowing from the north and has winter in it. You collect a pile of dry, dead cedar branches and build a small fire to warm yourself, smelling the perfume of the burning wood and hearing its excited crackle. The fire makes a dome of yellow light over you, and nearby you hear an owl screech and the barking of coyotes.

Hunched over the fire, you dip a rainbow trout in cornmeal flour and fry it crisp in bacon fat. Holding the trout by its head and tail, you nibble it off its backbone, finishing with the tail, crisp as a potato chip. You finish your meal with coffee and hot homemade biscuits smothered in butter. You're warm and relaxed and feel good all over. Something rustles the thicket. As it approaches you, you realize that no danger exists for you or it. What is it? Have a dialogue with it. Ask it to speak to you; ask how it represents a solution to your challenge. Pay attention and ask for clarification where necessary. When you are satisfied, thank it for its insights, and allow it to disappear back into the thicket.

You finish your coffee and eat an apple so crisp and sweet that it seems to explode with juice when you bite into it. The campfire burns low and the thicket rustles from a strange wind that stirs mysterious feelings in you.

The night begins to turn cold. You put on your insulated underwear and the warmth gives you pure ecstatic comfort. You pick up your kerosene lamp, trim the wick, and light it to make a golden butterfly of flame. The lamp gives you warmth as well as light, and you think that no pleasanter light was ever designed. This must be like the lamps the pilgrims used.

You take your lamp to the abandoned mine, lie on the ground, and peer into the shaft to its very source. When your eyes adjust to the darkness, you see something in the depths. What is it? Study it and then let it go, but remember what you saw.

As you get up and prepare to leave the mine, you notice a weather-beaten leather briefcase lying in the grass. You pick it up and open it. Inside you find a piece of paper folded in quarters.

As you unfold the paper, you see that on it is written a message in response to your challenge. You read the message. Contemplate the message and how it might help you solve your challenge.

When you are finished, return to your campsite. Take a deep breath and try to fix the images you received in your consciousness, then open your eyes and immediately write or draw your impressions and images.

Practice this exercise until you feel comfortable with it and images begin to appear freely and vividly. The images you invoke are clues to solutions. It may take time for the images and their import to become clear; sometimes you must wait for other images to furnish a context. Eventually, you'll find meanings for these slippery, dodging ghosts.

A community newspaper publisher wanted to make his newspaper unique and different.

He took a guided journey to The Dakotas. The images and impressions he recorded were: comfort, dogs, friendship, hunger, chickens, coldness, death, warmth, animals approaching in the dark, no danger from the animal, turning cold, dead pilgrims, and pleasant memories. The message that he found in the briefcase read: "Dead dogs are a comfort too."

He wondered, "How can dead dogs relate to my challenge?" He thought about pets, death, and grieving owners. Then the idea arrived.

The idea: An obituary column for pets. It's a journalism first and something no major publication could attempt or dare to emulate. Pet lovers liked it and, since most people have pets, circulation rose.

The obituaries are really about people's relationships with animals. The pet owners make them lively and personal by writing about what the pet did all day. For example, a typical obit reads:

> Jazz, my dog, in many ways was unremarkable. Like so many of us, she liked to spend her nights on the recliner watching television. Her favorite show was "Miami Vice." Wise potato chips were her favorite snack. Her occasional outbursts of temper, often brought on when others tried to share the recliner, were just her style, and everyone understood. Jazz lived to go on vacation just once.

You certainly don't have to use The Dakotas—you may feel more comfortable writing and using scenarios that center on beaches, vacations, voyages, space trips, mysteries, or whatever. The point of any scenario is to get as many of your senses involved as possible in an imaginary setting, and guide your imagination to actively search for messages and images from your unconscious.

Remember, it doesn't matter whether the cat is black or white, so long as it catches the mouse. Nor does it matter if ideas and insights come from your conscious or unconscious psyche.

Following is another of my favorite guided journeys, titled Storm. Use the same procedures that you used in The Dakotas. Relax, write your challenge, and ask your unconscious for symbols or images to help you resolve your challenge.

STORM

You had never seen such a sunset. The sun was like a dying coal, ringed with black long before it neared the horizon. After the sunset, the rim of the earth was blood-red for a few minutes, then the red was streaked with black. When you looked at the eerie sky, it seemed as if the world had turned upside down and the road that ought to be beneath your feet was now above your head. And then the sky turned black.

You are surprised by a flicker of light to the west—so quick that you do not recognize it as lightning. But it flickers again and again and soon is almost constant. Then comes the thunder, with a sound that seems to roll over you like boulders. The lightning begins to drive into the earth, with streaks as big as poles and terrible sounds.

The rain begins, pelting down in big scattered drops that at first feel good, but the drops grow bigger and soon the rain is falling in sheets, blown this way and that by the fitful wind. In a bright flash of lightning, you see something run in front of you. What is it? Study it and then let it go, but remember what you saw.

The water beats down more heavily, pounding you and running in streams off your hat brim. The rain is now so heavy that you begin to think you might be drowned. A stream of water pours down in front of your nose while another runs down your back. You are so cold and wet that you feel you might never get warm again.

The ground is covered with water and there is nothing to do but splash along. Suddenly, you begin to slide—you have stepped into a hole and you feel water rising up to your hips. You climb out and squish along again.

Soon you get too tired to think and can only hope for morning. But the night goes on and on. Finally, the lightning dies and the hard rain slows to a drizzle. You stop to empty your shoes of water. You drop one. When you stoop down to pick it up, you notice a bottle with a slip of paper in it. You pick up the bottle and put it in your pocket.

A little while later, dawn breaks and the rain stops completely. The sky is cloudless. The first sunlight sparkles on the wet trees and bushes and on the hundreds of scattered puddles. Cold and damp, you bend over a puddle and wash the mud off your clothes. Now that the sun is beginning to warm things up, you find a grassy hill that isn't too wet and start a small fire. Starved, you fry up some eggs and thick slices of bacon. Breaking the fried eggs with your knife, you eat them with slices of bacon as you warm your body by the fire.

Remembering the bottle, you take out the note and read it slowly. What are the images? Open your eyes and write or draw your impressions and images. Write whatever comes to mind.

If the images are cloudy, repeat the exercise daily until you are comfortable with it and the images grow vivid. Begin to imagine that you are going to experience a breakthrough and the images will flow.

A lawyer who was trying to find a new business niche experienced Storm several times. He kept seeing the image of a doctor in rags running from someone in the storm. He wondered what would make this doctor so poor and scared. "Malpractice suits," he thought and decided to provide a service to protect doctors from frivolous lawsuits.

The idea: A service that helps doctors avoid malpractice claims by identifying litigious patients in advance. He discovered that 35 percent of all people who file malpractice suits have been plaintiffs in previous civil actions. His idea is to computerize all civil actions in certain target cities back to a given date. He will then sell the information to doctors for an annual fee plus a service charge for each search. The flip side is that he also plans to computerize doctors' litigation histories and provide a search service for malpractice lawyers.

Those who deny the value of asking the unconscious for ideas are those who decline to taste it. They are like people who have been eating plain boiled asparagus for so long that they begin to deny the very existence of Indian restaurants.

JUST ASK

Once you are able to summon up images from your unconscious at will, you can simply ask your unconscious for answers. The basic procedure is:

1. Formulate a challenge.

2. Address it to your unconscious.

3. Ask for the answer to emerge as a mental image.

If you are adept at imaging, the answer will emerge spontaneously and effortlessly. If a chain of images emerges, often the first one is the most significant. Spend some time studying that image for meaning.

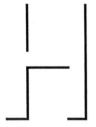

In the figure in the margin, the lines seem irrelevant. Some appear to form right angles, but the lines do not appear to represent anything meaningful.

Now, imagine that the lines represent the shadow of the block letter H illuminated from above. Imagine that you are looking down at it. Do you see how your imagination formed the H out of a seemingly irrelevant collection of lines? You have imagined it into existence.

This is why it's important not to censor or ignore mental images that seem irrelevant. Often, after considerable attention, your imagination will coax out a message. And once you imagine the message, it exists.

Guided imagery adventures such as The Dakotas and Storm put you in touch with your unconscious, giving it an opportunity to express itself. This technique helps you overcome "conscious cramp" (mental strain from overusing your conscious mind) and allows the images and messages that are always present to come into your consciousness. Once retrieved, they may almost seem like lonely and mysterious poetry that leads the way to ideas and insights in accordance with some secret design.

Another way to get in touch with your unconscious is The Three Doors.

The Three Doors

Formulate and write a definite question about your challenge. Relax. Breathe deeply and slowly. With each breath, your lungs fill with fresh, clean air and you feel yourself becoming lighter. Keep taking deep breaths until you feel everything become effortless and easy.

Imagine you are standing before a series of doors, one behind the other. Visualize yourself opening the doors one at a time. When you've finished, write down what you saw and felt, and what you did.

Many people feel The Three Doors leads them to deeper levels of their unconscious. Each door that is opened represents going deeper and deeper into yourself. The third door seems to reveal the most significant answers.

You can search for meaning in the images generated, or free-associate from those images to find ideas for solving your challenge. A city planner faced the challenge of improving city construction projects. The question he wanted resolved was: How can we avoid the chaos that city construction projects create? Tearing up pavement is unsightly, inconvenient, and causes financial harm to city merchants.

Using The Three Doors, he called up the following:

Door one: storm clouds.

Door two: long sidewalks.

Door three: long winding snakes.

The meaning he found in free-associating from these images led to a new idea for the installation of sewer pipes and cables.

The idea: Put underground cables and sewer pipes in modular concrete elements above the ground, molded as curbs (much like long concrete snakes winding through the city). These elements are easy, fast to install, repair, and will reduce the cost and inconvenience to the city and, in particular, to its merchants.

Summary

The unconscious is pure nature and, like nature, has great gifts for those who know how to find them. Songwriter and musician John Lennon taught himself to drop a hook into his unconscious and dredge up the images that he integrated into his music. He would relate the hooked images and messages to his challenge of creating original songs.

The logic of dredging for ideas is similar to the way treasure hunters search for lost booty. They suppose it's down there under the black, mysterious flowing water, and they work the grappling hooks back and forth, back and forth, back and forth, until they snag something and drag it to the surface.

You can too.

CHAPTER THIRTY-TWO

THE SHADOW

"Subtle and insubstantial, the expert leaves no
trace; divinely mysterious, he is inaudible."

SUN TZU

Close your left eye and shift your gaze over the target on the left until the target on the right disappears. This means that you have found your right eye's blind spot, a small area with no light receptors. By fixating your right eye on the left target, you become blind to the target on the right. Similarly, when you fixate on your conscious mind you become blind to the value of the unconscious.

We fixate on the conscious mind because we have been taught that it is the master of the universe. If you indulge yourself with this illusion about the heroic nature of the conscious mind and disregard the unconscious as you fish for ideas, you are like a fisherman who stands on a whale while fishing for minnows.

But how do you get in touch with your unconscious? It's one thing to say, "Let ideas roll out of my unconscious mind like mighty waters," quite another to work out the irrigation system. You need a technique.

Look at the shape that appears in the margin on the following page. Can you determine what it is?

The object is a kite, with the top of the kite at the lower right. Once you name the object, your perception changes and the figure becomes meaningful. When you name something, you create expectations and change your perceptions. Once the figure is given meaning by naming it, it is impossible to look at it and have the perception you had before.

In the same way, you can organize the irregular shapes from your unconscious into regular ones by personifying your unconscious. This technique is known as psychosynthesis, and it has incredible potential since there is no known limit to the capacities of the deep unconscious. Psychosynthesis has been used by geniuses, visionaries, artists, and inventors for centuries. Douglas MacArthur had numerous conversations with the personification of his hero-father, whom he would conjure up to discuss strategy in the Pacific. Mozart was a coarse, narcissistic boor; however, when he communicated with his personified inner self, the result was some of the most complex and sensitive music the world has ever known.

Buckminster Fuller once had a conversation with his inner spiritual guide who told him: "You do not belong to you. You belong to the Universe." Fuller went on to become an architect-engineer-poet-futurist who shook the world with his technological innovations and visions of global unity. Milton referred to his inner guide as his "Celestial Patroness, who . . . unimplor'd . . . dictates to me my unpremeditated Verse."

MacArthur, Mozart, Fuller, and Milton used imagination to create a route between the conscious and unconscious and back again. By creating and interacting with their inner advisors, they learned to collect information from their unconscious and used this information to solve challenges.

Stuart Miller, an authority on psychosynthesis, describes in *Dialogue With Higher Self* one way of initiating an interior dialogue:

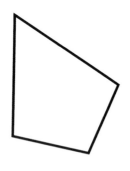

> Assume, with many ancient traditions, that you have within you a source of understanding and wisdom that knows who you are, what you have been, and what you can most meaningfully become in the future. This source is in tune with your unfolding purpose. It can help you direct your energies toward achieving increasing integration, toward harmonizing and unifying your life.

Having made this assumption, close your eyes, take a few deep breaths, and imagine that you are seeing the face of a wise old man or woman whose eyes express great love for you. If you have difficulty visualizing this, first imagine a candle flame, burning steadily and quietly, and then let the face appear at the center.

Engage this wise old person in dialogue, in whatever way seems best: use the presence and guidance of the sage to help you better understand whatever questions, directions, or choices you are dealing with at the moment. Spend as much time as you need in this dialogue, and when you are finished, write down what happened, amplifying and evaluating further whatever insights were gained.

You can create a personal adviser to help you create associative imagery while in a relaxed awake state. Choose anyone you like, alive or dead, real or fictional: Sun Tzu, Marie Curie, Socrates, Batman, Wonder Woman, Amelia Earhart, Napoleon Bonaparte, Leonardo da Vinci, Indira Gandhi, Thomas Edison, Cornelius Vanderbilt, Buddha, Eleanor Roosevelt, Henry Ford, or an imaginary, all-knowing, mythical figure or guru to help you with your question or challenge.

With so many possible advisors available, you need to make some choices. As you move toward forming a relationship, it is important that you clearly envision the kind of adviser you want to work with. By clarifying and defining the relationship, you will know what kind of experience you hope to share and in what areas you hope to get meaningful ideas and advice.

BLUEPRINT

To invoke your personal mentor, perform the following:

1. *Let go of your tension.* Consciously take your body into a state of deep relaxation. You may wish to use the technique described under "The Jell-O Syndrome" in chapter 22.

    Do not worry about achieving a deep enough level of relaxation. Just be passive and allow relaxation to occur at its own pace.

2. *Imagine that your body is surrounded with soft, glowing white light.* Let the light comfort you and bathe you in its soft radiance.

3. *Now imagine that you are walking into a favorite place (house, boat, mountain, forest, room, whatever).* Picture the details. What does it look like? Smell like? Feel like? What sounds do you hear?

4. *Picture your spiritual mentor walking toward you.* Look at his or her face. What do you see? Be aware of your emotions and reactions. Say to your mentor: "Be my guide. Introduce me to solutions and to new ideas. Lead me to the resolution of my problem." The more fully you create

the pictures in your mind, the more powerful the communication with your unconscious will be.

Have your guide answer, beginning a brief dialogue. Exchange names and details of your challenges and problems. Make it as real as possible. You may get immediate answers, but if not, don't get discouraged. The answers will come to you in some form later.

There is one important rule to remember when using this technique: Give your full attention to what the mentor says or does, just as much as you would if you met your mentor in the outer world. This will keep the experience from remaining a passive fantasy.

5. *Bring the conversation to a close.* Have your guide say to you, "Listen, I'm here for you. Call me up whenever you need me. Know that I'll help you whenever you need me." Feel yourself trusting that. Open your eyes and return to the outside world.

People have different experiences in meeting their guides. Don't be surprised if your guide seems eccentric or has a sense of humor or a flair for the dramatic.

Phil Pies, who is known by his friends as the King of Batavia, related this story to me about his inner guide, whom he calls "Shadow." Phil wanted to do something to help educate the disadvantaged. But what can one person do? Phil called up Shadow, who arrived with a bulldog. He asked Shadow, "How can I generate scholarships for those students who are unable to attend college without spending a tremendous amount of money?"

"What did people use before money?" asked Shadow.

"Well, I suppose they bartered goods and services," Phil replied.

Shadow smiled and said, "Exactly."

Phil mused about this for days. How could barter be employed to help educate the disadvantaged? Then it hit him.

The idea: A not-for-profit bartering organization. The concept is simple. A business agrees to donate goods (excess equipment or inventory) to the organization, which then locates a college willing to exchange tuition credit for the donated goods. The exchange is made, and the college issues scholarship credits to the not-for-profit organization. When a disadvantaged student applies to the organization for financial aid, it pairs the student with the appropriate college and the student is issued tuition credits in the name of the business which originally donated the goods. Everybody wins, as excess shelving, computers, and so on are turned into education for the disadvantaged. The businesses can write off their tax-deductible donations.

When you first try this technique, your mentor may be hard to understand, or you may not like him or her. If your mentor is confusing, ask for another spiritual mentor who is easier for you to understand. Your mind will oblige. If you feel good with your experience, then stay with your guide. If not, change your guide. You may change guides frequently, or you may stay with the same guide for years.

This is not a mysterious technique; it is a way of personifying your conflicting ideas and emotions in the form of a specific image, of activating your unconscious through concentration. Still, some people feel awed and magical and mysterious when they become expert at this technique.

A police detective investigating a murder faced the challenge of finding the murder weapon. He consulted with his inner advisor who simply said, "Ti lo." He got the same response every time he tried. Finally, he wrote it down and free-associated from it. He reversed it to "Lo ti," which he translated to "low-tide." He directed the search to the beach at low tide and the murder weapon was found. The message was based on a body of experiences that had some significance for his challenge, but that he didn't know was influencing him.

With practice, you will find answers and associations that are extraordinarily varied and novel. You may see the associative link immediately, or the message may not be readily understandable until later.

The CEO of a major company was confronted with serious financial difficulties. Since he viewed the company as the source of his happiness, he ignored the problems and refused to discuss them with other officers of the company. He began to project the problems on the other people involved. Finally, he tried to repress these projections as being disloyal to his friends.

Up against the wall, he created a personal spiritual advisor he called "Companion." Companion told him: "You drowned the employees of the company whom you feared. But now you are attacked by a greater enemy. If you had not drowned the employees, you might have received help from them, where without them you have little chance."

He chewed on this like a rubber meatball. After several days, he interpreted it to mean that he had covered up an increasingly bad situation for fear that the situation would not be solvable and would lead to the dissolution of the source of his happiness—the company. The greater enemy was the unconscious guilt, resentment, and anger that were overwhelming him and making it impossible for him to work. In the end, he revealed all the disturbing and negative aspects of the financial situation and, with help from the others, saved the company.

Summary

Your inner guide is a manifestation of the higher part of your unconscious. You can evoke your inner guide to come forth as a person or being who can help you meet and solve your challenges.

Your guide will assist you to:

1. Increase your access to unconscious data.

2. Make more fluent free associations. It will increase your ability to play with hypotheses, metaphors, and relationships.

3. Heighten your ability to use visual imagery.

4. Lessen your inhibitions and reduce your tendency to render negative thoughts.

5. Heighten your motivation.

6. Begin to experience existence in different ways with deeper levels of understanding.

You can call on your guide anytime you need or desire creative inspiration or solutions to challenges. Many people who have established a deep relationship with their guides meet them every day in meditation. Others create a whole constellation of distinct spiritual mentors and bring in four or five at a time to play different roles in problem solving.

Most of us have but an inkling of what is really within us. To realize more, we need to appreciate our unconscious dimension. Once you acknowledge this dimension, you gain an independence of thought. Those who see the light in themselves will never need to revolve as satellites around others.

—

CHAPTER THIRTY-THREE

THE BOOK OF THE DEAD

"Now the resources of those skilled in the use
of extraordinary forces are
as infinite as the heavens and earth;
as inexhaustible as the flow of great rivers."

SUN TZU

The Book of the Dead is an extraordinary technique based on a creativity exercise used by Professor Michael Ray in his creativity class at Stanford's Graduate School of Business. This exercise uses Egyptian hieroglyphics as a rich source of objects that invite your imagination to free-associate ideas, which you will find as if they were crustless sandwiches hidden under a cool tea towel.

The hieroglyphics used in this Thinkertoy are from the hieroglyphic transcript of the Egyptian Book of the Dead. This important work predates the Egyptian dynasties and contains spells, incantations, litanies, magical formulas, words of power, and words of prayer. Scholars are still entranced by the difficult allusions, symbolisms, and passages that guided the ancient Egyptians, whether king or servant, through life's problems. They lived with its teachings, were buried according to its directions, and based their hopes on its words of power. Scholars still debate as to whether the book is a library of classics, or of metaphysics, or religion, or the occult.

BLUEPRINT

1. *Write out the challenge you want to solve.*

2. *Choose one of the three sets of hieroglyphics.*

3. *Scan the illustration of hieroglyphics and then write out the challenge again.*

4. *Empty your mind of all distractions and concentrate on the challenge.* Close your eyes as you meditate on the problem for a few minutes.

5. *Open your eyes and "translate" each line of hieroglyphics.* Imagine that The Book of the Dead was written to help you with your specific challenge. Believe that each line was written especially for you and that the secret to the solution of your specific business challenge is in the interpretation of the images.

6. *As you interpret each hieroglyphic, free-associate from it.* A figure might look like a star, which reminds you of a friend who was an athletic star, which reminds you of his father who used to quote John Steinbeck, which reminds you of traveling with a dog, which reminds you of your neighborhood veterinarian who rides a bicycle, which reminds you of a fold-away bicycle, which might help you come up with an idea to solve your challenge, and so on. All the lines, shapes, and structures convey meaning.

   When interpreting the figures, be on the lookout for parts that puzzle you, seem to be missing, or that show up when you change your focus. Ask questions such as:

   "What is this?"

   "Why did they use this?"

   "What could this mean?"

   "What does the frequency of this figure mean?"

   "What figure comes closest to my challenge?"

   "Who could this be?"

   "What does this remind me of?"

   Among these questions, one may stand out as the key to resolving your challenge.

7. *Write out your interpretations.* Search for clues, new ideas, insights, and new lines of speculation. Combine the interpretations for the various lines into one all-inclusive interpretation. See if you can combine the various line interpretations into a narrative that may contain the solution to the challenge.

How many triangles can you see in the figure in the margin?

When you view this figure, you see the image as a whole and at the same time you see its parts. Your imagination tends to fill in the blanks, and so you think you can see as many as eight triangles as well as a six-pointed star made by combining the large white triangle and the one formed by V's. But there are no triangles. You have gone beyond the information given to see something that does not exist.

This is the way your mind free-associates. You see the images as a whole, and at the same time you see the parts. Your imagination will fill in the blanks, and you will go beyond the information given to create or reveal something new.

Following are three different sets of hieroglyphics from the Papyrus of Nekht, which contains a variety of material, including vignettes and hymns. Search them for your messages.

A professor wanted to start a business to generate extra income. He explored the images in set two, line one. He saw water, three circles between two lines, and a person offering something. The circles and water reminded him of oysters. The circles between the two lines reminded him of packaged oysters. The person offering something made him think of gifts and holidays.

He then associated oysters with lovemaking and lovemaking with Valentine's Day, and this inspired his idea. He started a mail-order business that will send your love a dozen fresh oysters for Valentine's Day.

You may get a single, straightforward narrative or idea that resolves your challenge, or you may get the essence of a continuing mystery, with a mere hint of interpretation. Your task is to apprehend the meaning of the drawings as they relate to your challenge and resolve the mystery.

SET ONE

SET TWO

SET THREE

A management consultant was asked to give a talk about the essentials of a good sales meeting to a group of high-powered sales managers. For inspiration, he consulted set one, line one of the Book of the Dead. His key images were a fish, a fishhook, three lines, and a person's face. The associations he made from the images were:

Fishhook: A sales meeting needs something that hooks or grabs.

Fish: A successful sales meeting needs the participation of the salespeople much as you need the participation of a fish to catch it.

Person's face: The presentation must be relevant to the salespeople.

Three lines: There are three stages to a successful sales meeting: attention grabber, participation, and relevance.

His interpretation told him to concentrate his talk on those three essentials of a successful sales meeting.

He gave each sales manager an envelope and started the meeting by asking them to open the envelope. They discovered a bit of nylon cord on the end of which was a fish hook. He explained that this was the first thing that made for a good sales meeting. He then proceeded to go around the room, questioning them about what they thought the hook represented. After several answers, he stopped and explained that the first point of a good meeting is represented by the fishhook . . . the *attention grabber.* But, more important, he told them he had gotten them to think about what he wanted them to think about and *participate* even before he started to speak. He got their attention and participation and made his message *relevant* to all the sales managers. In a few minutes, he had hammered home the three essentials of a good meeting.

In another case, a personnel manager for a life insurance company had the challenge of improving working conditions for white-collar employees. His interpretation of set one was:

Line one: A lot of stress.

Line two: You need a way to measure stressful activities.

Line three: We need to relax.

Line four: Inexpensive.

Line five: Something similar to seat belts for safety.

Line six: People play to relax.

Line seven: Complete program.

Line eight: Build morale.

He had a whole banquet of thoughts to nibble at, and his nibbling finally led to an idea. He concentrated on finding something that would be inexpensive and playful to measure and help alleviate stress. He researched the market and found something that would work—stress control cards.

The idea: He bought a stress control card for each employee. These cards work on the principle that the extremities go cold under stress—the card takes the temperature of one's thumb and registers one of four shades from black (stressed) to blue (relaxed).

On the back of the card is a ten-second relaxation exercise for stressed-out employees. The card acts as a reminder to manage stress and be careful, much like the seat-belt message in a car. The card is the first step in a stress program the personnel manager decided to develop.

His interpretations produced an idea that is effective, inexpensive, playful, motivating, and part of a complete program to manage stress in the corporate environment.

Summary

Everyone's imagination gets stale after a while, like those people who hang around a college town long after they've graduated. Providing unusual external images refreshes your imagination. Something in your interpretation may lead to an idea that will catch the sunlight like a silver spur.

PART THREE

—

THE SPIRIT OF
KOINONIA

In ancient Greece, Socrates and his friends spent years freely meeting and conversing with each other, having dialogues that helped shape Western civilization. They exchanged ideas without trying to change the other's mind and without bitter argument. They felt free to propose whatever was on their mind. They always paid attention to each other's views and established an extraordinary fellowship. Socrates and his friends bound themselves by principles of discussion to maintain a sense of collegiality. These principles were known as "Koinonia," which means "spirit of fellowship." The principles they established were to establish dialogue, be collegial, clarify your thinking, and be honest.

Establish dialogue. In Greek, the word *dialogue* means a "talking through." The Greeks believed that the key to establishing dialogue is to exchange ideas without trying to change someone's mind. This is not the same as *discussion,* which from its Latin root means to "dash to pieces." The basic rules of dialogue for the Greeks were: "don't argue," "don't interrupt," and "listen carefully."

Be collegial. All participants must regard each another as equal colleagues, even if they have nothing in common. When you look at the dots in the illustration below, your attention is drawn to the lone dot that stands separate and apart from the group of dots. The lone dot is the focus of your attention.

In the same way, if a participant feels that he or she is not an equal colleague with the rest of a brainstorming group, that participant will become the focus of the session, either consciously or unconsciously, and inhibit the creativity of the group.

Thinking of others as colleagues is important because thought is participative. Just the willingness to consciously think of others as colleagues contributes toward interacting as colleagues. We talk differently and more honestly with friends than we do with people who are not friends. Any controlling authority, no matter how carefully presented, will tend to inhibit the free play of thought. If one person is used to having his view prevail because she is the most senior person present, then she must surrender that privilege. If one person is used to being silent because he is more junior, then he must surrender the security of keeping quiet. Similarly, in the illustration below, the furthest tree seems much larger than the nearest tree. But to assume this would be wrong, as they are the exact same size.

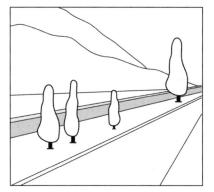

Clarify your thinking. To clarify your thinking, you must suspend all assumptions. Free thought is blocked if our thoughts and opinions are based on assumptions. For instance, if you believe that certain people are not creative, you're not likely to give their ideas fair consideration. Check your assumptions about everything and maintain an unbiased view.

The difficulty of effective collaboration has been demonstrated by experiments conducted by Howard Gruber at the University of Geneva. In one experiment, he used a box that allows two people to peer into it and see the shadow cast by what is to them an unknown object. Because of the angle, each viewer sees a different shape. Their task is to share the information about what they see in order to identify the object casting the shadow. For instance, if a cone is placed in the box, one viewer sees a circle, the other a triangle.

The idea was to encourage the viewers to collaborate like two astronomers taking a fix on the heavens from different positions, thus seeing the object in slightly different ways. They take respectful advantage of the fact that one sees it from here and the other from there, and they put together an idea of what's out there that is richer and more soundly based than what either one could reach alone.

But the opposite happened. Each viewer assumed that his view was the correct one and that the other person was confused, blind, or crazy. "How can you see a triangle? I see a circle." This was true of highly intelligent, educated adults. The assumptions made by the viewers made it difficult to collaborate about even a simple object, like a cone.

Be honest. Say what you think. Socrates and his followers believed Koinonia allowed a group to access a larger pool of common thoughts that could not be accessed individually. Through Koinonia, a new kind of thinking starts to come into being, based on the development of common thoughts. People are no longer in opposition but are participants in a pool of common ideas that are capable of constant development and change.

The notion that the collective intelligence of a group is larger than the intelligence of an individual can be traced back to primitive times when hunter-gatherer bands would meet to discuss and solve common problems. It is a commonly understood and accepted practice. What's difficult is the willingness of a group to discipline itself to brainstorm ideas openly and productively.

This part contains:

- Warming-up exercises.

- Brainstorming (American style)

- Orthodox brainstorming techniques

- Raw creative-thinking techniques for groups

WARMING UP

Imagine a gardener who plants a turnip. After a while, the turnip isn't developing as it should, and the gardener is unhappy. The gardener digs it up and examines the turnip to see if he can find any faults. He then cleans it, clips some hair, and replants the turnip using a different process, stunting its growth further. In effect, by trying to control nature, he has interfered with it and produces a poor turnip, if it grows at all.

If the gardener had relaxed and not interfered with nature, he would have found that nature would do all of the work after he planted the seed, and the turnip would grow. The same need for control is what freezes thinking and what prevents the free play of thought in brainstorming sessions. These exercises are designed to help participants forget control, relax, and have fun with thought.

BRAINSTORMING (AMERICAN STYLE)

Alex Osborne, an advertising executive in Buffalo, New York, formalized brainstorming in 1941 as a systematic effort and disciplined practice to produce ideas in a group. Osborne's idea was to create an uninhibiting environment that would encourage imaginative ideas and thoughts. The usual method is to have a small group discuss a problem. Ideas are offered by participants one at a time. One member records ideas and suggestions on a flip chart or chalkboard. All withhold judgment. After the brainstorming session, the various ideas and suggestions are reviewed and evaluated and the group agrees on a final resolution.

In the illustration below there are two circles of equal size. Circle A, with the black arrows, symbolically represents the creative energy of a group brainstorming in an uninhibiting environment. Circle B, on the other hand, represents the creative energy in an inhibiting environment. Circle A is expanding and liberating creative thought, whereas circle B is contracting and restricting creative thought. The restrictive nature of the forces in circle B make the circle appear smaller, even though the circles are identical in size. Which brainstorming group would you prefer to join?

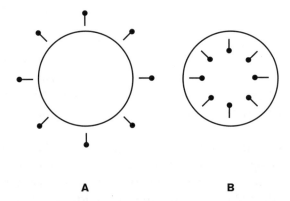

A   B

ORTHODOX TECHNIQUES

There are many problems with traditional brainstorming. Sessions can be undercut by group uniformity pressures and perceived threats from managers and bosses. Other sessions fail because people find it difficult to avoid judging and evaluating ideas as they are offered. Personality differences also come into play: Some people are naturally willing to talk, while others tend to be silent.

This part contains some of the most popular orthodox techniques that are designed to overcome the problems with the American style of brainstorming. The pattern of different ways of brainstorming is much more like that of a forest of different interdependent plants, or a city of different interconnected buildings, than of a single enormous building pile on a single foundation stone.

Read the following paragraph:

Aoccdrnig to rscheearch at Cmabrdige Uinvrevtisy, it deosn't mttaer in waht oredr the litteers in a wrod are, the olny iprmoetnt tihng is taht the frist and lsat ltteer be at the rghit pclae. The rset can be a ttoal mses and you can sitll raed it wouthit a porbelm. Tihs is besauae ocne we laren how to raed we look for the eenssces of the jmulbed ltteers. The huamn mnid deos not raed ervey lteter by istlef, but preecsievs the wrod as a wlohe. We do tihs ucnsoniuscoly wuithot tuhoght.

We have a raw natural talent to interpret the essences of things. We make sense out of these jumbled letters because we immediately see the essence. This raw talent is why we're all creative as children. A box could be a fort, a car, a tank, a cave, a house, something to draw on, and even a spaceship. When we were kids, our imaginations were not structured or restrained by rules and constraints of logic. We did not strive to eliminate possibilities—we strove to expand them.

Consider a child building something with a Lego construction set. She can build all kinds of structures and when she's finished she can pick up pieces and move them, add more pieces, divide structures into new structures, and so on. There are clear constraints on the set and construction: They cannot be put together any which way, they will not stay together if unbalanced, and gravity pulls them apart. These constraints are inherent in the objects and their design. It is the design of the pieces that imposes these limitations. The child quickly learns the ways Legos go together and the ways they don't go together. She ends up building a wide variety of structures that satisfy the Legos' design and constraints.

If the child was told to make something out of plastic and she had at her disposal every method of melting and molding plastic, the Lego constructions themselves would be only a "tiny" fraction of the possible products she would create. In fact, the child's Lego constructions would look contrived and trivial compared to what she could create with no constraints.

With Legos, it's the constraints inherent in the design that limit what can be built. With humans, it's the constraints inherent in the system of logic we were taught that limit our imagination and inventiveness.

Raw creative-thinking techniques are designed to remove the constraints of logic and free your imagination to be creative again. Pablo Picasso said it best when he said, "Every child is an artist. The problem is how to remain an artist once we grow up." The value of learning "raw" creative techniques is to do just that—to learn how to think like a child again.

CHAPTER THIRTY-FOUR

WARMING UP

"For the men of Wu and Yueh are enemies;
yet if they are rowing in a river in the same
boat and are caught by a storm,
they will come to each other's assistance
just as the left hand helps the right."

SUN TZU

If we toss seeds on hard-packed ground, the chances of them taking root and producing healthy plants is slim. However, if we plough and till the ground—mix it up, break it apart, and make it less solid and more loose—chances are that most of our seeds will find a way to grow in the loose soil.

In the same way, if we start a brainstorming session cold, with a serious, uptight facilitator throwing out questions and problems to a stiff, conservative group, the chances of producing healthy ideas is minimal.

WARMING-UP ACTIVITIES

Help brainstorming participants relax and loosen up by tilling their minds with these warming-up exercises. The group will open their minds to new ideas, which will allow them to seed and grow.

- *Baby pictures.* Have each participant bring in a picture of him or herself as a baby. Post them on a wall without labels. Ask everyone to match the pictures with the participants.

- *Symbol.* Ask participants to draw a personal symbol that represents their view about creativity. It can be anything—an eagle, a compass, a paintbrush, the moon, etc. Then each participant displays his or her symbol and explains how or why it represents their view.

- *Corporate symbol.* Ask participants to choose an animal, bird, insect, or fish as their corporate symbol. Have them defend their choice. Ask if the creature embodies both the strengths and weaknesses of the corporation.

- *"You're fired."* Sometimes, it takes a five-alarm wake-up call to jolt people out of their complacency. At the beginning of the meeting, ask the participants to imagine that they are fired. Now, ask them to reapply for their jobs. This should shock them and force them to think about their knowledge and competencies and, most importantly, what they need to do to improve. Or, print an imaginary newspaper of the future that announces your company's bankruptcy. Then ask the participants to imagine why the company went bankrupt. The element of shock wakes us up to see, hear, and experience our world anew.

- *Everyone's a consultant.* Ask each person to write a current job-related problem or concern on a blank sheet of paper. For example, "How can I get better cooperation from our warehouse employees in fulfilling orders on time?" or "How can we overcome the low price and discount program of our competition?" After allowing a few minutes to write out the problems, ask each person to pass his or her problem to the right. That person reads the problem just received and jots down their responses. They are given sixty seconds to respond to the individual sheet. Keep the process going until each person gets his or her sheet back. Then share and discuss the ideas.

- *Looking at somebody else.* With this approach, ideas and solutions come by looking for ideas in unrelated fields. As a pre-exercise for a meeting on strategies and tactics for selling luxury boxes for a NFL football franchise to corporations, sales and marketing employees were sent out to observe marketing and sales in unrelated retail operations such as designer-fashion stores, computer software franchises, fast-food restaurants, and bookstores. They came back with long lists of ideas and suggestions that could be applied in their own business.

- *Walking in the customer's shoes.* In this approach, people turn around to find out what it's really like to be someone in a different position. For example, a realtor sent his salespeople to car dealerships to help them improve their selling skills. Posing as customers, they walked through the entire sales process, recording particular behavior, words, and actions that critically affected their attitude as "buyers." At the sales meeting, they shared their experiences and talked about ways they could improve their own selling skills. It was an eye-opening experience that made the salespeople see that it's one thing to talk about walking in someone else's shoes—and another to actually do it.

SPACE CREATURE

Have a group imagine a creature living on another planet with a different atmosphere in a distant solar system. Ask them to draw a picture of the creature they imagine. Then have the group display their drawings.

You'll discover that most people draw creatures that resemble life as we understand it, even though we're free to think up anything. Namely, creatures with sense organs to see, hear, and smell, and arms and legs with bilateral symmetry. Rather than creating something that's idiosyncratic and unpredictable, most people create creatures that have a great deal in common with one another and with the properties of typical earth animals.

There is no reason animals on other planets would have to resemble animals on earth. People drawing space creatures could have tapped into any existing knowledge base (such as rock formations, tumbleweed, or clouds) to get an idea for the general shape of their space creature, and each person could access something different and novel. But most people do not, and so they wind up drawing creatures that have similar properties to creatures on earth.

This group exercise exhibits a phenomenon called *structured imagination.* Structured imagination refers to the fact that even when we use our imagination to develop new ideas, those ideas are heavily structured in highly predictable ways according to existing concepts, categories, and stereotypes. This is true whether the individuals are inventors, artists, writers, scientists, designers, businesspeople, or everyday people fantasizing about a better life.

WALKING IN SOMEBODY ELSE'S SHOES

With participants sitting at tables in groups of six to ten, tell everyone to take off their shoes. Then talk for a few minutes about how it feels to be sitting at a table in a serious business meeting with your shoes off. Talk about the fact that taking off your shoes is natural at home and on holiday but not usually done in business settings. Then ask them to try a few different things:

1. Ask them to exchange shoes—to actually put on someone else's shoes. Ask them to try to make a big change; men put on women's

shoes, for example. Talk about how that feels. Talk about social norms, and begin talking about what it is like to be a bit outside the box.

2. Next, tell them to put the shoes on the table in front of them. Let everyone sit there looking at all the shoes for a while. Watch the nervousness. This is typically a very weird and uncomfortable and antisocial thing for them to experience. Talk about what it feels like to have someone else's shoes up on the table in front of you. Talk about how we deal with discomfort, typically, by trying to reduce it. But point out that improvement implies change, and change nearly always brings discomfort. Innovative change must be really outside the box, which brings even greater discomfort, and so on.

3. Now, announce a contest in which the team that builds the highest structure of shoes will receive a big contract. The winner is determined by measuring the distance from the top of the table surface to the highest point of any shoe. Don't discuss the contest very much; just tell them what they have to do, say they have four minutes, and say, "Go." One solution might be to have the tallest person in the group stand on the tabletop and hold one shoe over her head. Or, you can make a rule that there be a continuous path of shoes touching shoes, like an electrical circuit.

Watch what the participants do during this exercise, so that you will have plenty to talk about when you debrief. You will be amazed at the creative solutions the groups develop. Look for how quickly or slowly the various groups get into the task. Look for the emergence of natural leaders. Look for cycles of buildup, deconstruction and reconstruction, etc. Just observe. A variety of talking points will emerge:

- Handling shoes bonds the team.

- The participants didn't know they would be asked to build a structure with the shoes but were allowed to warm up to the idea gradually. This may be a good strategy when implementing innovative ideas in general.

- Things are most uncomfortable when we think too much about them; just start doing it and a lot of the discomfort goes away.

- It's not stealing when you take an idea from observing another team. That is the basis of benchmarking in business improvement.

- When looking for solutions, it's often helpful to use things you didn't expect to use. (For example, I once saw a group make a sort of chimney out of the binders containing the workshop materials, and then filled the chimney with shoes stood on end. Someone always ends up taking off their belt to attach something to something else. And so on.)

- Innovation often happens through cycles of trying something, dismantling it, trying another tack, and so on. Rarely do you just sit and think about a problem and work it all out in your mind. Doing stimulates thinking.

- The thought processes involved in the most creative approaches are often the combinations of several ideas and concepts.

USE YOUR IMAGINATION

When we compare a problem to something unusual, we tend to have a need to try to make sense of it. Consequently, we break down the comparison and analyze the different parts to see if doing so allows us to understand the problem or make it somehow familiar. When this happens, we form new links and relationships that may lead to breakthrough ideas. For example, years back, a group of designers were looking for ideas for a new light fixture. They compared a light fixture to a monkey and imagined a monkey running around a house with a light. This thought led them to conceive track lighting.

Ask metaphoric questions to stimulate a group's imagination. For example:

- What animal is like the problem? Why?

- In what ways is a cold, half-eaten pizza like the solution to the problem?

- How is the problem like a flashlight battery? How can the similarities spark new ideas?

- If your problem were a lawn, what would the weeds be?

As part of an environmental science course, a group of students at St. Bonaventure University brainstormed for new ideas for recycling. The question they worked with was, *What famous historical figure comes closest to resembling the essence of the problem?*

One student suggested the Wright brothers because of their open minds with respect to aviation. Using this comparison, another student made the connection between the Wrights and his hobby of model planes. He explained how he used to blend old, leftover paints to create a unique beige color to differentiate his model planes from others. This sparked a thought in another student, who suggested the same principle be applied to recycling. They developed a service that picks up old paint, blends it, then sells it for $5 a gallon. They call the paint Earth Beige. They are now working on another service to pick up junk mail and convert it into fiberboard.

FAILURE 101

To demonstrate the value of risk-taking and failure, break a group into teams. Give each team a pile of ice-cream bar sticks. The exercise is to see which team can build the highest structure in twenty minutes using the sticks. After the exercise, ask the participants for their insights into every failure. You'll generally find that those who follow a fixed, logical idea from the outset don't wind up with the highest structure, and those who wind up successful went through the most failures. The lesson is to free oneself of preconceived notions about failure, open oneself up to surprise, and learn to play like an open-minded child again, with perspective and context.

IS THAT A YELLOW OR BLUE QUESTION?

Trigger your spirit of inquiry by using "color questioning," based on the work of Jerry Rhodes, who did extensive research on managers and management styles. Rhodes developed a fairly extensive scheme for the kind of questions one might ask. At the core are four types of questions that are identified as "colors of the mind." The color questions are:

- *Yellow questions.* Think of the color yellow as neutral and objective. The question should be a description of face. Ask, "What is?" For example, "What is the most significant problem or concern that we face?"

- *Green questions.* Think of green as fertile and creative. The question should be imaginative and ingenious. Ask, "What if we . . . ?" or "Suppose we . . . ?" Come up with the most inventive question you can.

- *Blue questions.* Think of blue as hopeful and positive. The question should be based on an opinion or judgment of some value or need. Think about what needs to be done or added. Ask, "What can we do?" or "What should we do?"

- *Black questions.* Think of black as negative. Ask, "What can't be done?" or "What's not possible?"

When brainstorming for ideas and solutions about a particular subject, label four separate sheets of paper: yellow, green, blue, and black. Have the group think of as many yellow, green, blue, and black questions about your subject as they can, and record them on the appropriate sheets. You can post them in columns on a large sheet of paper. You can also write them on index cards and tape them to the wall under the appropriately colored card. Whenever you have a negative question, write it on the black question sheet. At a later stage, review the black questions and try to look for ways to overcome them. Prioritize the questions after listing as many as you can to decide which questions to answer first.

TAKE A DIFFERENT PERSPECTIVE

Write the alphabet vertically on the chalkboard. Then ask for names of famous (real or fictional) people for each letter: A = Neil Armstrong, B = Alexander Graham Bell, C = Charlie Chaplin, D = Leonardo da Vinci, E = Albert Einstein, F = Fred Flintstone, G = Boy George and so on. Have each person in the group pick a name that has the same letter of the first letter of their last name. One might end up with Albert Einstein or David Letterman. Then have each person think about how that famous person might approach the problem. Suppose the problem is how to encourage employees to submit more ideas. How, for example, would Charlie Chaplin encourage employees? How would Alexander Graham Bell? Finally, have the group share their perspectives.

ONE + ONE = ONE

When one drop of water is added to another drop, they make only one drop not two. Anecdotally, when you add one concept to another, they make one concept not two. Consider how you readily understand verbal combinations such as "conference call," "home page," "party girl," "finger lakes," "religious right," and "race card." These examples of verbal blending represent how a new concept is formed by consolidating and articulating two concepts as one. "Religious right," for instance, refers to a group of people with strong religious beliefs who try to influence the political process.

Gregory Murphy of the University of Illinois had people rate how true certain properties were of individual concepts and their combinations. One set of concepts consisted of the individual words "empty" and "store" and their combination "empty store." Consider the property "losing money." Like subjects in Murphy's study, you probably recognize that losing money is typical of "empty stores," but not of "stores" in general or of things that are "empty." Meaning changes when we combine concepts, and the more novel the combination, the more novel the new meaning.

Much of creative thinking involves combining previously unrelated ideas, goods, or services and turning them into something new. The printing press was created by Gutenberg, who combined the coin punch with the wine press. The process of combining ideas or elements or parts of ideas is called *synthesis*. Synthesis is regarded by many to be the essence of creativity.

Ask participants to think of the name of an object that begins with the same letter as their last name (for example, M = meal, A = apple, C = credit card, D = diamond, E = energy bar, and so on). Write the name on a sticky note and post it on their forehead. Now ask the participants to mingle around the room and combine their object with someone else's to create something new. For example:

- Rock + Chair = A spongy mat that you can put on top of rocks to transform any rock into a chair.

- Deck + Legos = A put-it-together adjustable wooden deck that can be dismantled and stored.

- Desk + Treadmill = A treadmill desk. You can walk at a one-mph pace while you work at your computer, guaranteeing weight loss without dieting.

- Bomb + Bath = Doggie bath bombs. The bombs are made of pet shampoo that has been molded into a solid form. You throw the bomb in the water and it bubbles and fizzes, saving you the trouble of trying to hold on to the slippery shampoo bottle and your squirmy dog at the same time.

- Dog + Shovel = A new pet-related business. For a fee, pick up dog poop with pooper scoopers for institutions, corporations, golf courses, and estates.

You'd be surprised at the new ideas, products, and business possibilities people come up with using this simple exercise.

I Am a Camera

This is an activity in learning how to see without preconceptions. Pretend you're a camera while another person plays the photographer. The photographer stands behind you. Your eyes are the lens and your right shoulder is the shutter. Keep your eyes (lens) shut until the photographer takes a photograph by tapping you on the right shoulder (shutter). Open and close your eyes quickly, just as the shutter of a camera does.

The photographer walks you around, guiding you by your shoulders and positioning you so that different scenes will be in your line of vision. Do this a few times, so you keep moving and snapping. The camera's task is to record every detail of the picture perfectly, with no distortion. Open your eyes only for a second. All you have to do is see what's in front of you without any preconceived notions for each of the pictures you take. The reason for doing this is that a rapid series of recorded impressions gives you the experience of seeing what is, without that perception being filtered through your expectations. It's the seeing without any predetermined concepts that's important. Learning how to reduce your preconceptions when you face a new problem is a vital element in the creative process.

Another activity to help you practice getting rid of preconceptions is to create different names for things. For example, *rainbow* might be named "painted rain." In a group, have people create different names for:

- Mountain
- Cloud
- Ocean
- World
- Painting

Next, have the participants rename the subject of the meeting with a different name. For example, if the meeting is about office morale, *morale* might be named "a spring flower" or "a warm hug," and so on.

Are You a Hammer or a Nail?

This is a fun go-around-the-room discussion. Ask the group questions about what best describes them and then have them explain why they think so.

1. What comes closest to describing you in general:
   - Hammer or nail?
   - Cloud or rock?

2. At work:
   - Tree or wind?
   - Saltshaker or catsup bottle?

3. At meetings:
   - Handshake or kiss?
   - Watch or compass?

4. Your creativity:
   - Snowflake or boiling water?
   - Thunderstorm or the smell of leaves burning?

THE MARTIANS HAVE LANDED

Even though words evolved from pictures and symbols, that does not mean that words are more advanced. The latest advance in computer technology is the graphic symbol. Many professions rely on graphic languages: Physicists draw diagrams; executives employ charts; football coaches draw X's and O's; and corporations are known by their trademarks.

Visual and verbal thinking are, in fact, complementary. As you focus on the figure at the left, you will notice the faces interchange places. First, the left side will look like the outside, and the right side will look like a face; and then the right will be a face, and the left will be outside. And so on.

This is the way visual and verbal thinking works. What we call verbal thinking is always the outside out. But the inside visual thinking is always there, and when we turn our thinking inside out, we call that thinking, too.

Try this exercise with a group. Imagine that a delegation of Martians has just landed on your company's parking lot. You welcome them inside. They do not understand any Earth languages—only graphic symbols. They are curious about your company and about you. They want to know what the company does and what you do.

- Tell the participants to create a short speech composed of graphic symbols to welcome the Martians and to explain what the company does and their roles in the company (i.e., their jobs).

- Tape the speeches on the walls. Have participants wander around reviewing all the speeches.

- Select the one speech you would present to the Martians.

CROSSBREEDING

A Japanese woman created a novelty item that's become a big hit in Japan. It is a key-chain plant: a clear plastic micro case where plants grow in their own miniature arboretum until they get too large, at which point they can be transplanted into bigger pots. How in the world did she get the idea?

She got it by playing with different ideas and by crossbreeding ideas and objects in her mind until she got the right combination. One day she was thinking of a house key while looking at a sunflower. She thought if I could crossbreed the key with a flower my key would always be readily available as a flower in the garden. She laughed as she thought of carrying her key flower with her during the day. Then she experienced an "aha!" moment as she thought of miniaturizing the key and flower into a key-chain plant.

Get imaginations moving with the bizarre activity of idea crossbreeding. What would you get if you crossbred the president of the company with a sunflower? The human resources director with a baseball? The sales manager with a submarine? The vice president of marketing with a gecko?

Encourage the group to experiment by crossbreeding plants, objects, animals, and people.

1. Provide four boxes containing slips of paper with random names of plants, objects, animals, and job descriptors. Try to use objects that are business-related, such as a copy machine, product, phone, paperwork, desk, meeting room, and so on.

2. Ask each participant to take one slip each, then make hybrids out of them. Examples:

    - bird x supervisor
    - pony x salesperson
    - customer x door
    - watermelon x receptionist
    - paperwork x key
    - customer service x ballet dancer

3. Ask the group, what does each hybrid look like? Draw a picture. Label and post them on a wall.

4. Ask the group to think about what each hybrid does. What sound does it make? What are the unique strengths of each (at least three)? What are the unique weaknesses of each (at least three)?

IMPOSSIBLE HYBRIDS

Another exercise to stretch the imagination focuses on creating impossible objects. Creativity involves the synthesis of unlike concepts, particularly when the concepts are not normally seen as overlapping. Below are unusual combinations of objects. Try to imagine each object, describe it as fully as possible, and draw a picture of it.

- A piece of furniture that is also a fruit.

- A vehicle that is also a fish.

- A food that is also a rock.

- A fruit that is also a human dwelling.

- A bird that is also a kitchen utensil.

- A food flavoring that is also a tool.

- A computer that is also a teacup.

- A cooking stove that is also a bicycle.

- A lampshade that is a book.

For example, for the first one you might draw a giant pineapple carved into a chair. For a vehicle that is also a fish, you might picture a dolphin pulling a boat. A cooking stove that is also a bicycle might involve filling the tubes of a bicycle frame with steam that could be released to do the cooking, while the pedaling creates the energy source. A food that is a rock might mean that the minerals in a rock provide a source of nutritional supplement.

SUMMARY

These kinds of exercises help to free imaginations to create off-the-wall ideas. One middle school principal told me of an idea she and the school caretaker came up with to solve the problem of lipstick on mirrors. The girls were fond of leaving lipstick kisses on the mirrors. She invited a group of them to join her in the bathroom so they could see how difficult it was for the caretaker to clean the lipstick off the mirrors. She introduced the janitor, who stepped up with a sponge squeegee, which he took into a toilet cubicle, dipped it into the toilet bowl, and then used it to clean the lipstick from the mirrors. After that demonstration, there was no more lipstick on the mirrors.

BRAINSTORMING

"The clever combatant looks to the effect of
combined energy, and does not require too
much from individuals."

SUN TZU

Brainstorming is a little like a group of people meeting to make a sculpture. Everyone brings a piece of clay to the meeting and places it on the table. The pieces are molded together into a core and then the sculpture is turned, rearranged, modified, reduced, expanded, and otherwise changed until the group agrees on the final sculpture.

Developed in 1941 by A. F. Osborne, brainstorming was designed to encourage a group to express various ideas and to defer critical judgment until later. Everyone offers ideas that are listed, combined, improved, and changed into various other ideas. In the end, the group agrees on a final resolution.

The idea is to create an uninhibiting environment that will encourage imaginative ideas and thoughts. The usual method is to have a small group (six to twelve people) discuss a specific problem. One member records the remarks and suggestions. All withhold judgment on all suggestions. After the session, the various ideas and suggestions are reviewed and evaluated.

The two basic principles of brainstorming are:

1. *Quantity breeds quality.* A ship should not ride out to sea with a single anchor, nor should you attempt to solve a challenge with a single idea. The more ideas you come up with, the more likely you are to arrive at the *best* solution.

2. *Defer judgment.* In the illustration on the next page, most people would instinctively and immediately judge the dot to be above the

center of the triangle. They would be wrong. If you measure it, you will find that the dot is, in fact, in the exact center.

This is how we evaluate new ideas. We judge them instinctively and immediately and are often incorrect. Yet, in other matters we defer judgment. For example, when shopping for a new shirt or sweater, you don't usually buy the first one you see—you look over the entire selection and then go back and evaluate. This is the natural thing to do when shopping for clothes, and it is the way we should shop for ideas.

Constructing a railroad is a complex feat of engineering requiring imagination, intelligence, effort, and skill. Yet, a single person can derail an entire train by pulling up one track. Pulling up a track is not a particularly skillful act, but the result is immediate and devastating.

A negative thinker can derail a proposal by focusing on a fraction of it. Showing that one part of the whole is absurd, he or she implies that the whole is equally absurd. By destroying a part, a person can destroy the whole and feel a sense of achievement without taking the time or making the effort to create anything.

When we collaborate and attune ourselves to a common purpose, our energies must be channeled in a constructive direction. The success of any brainstorming session depends upon all members understanding the importance of creating a positive environment. To encourage this, avoid making negative or judgmental statements about ideas, such as:

- It's against all our combined logic.
- It can't be done.
- Someone must have already tried it.
- You're on the wrong track.
- The market is not ready yet.
- Not enough return on investment.

Whenever someone says, "Yes, but . . ." you should make them to change that into "Yes, and . . ." and continue where the last person left off. Whenever someone says, "It won't work" or "It can't be done," make them or the group come up with three ways to make it work or get it done.

A brainstorming session that reflects a spirit of fellowship and good will allows the group to grow a new kind of communal mind that is based on the development of common thoughts. People are no longer in opposition. They become participants in a pool of common ideas, which are capable of constant development and change. Think of your brain as an enchanted loom, perpetually weaving and reweaving new ideas, conjectures, and concepts. The communal mind is an immensely larger loom and contains the means to construct new ideas, conjectures, and concepts immeasurably more diverse than the products of any solitary genius.

THE MEETING

Idea ticket. In advance of a meeting, frame a problem or issue to address. Ask each person to bring at least one new idea or suggestion about the problem as their ticket of admission to the meeting. Have the people write their ideas on index cards and collect them at the door. No one gets in without a ticket. Start the meeting by reading everyone's contribution.

It's showtime. Stagecraft counts for a lot in today's fast-paced, visual world. Think of your meeting as a theatrical production, with sets (colorfully decorated classrooms), props (well-designed materials), and plotlines (themes), and with the manager as the director. As the director, the manager manipulates the participants' perceptions. The director prods, provokes, inspires, and challenges the people who feel stuck and stymied. For example, in a workshop for sales supervisors, the sales manager wore a football jersey and carried a football. When he asked a question, the manager would throw the ball to the person that he wanted to respond. When the manager wanted to change the topic, he would blow a whistle and make a change. The walls were decorated with goal posts displaying quotes from successful football coaches. At the end of the meeting, participants received a miniature football as a reminder that they now had to carry the ball into the field.

The sounds of success. Just like in the movies, in meetings, music can help set the tone and heighten the experience for participants. For example, play soft classical music when the group is brainstorming or light jazz during coffee breaks. The sound track doesn't have to be music. You may want to use the sound of roaring crowds to cheer people on, laugh tracks to loosen people up when they get uptight, jungle noises when someone becomes too negative, bells and gongs when a consensus opinion is reached, bombs blowing up when ideas are discarded, and so on. The possibilities are endless.

1. *Select your problem.* Write the problem as a definite question, as specifically as possible.

2. *Choose the participants.* The ideal number of participants is between six and twelve. Participants should have a positive attitude and be fluent and flexible thinkers. They should be strong, independent personalities who are excited about participating and feel a genuine need to improve goods and services. Someone who has the power to make and implement decisions should also be present.

   A note of caution about the invited decision-maker: It's important that the group leader control and put in perspective the decision-maker's opinions, as nothing subdues a subordinate faster than the strong opinion of authority.

3. *Choose the environment.* The preferred location is a comfortable room off-site. The meeting leader should communicate a strong sense of urgency and a hunger for innovative ideas, but should allow for frequent breaks.

4. *Select a group leader.* The group leader should have strong interpersonal skills and be able to paraphrase and find analogies for suggestions. The group leader should:

   - *Prepare in advance as much as possible.* Ask each participant to become as familiar as they can with creativity exercises. Plan the meeting carefully.

   - *Invite people from diverse areas:* non-experts as well as experts on the situation, and people who can make decisions about ideas generated by the group. Discourage observers, onlookers, and guests. Just as a piece of shell can take all the fun out of an egg salad sandwich, observers can spoil a session. Every attendee should be a participant.

   - *Write an agenda and send it to all invitees.*

   - *Employ a variety of creativity techniques to get ideas flowing.* Use humor and bizarre examples to loosen people up.

   - *Focus on the challenge.* Be specific about what decisions have to be made and continuously summarize the group's progress throughout the meeting.

   - *Encourage any and all ideas, the more bizarre the better.* Pay attention to the *ideas,* and avoid identifying specific ideas with the person who suggested them.

- Be prepared to go back and manipulate ideas. Creativity always involves manipulation. Use questions that are designed to manipulate the subject in some way so as to change its position, rearrange its components, exaggerate some part, or alter the attributes to produce a series of ideas in a short time. Use the questions in chapter 9, SCAMPER.

- Emphasize each person's unique contribution to the meeting.

5. *Select a recorder.* Assign someone to record all ideas the group suggests. If the ideas are not recorded, they will vanish completely.

    After brainstorming, the group leader or the group as a whole should arrange the ideas into related groups to prioritize and evaluate them. In the evaluation stage, some will be discarded, some will stand out as worthwhile, and others will lend themselves to further modification and manipulation.

    Try using generative graphics such as large wall-mounted scrolls of paper to facilitate group problem-solving. Record the ideas with a cartoon, diagram, or written phrase using large colored felt markers. The idea is to stimulate full and energetic participation, and to find colorful, stimulating, and graphic ways to portray ideas and illustrate the group's thinking. For many of us, this method of sketching ideas is closer to how our thoughts naturally grow. Later, your generative graphics can be translated and recorded.

    A home construction company brainstormed new garage designs by using generative graphics. They stimulated quite a few unusual designs and decided to focus on designing a home double-deck garage, ten feet wide and twenty feet high. One car is hoisted on a lift. This is an ideal design for those who have limited lawn space or own classic or rarely driven cars, since the roof completely obscures the car on top. The construction company then created a program to maintain the lift arrangement for an annual fee.

6. *Follow up.* Directly after the meeting, have a lunch, dinner, or cocktail party to celebrate the group's achievements. Write letters to the supervisors of participants acknowledging each individual's contribution to the session.

    It's a good idea to send each person a categorized list of the ideas that the group generated so that they can continue working on those ideas and keep the momentum of the brainstorming session going.

Another good follow-up is to ask each participant to report back on at least one idea he or she thinks is worthy of action, and four or five recommendations for implementing the idea.

A shopping mall staff brainstormed ways to generate more traffic for its stores. One of the ideas was a simple message board for shoppers. Two days after the meeting, a participant forwarded plans and detailed drawings for an electronic message and information center with user-friendly computer message stations. Responding to a series of options the computer gives you, you can read a message from a friend, respond to it, or leave a new one for a specific person (secret passwords can be used) or for the world. Press a button and you can get a printout. All for free. The idea is to turn the mall into more than a shopping mall—it becomes a central message station, which generates customers for the stores.

7. *Evaluate the ideas.* If you try to get hot and cold water out of a faucet at the same time, all you get is lukewarm water. If you try to evaluate ideas as they are being generated, you will not get the ideas hot enough or the criticism cold enough. Do not evaluate ideas until the end of the session.

At the end of a brainstorming session, make three lists: ideas of immediate usefulness, areas for further exploration, and new approaches to the problem.

The leader can categorize the ideas alone, or he or she can have the group evaluate the ideas by voting on the most useful.

Strive for quantity. List *all* ideas as they pop up no matter how similar they may seem. In the figure in the margin, a series of arcs are placed, one on top of the other, to form a column. Each arc is exactly the same size, so they should form a perfectly straight column. Yet, the top of the column appears wider than the bottom.

By repeating a simple arc, we produced an illusion, a distortion in perception. We see something different from what is actually presented on the page. In the same way, when you list ideas, no matter how similar, someone may perceive something new and different.

One group brainstormed the problem of unwanted telephone calls: obscene calls, heavy breathers, salespeople, and so on. Their challenge was: "In what ways might we eliminate unwanted telephone calls?"

One idea offered was: "Why can't we trace the calls and make revenge calls to get even?" After other ideas were listed, the group came up with the revenge telephone. A revenge telephone is actually an answering machine with prerecorded fight-back messages. You can access any message by selecting a key when you pick up the phone. Press one key and the offending party gets a 100-decibel blast. Another key and a threatening male voice shouts, "What the hell do you want?!"

Each member of the group should think of ways to improve ideas or to combine two or more ideas into one better idea. The group leader should keep asking, "what else?" and "how else?"

Another member suggested: "Instead of an answering machine, why not develop a telephone screening box that would provide protection not only from obscene telephone callers but from salespeople as well?" The group came up with a simple screening device you can hook up yourself. It can screen calls before ringing the telephone by asking the caller to enter their secret code. If the caller did not have the code, they would have to leave a message. The phone would not ring for these calls. You could have a variety of codes: one for close friends and relatives, another for business that would only ring the phone during business hours, and so on.

Another member said: "Something somebody said gave me an idea. The idea has nothing to do with obscene telephone calls, but I think it should be explored. Why can't we develop a two-headed public telephone?"

The idea as she described it: "Suppose you and your friend are in town and want to meet a third friend. You have to decide where and want to discuss it together. If you had a public telephone with two receivers, one person could listen as the other takes down directions. A two-headed public telephone would probably generate more money, as the conversations would tend to last longer.

Tag on to ideas and make new ideas out of previous ones. It's much easier to build on ideas than to keep creating new ones. Keep asking "what else?"

Another person offered: "Let's get back to the answering machine. How about a machine that doesn't record messages? You could design a machine that performs like a real secretary. The machine would have a variety of different prerecorded responses that a person could use to fake the caller."

The idea: An answering machine that allows you to monitor incoming calls, ask questions, and give the appropriate response without ever picking up the phone. For instance:

"Hello, this is the office of Richard Stratton. Who's calling, please?"

"Hi, this is Alan Spiegel from the Acme Energy Co. May I speak to Mr. Stratton, please?"

Now, Mr. Stratton does not know who Spiegel is or what he wants, so he pushes the response button that says: "Could you please tell me what you want to talk to Mr. Stratton about?"

"I want to show him our new line of energy-saving windows."

Ah! A salesman whom Stratton does not want to talk to, so he pushes another response button, which says: "I'm sorry, Mr. Stratton is out of town and won't be back for six months."

The caller thinks he's talking to a real person, and Stratton is able to respond with various messages while he monitors his incoming calls with impunity. To make it particularly human, the machine doesn't take messages.

Once this group started listing and manipulating, they came up with four new products: The revenge telephone, the telephone screening device, two-headed public telephones, and the receptionist answering machine.

The power of association is that it is a two-way street. When a group member suggests an idea, he almost automatically steers his imagination toward another idea. At the same time, his ideas stimulate other participants' imaginations and associative powers. A spark from one mind will likely light up ideas in others, much like a string of firecrackers.

A fruit wholesaler and his staff brainstormed ideas for a unique gift business.

One person's idea was to promote an atypical fruit as a gift item, such as a watermelon. This triggered another person to remember that watermelons can be grown into any rectangular or pyramidal shape. Another member offered ways to add personal messages grown into the skin by using masking tape. The idea they finally settled on: custom-shaped watermelons with personal messages grown into their skins.

LORDS OF DISCIPLINE

Sometimes meetings stall because participants are too tightly focused on the problem and on structured ways of doing things. I call these people the Lords of Discipline.

If a meeting is peopled by the Lords of Discipline, a group leader has to move them away from their disciplined way of looking at problems. Doing so could be likened to helping them make the transition from driving on the left side of the road to driving on the right.

Suppose your challenge is to create an advertising program for a new movie. Your meeting is staffed by Lords of Discipline who can't move beyond the traditional ways of advertising and marketing movies. Their thinking is constrained by focusing too much on the problem and not enough on the process. By asking a series of abstract questions, you can sometimes loosen their focus. These questions might include:

- "What catches people's attention?"

- "What surprises people?"

- "What shocks people?"

- "What do people enjoy?"

- "Whom do people respond to?"

- "What do people respond to?"

- "Who do people admire?"

- "Whom do they want to talk to?"

Have them list their responses, then use those responses as stimuli for new ideas.

An advertising agency was given a contract by a foreign brewery to reinvigorate American sales. The challenge was to reach men ages twenty-one to twenty-nine. The agency's research showed that these men are not sitting in front of the TV. They are playing video games; they're in bars.

The agency started the session with the general question: What catches the attention of young men? Responses included: nude girls, beautiful women, NASCAR, football, free drinks, celebrities, bodybuilding, and so on.

They listed the responses and free-associated from them. Beautiful women and free drinks reminded them of young people using pickup lines in bars. This stimulated the idea for the brewery to spend its advertising money to dress beer bottles in agency-designed back labels, novelties meant for frisky barflies to use as icebreakers. "I'm with the band," says one. "Of course they're real," reads another. Who could resist, "I'm a hottie magnet." This radical approach increased sales by 40 percent—with no television advertising.

BRAINSTORMING BULLETIN BOARD

Use a bulletin board to brainstorm creative ideas at your office. Place the bulletin board in a central location, write the problem to be solved on a piece of colored paper, and place it in the center of the board for all interested parties to see. Anyone with an idea or suggestion about the problem writes it on a white piece of paper and places it under the problem on the board.

The advantages of this technique are:

1. The problem is visible and, thus, will be on the minds of all interested people.

2. It spurs ideas by association. As one person reads the problem and ideas on the board, he or she is likely to think of a new idea.

3. You can leave the problem up as long as you like. This gives people sufficient time to consider it.

4. If few or no people offer ideas, you might consider ways to encourage workers to become more creative.

One company in Rochester, New York, put up such a board and announced that it would pay $100 to anyone who came up with an idea that could save the company money immediately. The first winner was an employee who suggested that the award be cut to $50.

The next challenge posted was: "In what ways can we improve our advertising?" The winner was an employee who suggested that a better way to advertise was to give people small packets of tissue paper with the company's message on them. This is a practical item that people will carry around with them and use often. It was their best promotion ever.

SOLO BRAINSTORMING

Take a pack of index cards and write your ideas on the cards. Jot down one idea per card, put it aside and write your next idea on the next card and so on until you run dry. Write the ideas as they occur to you—good ones, bad ones, bizarre ones, exotic ones, all mixed up together without regard to logic or value. The two keys to this technique are: (1) produce the greatest possible quantity of ideas, and (2) do not evaluate any idea until you have listed everything you can think of.

When you are finished, take your pack of idea cards and:

- Sort and evaluate them.
- Combine ideas.
- Free-associate from the ideas to create other ideas.
- Imagine how an idea would work and change it.
- Reverse it to see what the opposite idea is.
- Rearrange, adapt, transpose, or substitute for the ideas.
- Consider each idea from another point of view.
- Draw or diagram the idea.

- Make a metaphor out of it.

- Force connections between two or more ideas.

- Imagine what a critic would say about an idea and modify it accordingly.

- Sleep on it.

Assume your challenge is to come up with ways to differentiate your bank from other banks. The first idea that occurs to you is, "Why not make the bank comfortable and homey?"

Rather than rejecting this idea as being impractical, by working with the concept, you could come up with a new process of handling banking transactions. For example, you could create a bank where you hand your money and forms to a receptionist, who passes them to a row of clerks for processing. Instead of being frustrated while you wait in line, you can then sit in a homey atmosphere in a comfortable chair, watch TV, read magazines, and sip coffee. The clerk would call your name when your transaction is complete.

BRAINSKETCHING

What's darker: a Christmas tree or a frozen pea? Does a lobster have a mouth? How many windows are there in your living room? If the letter "D" is turned on its back and put on top of a "J," what does this remind you of? Many of us think visually and not verbally. You might ask each participant to draw a sketch of their idea on how to solve the problem. Sketching ideas provides visual stimuli to spark your imagination.

During a rehearsal of Debussy's *La Mer*, Arturo Toscanini found himself unable to describe the effect he wished from a particular passage. After a moment's thought, he took a silk handkerchief from his pocket and tossed it high into the air. The orchestra, mesmerized, watched the slow, graceful descent of the silken square. Toscanini smiled with satisfaction as it finally settled on the floor. "There," he said, "play it like that."

Image board. This is one technique that the Ford design center uses to inspire new car designs. When setting out to design a midpriced car for upwardly mobile families, the designers put together a wall-size board of photographs and drawings. They use pictures to answer such questions as: What kinds of these houses do these car-buyers live in? What kind of watches do they buy? Where do they go on vacation? What kind of art do they hang on their walls? What do their coffeepots look like? How do they dress?

As the board of pictures grows, an understanding of who is going to buy this car and what might appeal to them begins to emerge. As the design process moves along, the fresh new car designs that are created can be checked against the information the image board contains. Because it's visual, this check-off can be done quickly and—again, because it is visual—the experience is not hidebound or restrictive.

As you are working on a problem, if you find pictures, photographs, or diagrams that are relevant to your target, pin them up on the wall in front of you. Add to this image board as new pictures become available. Mix your sketches of ideas in among them.

Automobile designers at Mercedes-Benz had a large image board where interesting shapes and images were tacked on. One designer was enthralled with the shapes, textures, and colors of exotic fish. The designers became enthralled with the boxfish. Despite its boxy cube-shaped body, the designers discovered the boxfish is in fact a perfect example of an aerodynamic streamlined shape. The structural shape of the boxfish was adapted by the designers to create the efficiently designed DCX, which gets seventy to eighty-four miles per gallon.

SUMMARY

Next time you see geese flying along in V formation, you should consider what science has discovered about why they fly that way, which provides a good model of teamwork. As each bird flaps its wings, it creates an uplift for the bird immediately following. By flying in V formation, the whole flock adds at least 71 percent greater flying range than if each bird flew on its own. The geese get where they are going more quickly and easily because they are traveling on the thrust of one another.

When a goose falls out of formation, it suddenly feels the drag and resistance of trying to go it alone—and quickly gets back into formation to take advantage of the lifting power of the bird in front. If we have as much sense as a goose, we will stay in formation with those people who are headed the same way we are.

When the head goose gets tired, it rotates back in the wing and another goose flies point. It is sensible to take turns doing demanding jobs, whether we're talking about people working in an organization or geese flying south. Geese honk from behind to encourage those up front to keep up their speed. We should encourage our leaders as well with shows of encouragement.

Finally, when a goose gets sick or is wounded by gunshot and falls out of formation, two other geese fall out with that goose and follow it down to lend help and protection. They stay with the fallen goose until it is able to fly or until it dies, and only then do they launch out on their own, or with another formation, to catch up with their group. We should help others keep up with the rest at work by working with them.

CHAPTER THIRTY-SIX

ORTHODOX BRAINSTORMING

"The general that hearkens to wise
counsel and acts upon it will conquer."

SUN TZU

When you look into a kaleidoscope, you see a pattern formed by colored crystals. If you then add a new piece of crystal and manipulate the drum, you have a multitude of new patterns. Likewise, when a group brainstorms for ideas, they produce a number of ideas. These ideas produce a number of random combinations linking variations together; it's like adding crystals to a kaleidoscope. You create a multitude of new possibilities.

Following are some of my favorite orthodox brainstorming techniques that can help lead you to a multitude of new ideas.

SILENT TECHNIQUES

Brainwriting. Horst Geschka and his associates at the Batelle Institute in Frankfurt, Germany, developed a variety of group creative-thinking techniques called "brainwriting." In traditional brainstorming groups, people suggest ideas one at a time. This is *serial* processing of information, in that only one idea is offered at a time, in series. Brainwriting, in contrast, allows multiple ideas to be suggested at the same time. This is *parallel* processing of information, in that many ideas can be produced at once, in parallel. Thus, brainwriting increases idea production dramatically. If a brainwriting group has ten members, up to ten ideas will be generated for every one generated in a typical brainstorming session of ten members.

The basic guidelines are:

1. First, discuss the problem to clarify it. Write the problem in a location visible to all group members.

2. Distribute three-by-five-inch index cards to each participant and instruct them to write their ideas on the cards, one idea per card. Where group brainstorming involves participants shouting ideas out loud, brainwriting has people generate ideas by silently writing them down. As participants complete a card, they pass it silently to the person on the right.

3. Tell the group members to read the cards they are passed and to regard them as "stimulation cards." Tell them to write down any new ideas inspired by the stimulation cards on blank cards and then pass them to the person on their right. Within a few minutes, several idea cards will be rotating around the table.

4. After twenty to thirty minutes, collect all cards and have the group members tape them to a wall. The cards should be arranged into columns according to different categories of ideas, with a title card above each column. Eliminate the duplicates.

5. Evaluate the ideas by giving each participant a packet of adhesive dots and have them place the dots on the ideas they like. They can allocate the dots in any manner desired, placing them all on one idea, one each on five different ideas, or any other combination.

Brainwriting ensures that the loudest voices don't prevail, participants feel less pressure from managers and bosses, and ideas can't be shot down as soon as they are offered.

You can design your own brainwriting format based on the two principles: (1) idea generation is silent, and (2) ideas are created spontaneously in parallel. Some examples are:

- *Idea pool.* Ask participants to silently generate ideas on three-by-five-inch cards and place their cards in the center of the table instead of passing them to the person on their right. Whenever a participant wants or needs a stimulation card, they simply exchange their cards for cards from the pool.

- *Gallery.* This technique reverses the process. Instead of moving ideas around for people to examine, the gallery moves people around. Post sheets of flip-chart paper around the room, one per participant.

Participants stand silently and write their ideas on the sheets (one sheet per person) for ten to fifteen minutes. Then the participants are allowed fifteen minutes to walk around the "gallery," look at the other ideas, and take notes. Now, using the other ideas to stimulate further thought, participants return to their sheets and add to or refine their ideas. After about ten minutes of additional writing, the participants examine all the ideas and select the best ones.

- *Drawing ideas.* Another option for the gallery technique is to ask participants to draw or diagram their ideas instead of listing them. Drawing and diagramming is useful in creative thinking to recover information from memory that might otherwise be unavailable. For example, how many windows are there in your house? Diagramming your house allows you to inspect and count the windows. Creative insights sometimes occur as a result of drawing or diagramming a problem, because they help us notice certain features that may be overlooked. Post sheets of flip-chart paper and then ask the participants to draw a sketch or diagram of how the problem might be solved. Then the participants are again allowed to walk around the "gallery" and take notes. Using the notes, they return and refine their own sketches. The group then examines all the sketches and constructs a final solution from parts of different sketches.

- *Three plus.* Each participant silently writes three ideas on the tops of sheets of paper, one idea per sheet. The sheets are passed to the person on their right. That person writes down an idea that improves on the one listed at the top of the sheet. If participants have difficulty improving on the idea, ask them to list new ones. Do this for all three ideas. After five minutes or so, the idea sheets are again passed to the right. Continue the process until all members receive their original papers.

- *Airplanes.* Have each participant construct a paper airplane. Each participant writes down an idea on the airplane and sends it flying to another participant. Upon reading what's been written on the airplane, he or she writes down a modification or improvement of that idea, or an entirely fresh possibility and sends it flying to someone else. Continue the exercise for twenty minutes, then collect and categorize the ideas.

- *Wall of ideas.* Each participant silently writes ideas on sticky notes. While the group writes ideas, collect and paste them on a wall. When everyone is done, organize the ideas as a group. Ask the group to come to the wall and sort out the ideas in a meaningful way. Eventually, the ideas will be clustered into different themes and categories. Label each set of ideas with a topic card and paste it over the idea set. Do this for each set. Participants can elaborate or express concerns by writing their thoughts on additional sticky notes and pasting them next to the idea or set of ideas. Prioritize the ideas by giving each participant ten adhesive dots. The participants prioritize the ideas by placing a dot or dots on the ideas they like. They can place as many dots or as few as they wish on an idea. The group discusses the most highly rated ideas.

Reynolds is the leading provider of integrated solutions that help automotive retailers manage change and profitability. After brainstorming, a group of managers broke down the barriers between sales and customer service by creating Voice of the Customer, or VOC. VOC regularly surveys customers to measure satisfaction and uncover issues. Any negative response is immediately sent to the "issue owner" in sales for resolution. For example, a customer expressed dissatisfaction with the profitability of a particular Reynolds solution. VOC reported the problem to the issue owner in sales. A sales team created an action list in a face-to-face meeting with the customer and began tackling the issues one by one. They and the customer identified lack of training as the common denominator for the failed issues, which was quickly and easily corrected to the customer's satisfaction. VOC follows up to see if the customer is satisfied, and if they are not, VOC escalates the issue to the next level of management.

NOTEBOOKS

Brainstorming in notebooks is a technique widely used in the intelligence business. A group of analysts collaborates on a work by having each person working on it separately at different times. The result is usually a remarkable product that reflects several different points of view combined into something different over time. Collaboration over time creates different dimensions and different understandings of a subject. The guidelines for this technique are:

1. The coordinator gives each participant a notebook containing problem information and instructions. Each participant writes at least one idea per day in the notebook for one week.

2. The participants exchange the notebooks with each other every week. Participants can then use the ideas in the other notebooks to trigger new ideas through association.

3. The exchange of ideas should stop after four weeks, even if all notebooks haven't made the rounds. The coordinator collects the notebooks, categorizes the ideas, and prepares a summary. The participants gather in a group to discuss the ideas generated.

THE STRAVINSKY EFFECT

This technique combines generating ideas silently with the random clustering of people and ideas. It was inspired by the work of Igor Stravinsky, the genius of modernism in music, who never lost his eagerness to try something new. His *The Soldier's Tale* created a landmark departure from traditional performance styles by introducing the concept of clusters of performers (dancers, instrumentalists, and narrator) who saw themselves uniquely re-creating the composer's work, each performance being a new experiment.

The guidelines for using this technique in brainstorming are:

1. The facilitator posts a problem or challenge for discussion. For example, "In what ways might we create a more innovative corporation?"

2. Each participant writes eight responses or ideas on three-by-five-inch index cards, one idea per card.

3. The facilitator collects all the cards and shuffles them.

4. The facilitator randomly distributes three cards to each participant. Make sure that no participant receives his or her original cards. Ask everyone to study the cards and arrange them in order of personal preference. The facilitator spreads the leftover cards on a table face up.

5. The facilitator asks the participants to exchange the cards they don't like with those on the table. Participants go to the table and exchange any or all the cards with the leftover cards.

6. Next, the participants exchange cards with each other. Every participant must exchange at least one card and may exchange more if they choose to.

7. The facilitator asks the participants to form clusters. There is no limit to the number of participants who may join the same cluster, but no cluster may keep more than three cards.

8. The facilitator asks each cluster to prepare a creative way to present their three ideas to the group. They might create a graphic poster, bumper sticker, slogan, logo, T-shirt, television commercial, song, and so on.

A group of waste management experts met to come up with ideas on how to dispose of cell phones in environmentally friendly or socially responsible ways. They used the Stravinsky effect as their technique and came up with the idea to make the cellular phone casing of a biodegradable polymer, which comes embedded with sunflower seeds. The casing degrades in the compost and releases the seed from its viewable capsule.

They also came up with an idea to raise funds for local food banks through the process of recycling used cell phones and printer cartridges.

SIL

Three artists who have nothing in common with each other paint a picture of the same dog. The paintings are all done with different perspectives in different styles, yet each captures certain things about the essence of the dog. Each painting adds one perspective that adds to our understanding and perspective about the dog. The next technique is designed to do just that with ideas.

SIL is a German acronym that means "successive integration of problem elements." It first involves people silently and individually generating ideas about a previously stated problem. It differs from most other methods in that ideas are generated by progressively integrating previous ideas. The guidelines are:

1. The group silently writes ideas individually.

2. Two of the group members read one of their ideas out loud.

3. The remaining group members try to integrate the ideas into one idea.

4. A third member reads an idea, and the group attempts to integrate it with the one formed in the previous step.

This process of reading and integrating ideas continues until all the ideas have been read and integrated into one final solution. While it may not be possible to integrate all ideas, at least the process ensures that all ideas get a fair hearing.

OPEN MEETINGS

Don't get trapped into mediocrity by always having the same style of brainstorming meeting. A fun and lively format for a change of pace is the open meeting.

Open brainstorming meetings give all employees—from janitors to CEOs—the opportunity and the motivation to suggest ideas. The purpose behind the formlessness of an open meeting is to let ideas take their own shape, undistorted by status or personal politics. Open meetings are governed by a few simple guidelines, a general theme, and very loose time limits.

There is no agenda for the meeting. Someone reads the meeting's general theme aloud and invites everyone to identify a related issue for which they assume responsibility. When someone suggests an issue, that person writes it on a large sheet of paper, reads it aloud, and posts it on one of the walls. This process continues until all the issues have been posted.

The next phase is known as the "idea marketplace." Everyone is invited to sign up on one of the large "issue sheets" to discuss the issue. Participants can sign up for as many groups as they wish. Sponsors of each issue convene their groups to side rooms, discuss the issue, and record any ideas or other information suggested. Ideally, several smaller rooms near the larger meeting room should be available where the small groups can convene and pursue their issue. Each small group should honor the "law of two feet," which means that if any participant becomes bored or has nothing to contribute to the group, that person should honor the group and walk away.

A group of selected government employees held an open meeting with the theme of "conservation of energy." Some of the issues posted were: "automobile design," "civic promotions," "electricity," "alternative energy sources," and "public education."

One group convened to discuss the conservation of electricity. The discussion concentrated on public education and awareness. One of the engineers suggested some kind of home display of the cost of electricity as it is being used. A prototype for an electricity home monitor was made and perfected. The monitor displays the cost of electricity being used on a portable easy-to-read LCD monitor inside your home. People will soon learn how much it costs to operate electrical appliances and begin to think of ways to save money and conserve energy.

STORYBOARDING

In 1928, Walt Disney and his artists were working on his first talking cartoon, "Steamboat Willie." Disney wanted full animation. To animate everything required thousands of drawings. They were piled in stacks all over the place. It was hard to know what had been finished and what still needed to be done. They had to have meetings all the time, just to find out what was going on.

Walt Disney came up with the idea of having his artists pin their drawings on the walls of the studio in sequence so he could see in a glance how far along the project was. Each scene was then used as a point around which a complete story could be told. The story was told on a wall covered with a special kind of board, hence the term "storyboard."

Storyboarding quickly became a routine part of Disney's planning procedure for both animated and live-action films. He could walk in at any time of the day or night and see progress on any given project at a glance. Storyboards kept branching out into many uses. Disneyland and Walt Disney World were both operationally planned using storyboards.

Storyboarding was refined into a brainstorming technique, and a variety of related procedures for generating ideas have evolved since then. Although there are some significant differences among the procedures, all of them share the common feature begun by Walt Disney: laying out key concepts that are linked together to form a complete whole.

Storyboarding can be likened to taking your thoughts and the thoughts of others and making them visible by spreading them on a wall as you work on your problem. Following are basic guidelines used by many storyboarding methods:

1. *Topic.* Tape or pin the topic card on the wall. In our example, the topic is to "create a new restaurant."

2. *Purpose.* Normally most people start with a "purpose" header, which helps the group brainstorm the purposes for pursuing a particular topic. Each brainstormed purpose is written on a card and posted beneath the "purpose" card. For example, among the possible purposes for starting a new restaurant are making money, fulfilling a need, and serving the customer.

3. *Headers.* Identify and list headers, which are primarily the major issues, attributes, or solution categories of the process. Each one is written on a card and posted. Our example has the headers: purpose, location, name, theme, environment, menu, entertainment, marketing, and miscellaneous. Arrange and rearrange the headers until you come up with the sequence that best tells the story.

4. *Miscellaneous.* It's a good idea to include a miscellaneous header to contain all those items that don't fit within the other categories. Place thoughts in this column as the rest of the columns are brainstormed. Some of these may become separate headers themselves if enough similar items appear in the miscellaneous column. In our example, suppose participants listed several advertising and marketing suggestions and ideas. These ideas would create additional headers or, if significant enough, might merit separate storyboards.

5. *Brainstorming.* Group members use each category as a stimulus for problem solutions and write these ideas, solutions, and thoughts on cards. Each card is posted beneath the appropriate header card. For example, all the brainstormed names for the new restaurant would be posted underneath the "name" header, and all the suggested menu items would be listed under the "menu" header and so on.

6. *Hitchhiking.* During a storyboard session, consider all ideas relevant, no matter how impractical they appear. Encourage the group to think positively and defer judgment until a later time. Once the ideas start flowing, those working with the storyboard will become immersed in the problem and will hitchhike onto other ideas to create more new ideas. Encourage participants to examine the solutions and try to generate additional ideas from them or combine solutions across categories and use them as stimuli for new ideas.

7. *Flexibility.* Keep the storyboard flexible and dynamic. As ideas and suggestions accumulate, you may find it necessary to add more headers. For example, in our restaurant example, "environment" could be split into "physical environment" and "atmosphere." Think of the storyboard as a living, dynamic thing that is constantly evolving toward the ideal solution.

8. *Incubating.* The process continues until the group generates a sufficient number of ideas or time is called. It's usually a good idea to brainstorm for ideas using a storyboard over a time period of a few days or weeks to allow the ideas to incubate and cross-fertilize.

You can use a wide variety of materials to create your storyboard. Cork-boards, white boards, chalkboards or walls, anything that provides a surface where you can add, delete, or move things around. You can use different colors to distinguish headers and columns. Depending on which system you use, you may need pushpins, scissors, wide marking pens, chalk, a supply of cards, sticky notes, or other types of paper. Take a photograph of the completed board so it can be reconstructed and reworked in the future, if necessary.

The beauty of storyboarding is in its flexibility and adaptability to your needs. You can modify the guidelines to meet your requirements. It's a good idea to keep the process simple at first. After you've become comfortable with it, you can expand it at will.

COMBINING THINGS

In the illustration on the following page, the lines of dots above the A are equal in length. When I combine the lines of dots with two diagonal straight lines below B, the lines now appear to be unequal in length. The bottom line is now smaller, yet they are still equal in length. Combining the lines of dots with diagonal lines creates a different perception of the pattern with new properties. The lines of dots have not changed. Combining the dots with the lines changes the way you look at them, and when that happens, what you're looking at also changes.

Think for a moment about hydrogen and oxygen. Blend them together and you create water, a product with properties quite different from either of the component gases that make it up. Who could have predicted the

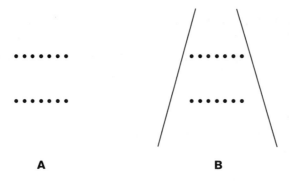

A   B

emergence of water from two simple gases? Alone, they have known and obvious properties. Put them together, and seemingly magical transformations occur. But it is not magic; it is the very essence of creativity.

Suppose you want to invent something new. Select twenty objects at random. You can select any objects—objects at home, objects at work, or objects you might find walking down the street. Or, you can imagine you are in a technologically oriented science museum, walking through the Smithsonian Institute or browsing in an electronic store, and make a list of twenty objects that you would likely see.

On a sheet of paper, make two lists of ten objects each, one column on the left side and one on the right. Pick one item from the left and combine it with one on the right. Play with the combinations until you find a promising new combination, then refine and elaborate it into a new invention.

Following is an example from a recent workshop. Two participants went to the front of the room. One listed the first ten objects that came to her mind for column A, while the other did the same for column B.

A	B
computer	slicer
coffeemaker	sculpture
bagel	hammock
sunglasses	beeper
doormat	windows
bathtub	vacuum cleaner
cell phone	automobile
suntan lotion	ticket
bedroom	soda can
television	insect repellent

In the example, the illustrated combinations yielded the following ideas:

- Combining "bagel" with "slicer" became a bagel slicer with plastic sides designed to hold the bagel and prevent rotation when slicing.

- "Bathtub" and "hammock" combined to make a baby tub. It's a simple hammock in the tub with a headrest to hold the baby's head securely, leaving the parent's hands free to do the washing.

- "Suntan lotion" and "insect repellent" combined to form a lotion that protects against both the sun and insects.

- "Coffeemaker" and "sculpture" combined to form a coffeemaker with a top that resembles a sculpture of the top of the volcano Mount Vesuvius. When the coffee is done, the top glows red.

- "Doormat" and "vacuum cleaner" combined to form a doormat with built-in suction. When you step on the doormat, the doormat sucks the dirt and debris from the bottom of your shoes.

- "Cell phone" and "soda can" inspired the idea of utilizing cell phones as devices that, with sensors, would enable users to dispense soda and other products from vending machines with the expense charged back to the vendor via the carrier.

Attributes. Take one object from column A and one from column B. Break each subject down by listing its attributes and then randomly combining the attributes. Make two lists of the object's attributes or characteristics and randomly combine them to trigger ideas. For example, we select "bedroom" and "automobile" from our columns above. Some of their attributes are as follows:

Bedroom	Automobile
bed	passengers
place to sleep	moves
window shades	wheels
located near bathroom	different colors
sense of security	automatic door locks

Combining "sense of security" and "automatic door locks" inspires the idea of a master lock near the bed that locks and unlocks all windows, doors, computer systems, and everything else in the house with one key.

Combining "window shades" and "moves" triggers the idea of incorporating light sensors that automatically raise or lower the shades according to the intensity of the outside light into window shades.

I know a physicist who makes systematic use of the idea that new associations may be formed by accidental combination. He cuts up indexes of physics textbooks and then throws the fragments into an empty fishbowl, then pulls out several scraps at a time to see whether any new useful combinations emerge. This simple technique has produced insights and ideas that he could not generate using his usual way of thinking. Cut up an index of a book in your field (e.g., a marketing book if you are in marketing) and try the same technique.

Combining Ideas

No program can generate a number more complex than itself, any more than a one-hundred-pound pregnant woman can give birth to a two-hundred-pound child. An idea grows by annexing its neighbor. Two ideas can cross-catalyze each other, but both need to be present in order for a new concept, product, or idea to form, like two chemicals forming a new compound.

Scientists at the University Medical Center at Bern, Switzerland, combined the technology of computed topography (CT) with the technology of magnetic resonance imaging (MRI) to create three-dimensional computer images of a corpse's internal organs. This virtual autopsy provides a head-to-toe cyber-corpse that a pathologist can view—wounds and all—from any depth and angle, including inside out. This, in effect, is a bloodless approach to an otherwise messy job with the added benefit of digital permanency.

Combining ideas to create more—and better—ideas will help your mind work to the peak of its creative efficiency. Try this strategy for combining ideas:

First, collect all your ideas and put them into two columns, column A and column B. Either list them on paper or write them on cards and put the cards into two piles or tape them onto the wall in two columns. Randomly connect one idea from column A and one idea from column B. Then try to combine the two into one idea. See how many viable combinations you can make.

To use this technique in a group brainstorming session, ask each participant to silently write five or six ideas on index cards. Then have each participant prioritize their ideas and select one. Collect and place the leftover cards face up on a table. Next, ask the participants to come to the table, review the leftover ideas, select one, and then return to their seat. This is also done silently and should take about five to ten minutes. Finally, ask each participant to combine his or her idea with the one they selected from the leftover pile into a new idea.

COMBINING SUBJECTS FROM UNRELATED FIELDS

Jacque Hadamard, the brilliant French mathematician who proved the prime number theorem, argued that invention, including mathematical invention, requires the discovery of unusual but fruitful combinations of ideas. To find such novelties, it is necessary to construct numerous random combinations. It is the random combinations of variables from different domains that allow new and exciting ideas to form.

Among combinations, the most fertile ideas will often be those formed of elements drawn from fields that are far apart. Suppose you wanted a new advertising campaign. Select two advertising campaigns from different fields that you like (e.g., an advertising program for a political campaign and an advertising program for the Red Cross). List the attributes of each in two columns and then make random connections until you create ideas for a new campaign.

Or, suppose you want to improve office morale. Identify two organizations from different fields that have terrific morale (e.g., the Super Bowl and a church), list the attributes of each, and then make random connections to come up with new and different ideas to improve morale in your office.

One entrepreneurial software engineer for a company that specializes in LCD products sat down one day and listed household objects (broom, refrigerator, telephone, lamp, etc.). The salesperson then combined each with various LCD products and, when he combined refrigerators with LCD, he got his "aha!" inspiration: poetry-generating fridge magnets. Each magnet has an LCD that displays a word selected at random from a three-hundred-word vocabulary. The magnets communicate with each other to make allegedly poetic phrases such as "the wet crows ruffled coherently" and "yellow flowers are shy smiles."

COMBINING PROBLEMS

Thomas Edison's lab was a big barn with many worktables holding separate projects in progress. He would work on one project and then another. His workshop was designed to allow one project to infect a neighboring one, so that moves made in one could also be tried in an adjacent project. This method of working allowed him to consistently rethink the way he saw his projects.

In the same way, you can tackle multiple problems using a notebook. Work on two or more unrelated problems in parallel. When you're stonewalled on one problem, move to the next. When you come up with ideas or moves that work for one problem, try the ideas or related ideas with the other problem as well. Masura Ibuka at Sony worked on two problems simultaneously. One problem was miniaturizing the stereo; another was working on entertainment systems that used headphones. Working with engineers on one and then with different engineers on the other, he combined the two projects into the Walkman radio.

COMBINE ELEMENTS OF EXTREME IDEAS

Leonardo da Vinci believed that to really know how things work, you should examine them under critical conditions. He believed in pushing concepts to the extreme in his imagination. Create two opposite extreme ideas. For instance, what idea would you create if you had all the resources (people, money, time, etc.) in the world? Then ask what idea would you create if you had no resources? And then try to combine the two into something practical. Also, think of the elements and attributes of each extreme and then make random connections between the two lists of extremes.

Suppose, for example, you want to reward employees for ideas that increase productivity. One extreme would be to award each employee one million dollars for each idea. The other extreme would be to award each employee a penny. The combination of the two extremes inspires a "Penny for Your Ideas" campaign. Buy a gum-ball machine and place it in your office filled with colored gum balls. For every idea (or every five or ten ideas) award the contributor a penny for use in the machine. Award a cash prize according to the color of the gum ball that comes out ($2 for green, $5 for yellow, $100 for red, etc.)

COMBINE DOMAINS

Many breakthrough ideas are based on combining information from different domains that are usually not thought of as related. Engineers at a pilot plant in Britain have combined the domains of housing and waste disposal into an innovative idea that could solve two problems at once by increasing housing and reducing waste. The plant uses household waste, dredge sludge, treated sewage, and incinerator bottom ash to produce coated pellets that can be used in a variety of construction applications. "The beauty of this process is that it takes waste that would otherwise go to a landfill and, using energy in the waste, turns it into useful building materials that would otherwise have to be quarried," says Darryl Newport of the University of East London, which is developing the pilot project. "It is a win-win-win situation."

Suppose you want to create a new product or service that would increase company efficiency. First create two lists of activities, one that's pertinent to the organization and one that's pertinent to the non-business world.

1. First, list business activities. The business list should be specific activities like "photocopying," "handling customer complaints," "coffee breaks," or "shipping." List ten to twenty activities you know about.

2. Next, focus on one activity. Based on what you know about it, try to develop a new product or service. For example, perhaps you can come up with a way for people to be educated or motivated while waiting in line to use the photocopier.

3. Now make a new list of activities, this time a list of ten to twenty activities that you know about outside the organization (e.g., bowling, singing, volunteering, mowing the lawn, etc.).

4. Finally, combine the two using your expertise in those areas—the business activity and the non-business activity. For example, combining the activities of singing and photocopying might inspire the idea to build a stereo or karaoke screen by the photocopier. Rather than song lyrics, this screen could have a running display of news and information about the company, such as awards, people, job openings, and so on.

A New Zealand company has combined the fields of passive lighting and construction materials. This combination has created passive emergency lighting, a photo-luminescent strip of natural or artificial light that guides people safely up and down steps, corridors, handrails, aisle markers, and seat numbers in stadiums. The patented Ecoglo technology bakes a photo-luminescent material into an aluminum extrusion. The product requires no energy to run, thus it can work in a complete power outage, and can be used to replace emergency lighting. Their product is nonradioactive and nontoxic, and responds to both indoor and outdoor (solar) lighting.

Left Brainers and Right Brainers

Here is a picture of coffee beans. A man's head is hidden somewhere in the beans. See how long it takes you to find it.

According to some recent cognitive research, if you can find the man's head within three seconds, your right brain is more developed than normal people. If you can find the man's head within one minute, your right brain is developing normally. If it takes you longer than two minutes, your left brain is more developed than normal. If you still can't find it, look in the lower left between the middle and side.

Here is a fun way to brainstorm by combining both the left and right brains of participants. Divide the group into left-brain (rational) thinkers and right-brain (intuitive) thinkers. Ask the left-brainers to come up with a practical, conventional, and logical idea; ask the right-brainers to come up with a far-out, unconventional, and illogical idea. Then bring the group back together and combine the left-brain idea with the right-brain idea to see what you get.

One group brainstormed for ways to encourage Americans to conserve fuel. The group was divided and eventually brought back together. The left-brainers suggested an advertising campaign to encourage people to buy and ride bicycles. The right-brainers suggested that environmentally-friendly electric cars automatically get the right of way on all roads, are exempt from traffic fines, and get free car washes, free coffee and newspapers at rest stops, and access to private, spacious bathrooms at all interstate toll roads.

They combined the two approaches into one idea: bicycle stations. Bicycle stations are facilities where people can park their bikes, stow their riding clothes, clean up, and emerge ready for work. The stations would also be social spaces, where people could take a coffee, pick up a newspaper, rest, or get a snack. The stations would be built along the existing commuter rail lines, and they would provide services from simple covered parking to full multimodal transit hubs that would eventually integrate a variety of clean transport options, giving commuters the opportunity to connect with electric vehicles, car shares, and rental bikes. By providing these types of benefits to cyclists, the city would have cleaner air and increased mobility.

SUMMARY

Years back, I participated in a session with a number of academics about educational reform. After the session, I discussed my disappointment with the results with Father Tom, a Franciscan monk who taught at St. Bonaventure University. I had discussed the issue with many in the group before the session, as I knew they had many unusual and unique ideas, yet they held back and offered only the same old conservative ideas. Father Tom laughed and said the professors were hoarding their ideas for their own publications. Academics are paranoid about original ideas and feel others want to steal them. They attend meetings of this type in order to find out what the others have done. He then told me a tale about a Franciscan missionary.

Many years ago in Japan, a missionary decided it would be nice for the village to celebrate the New Year with a big crock of hot sake wine. The monk asked the ten richest men to each bring one large jug of wine for the huge heating bowl, since none could provide for all. On the way to his wine cellar, each man thought, "My wine is too valuable to share! I'll just bring a jug of water instead, and since everyone else is bringing wine, no one will know the difference." And so, when the ten richest men gathered, each of them ceremoniously poured the contents of his jug into the big bowl. They looked sheepishly at one another as they heated and poured hot water for all.

CHAPTER THIRTY-SEVEN

RAW CREATIVITY

"All we need do is to throw something odd
and unaccountable in his way."

SUN TZU

The brain, like a musical instrument, has great emergent properties. Some older string instruments have special strings known as sympathetic strings. These strings are not played but resonate due to the vibrations of the other strings. Thus, the strings create musical sounds beyond the chords that can be played with surface strings. The sounds seem to be created out of nothing. Similarly, I think that there are resonating elements in our brains that, much like the sympathetic strings in stringed instruments, increase the capacity of the brain and our ability to make indirect complex associations.

We have the capacity to imagine and create new things from pieces of things, properties of the external world, essences, remote thoughts, and remote things. Through indirect associations (our brains' "sympathetic strings"), we conceptually blend together dissimilar subjects into new ideas or inventions. Humans began by combining animal bones and the activity of killing animals to create weapons made of bone. By the same process, over time, we invented the light bulb, television, space satellites, and other technology.

This way of thinking is so raw and natural to us that we don't even notice how fantastic it is. A good example of conceptual blending is the ordinary metaphor. If you look at a metaphor like "They are digging their financial grave," you know immediately what is meant. Yet there is no connection whatsoever between digging a grave and investing money. There is no logical way to connect graves and money. How do we know what this means?

The mind takes one input (grave digging) and another input (financial investment) and blends them together without effort. But the meaning isn't contained in either input; it's created by the combination of the two. The combination develops a structure not provided by the inputs, creating an emergent new meaning. With seemingly no effort, our minds merge dissimilar subjects, choreographing vast networks of indirect associations. When blended, the emergent thoughts and ideas appear simple and straightforward on a conscious level.

Raw creativity means responding to the essence of things. In the above metaphor, we make a connection between grave digging and financial investment because we unconsciously are responding to the essence of the metaphor, which is a connection between the loss of life and the loss of money.

Take the example of the scientist who was assigned the task of developing glues that can be used in medicine and surgery. The essence of his task is adhering things to each other. He looked for ways things adhere to other objects. One day while repairing the dock for his boat, he observed how strongly mussels adhered to his pier. He discovered that mussels excrete a substance that lets them anchor themselves firmly to any object and remain there while being buffeted by the ocean's waves. Today, the scientist is mimicking the cellular make up of the substance and developing a mussel-inspired glue that will one day be used to repair shattered bones.

WHAT IS THE ESSENCE?

An enlightening experiment was done by Gestalt psychologists with a group of dogs. The dogs were trained to approach something when shown a white square and avoid it when shown a gray square. When the dogs learned this, the experimenters switched to using a gray square and a black square. The dogs immediately shifted to approaching the object when shown the gray square (which had previously triggered avoidance) and avoiding the object when shown the black square (which had not previously been associated with an action). Presumably, rather than perceiving the gray, white, and black as an absolute stimuli, the dogs were responding to a deeper essence—lighter versus darker.

Many of us have lost the raw sensitivity to essences because we have been educated to focus on the particulars of experience as opposed to the universals. For example, suppose we were asked to design a new can opener. Most of our ideas would be driven by our experience and association with the particulars of can openers we've used, and we would likely design something that is only marginally different from existing can openers.

If we determine the essence of a can opener to be *opening things*, however, and look for clues in the world around us, we increase our chances of discovering a novel idea. Think for a moment about how things open. Some examples are:

- Valves open by steam.
- Oysters open by relaxing a muscle.
- Pea pods open when ripening weakens the seam.
- Doors open with keys.
- A fish's mouth opens when squeezed at the base.
- A car's accelerator opens when a pedal is pushed.

Our raw creativity allows us to make thousands of indirect associations, some of which may lead to an original, novel idea. For example, you can take the pea pod and work it into a new way of opening a can. Instead of creating a can opener, design the can with a weak seam that opens the can when pulled. This novel idea results from thinking about and approaching the problem in a different way than you've been taught.

Creative people in the arts, sciences, and industry often use this thinking strategy. Fred Smith, founder of Federal Express, said people in the transportation of goods business never really understood why and how he became so successful. He became successful, he said, because he understood the essence of the business, which is peace of mind, and not just transportation of goods. Grasping this essence, he was the first to make it possible for customers to track packages right from their desktops.

Martin Skalski, director of the transportation design sequence at Pratt Institute, teaches his students to tackle problems in terms of essences. For example, he doesn't tell students to design an automobile or study various automobile designs on the market. Instead, he begins the design process by having them create abstract compositions of things in motion. Then by progressively making the process less abstract, he eventually has them working on the real problem—designing forms of transportation—by creating connections between the abstract work and the final model.

World-renowned architect and designer Arthur Erickson also uses this thinking strategy with his students to help them avoid visual and functional preconceptions and to unlock creativity. For example, if he is looking for a new chair design, he will first ask his students to draw a picture of a figure in motion. Then he will ask them to build a wood, plastic, metal, or paper model of a structure that supports that figure in motion. Finally, he will have them use the model as the basis for a new chair design.

Erickson teaches his students the importance of finding the essence of designing furniture. As he puts it, "If I had said to the students, 'Look, we're going to design a chair or bed,' they would have explored the design on the basis of previous memories of chairs or beds. But by approaching the model from the essential direction, I was able to make them realize the vital essence of furniture."

In one group exercise, Erickson had his assistants generate a list of how to store things, a list of how to stack things, and a list of how to organize large objects. Then he gave his assistants the real problem, which was to design a parking garage using the ideas and thoughts from the three different lists.

The mind gets into ruts very quickly, particularly when it stalls and spins its wheels. It gets mired in the details of some perception. Charles Darwin asked the grand question "What is life?" instead of getting mired down classifying the mite or fungus. Getting right to the essence of the problem creates space between thoughts sunken into each other. It forces you to test assumptions and explore possibilities.

Suppose you want to improve the design of the umbrella. The essence of an umbrella is *protection from the rain.* When you examine the essence, you are likely to explore more creative possibilities for rain protection, such as a new kind of raincoat or even a new type of town design where there are arcades everywhere and umbrellas are no longer required. Or, consider the bookstore owner who viewed himself as a seller of books—a very specific idea. The trend toward the electronic media put him out of business. However, if he had viewed himself as a "provider of information and entertainment"—a more abstract and general characterization—the switch toward electronic media would not have been threatening; it would have opened up new opportunities.

BLUEPRINT

1. *First, describe the problem and determine its essence.* Ask the group, "What is the principle of the problem?"

    Example: Our problem is how to protect rural designer mailboxes from theft and vandalism. The essence is "protection."

2. *Ask the group to generate ideas on how to protect things.* Give the group an idea quota of sixty or more ideas. Don't mention the real problem, which is how to protect rural mailboxes.

    Examples:

    *   Place in a bank.
    *   Rustproof, to protect from weather damage.

- Provide good maintenance.

- Get an insurance policy.

- Put a chip in it so you can track its whereabouts.

- Protect it with an armed guard.

3. *After you've generated a number of different ideas, restate the problem for the group so that it is slightly less abstract.* For example, think of ways to protect things that are outside and vulnerable. Again, generate as many solutions as you can.

   Examples:

- Hire a guard.

- Watch it constantly.

- Drape it with camouflage.

- Put a fence around it.

- Keep it well lighted.

- Install an alarm system.

4. *Finally, address the group with the real problem.* Review and discuss the ideas and solutions to the two previous abstractions and use these as stimuli to generate solutions.

   Example: The real problem is how to protect rural mailboxes from theft and vandalism. The idea triggered from "get an insurance policy" is to offer an insurance policy to owners of rural mailboxes: $5 a year or $10 for three years to cover the mailbox from theft or destruction.

Scientists at Gillette wanted to develop a new toothbrush. They decided that the essence of a toothbrush is "cleaning." Among the things studied were:

- How are cars cleaned?

- How is hair cleaned?

- How are clothes cleaned?

- How are arteries cleaned?

- How are waterways cleaned?

They got excited when they studied car washes. Cars are washed and cleaned in a car wash. Car washes use multiple soaping and brushing actions in different directions. They incorporated the principle of multiple brushes brushing in different directions into the toothbrush known as the Oral B, which is the leading selling toothbrush in the world.

WHAT IS THE ESSENCE OF A CRAZY IDEA?

Nobel Prize–winning physicist Wolgang Pauli, the discoverer of electron spin, was presenting a new theory of elementary particles before a professional audience. An extended discussion followed. Physicist Niels Bohrs summarized the discussion to Pauli by saying that everyone agreed that his theory is crazy. The question that divided them was whether it was crazy enough to have a chance of being correct. Bohrs said his own feeling was that it was not crazy enough.

Logic hides in Bohr's illogic. In creative genius, there is a tolerance for unpredictable and playful avenues of thought. The result captures the whole paradoxical process of mixing unpredictable thinking and intentional tactics.

You can actively seek the accidental discovery by deliberately exploring the odd and unusual. It is this freedom from design or commitment that allows you to juxtapose things that would not otherwise have been arranged in this way, to construct a sequence of events that would not otherwise have been constructed.

BLUEPRINT

1. *First, discuss the problem with the group.* Suppose the problem is poor office morale. Now, ask the group to generate the most absurd or crazy ideas about the problem. The crazier the idea the better.

   Examples:

   - Pay people to stay at home and work on their houses and lawns.

   - Take all employees on a trip around the world.

   - Create a giant commune where all employees live. The men and women are intermixed and live in dormitories. Everything is shared equally, including the raising of children.

- At the end of every year, spray every employee with a special mist. The mist makes employees younger and more beautiful.

2. *Next, select one of the absurd ideas.*

    Absurd idea: Pay people to stay home and work on their houses and lawns.

3. *List the features and aspects of the absurd idea.*

    - Employees wouldn't have to spend free time working on their properties.

    - The maintenance of the property will increase its value.

    - It would free up employees' weekends as household chores are completed at home during the week.

    - Employees would save money staying home.

    - Word of mouth advertising. Employees would tell friends and relatives about this great deal.

4. *Select one of the features and extract the principle or essence of the feature and build it into a practical idea.*

    Principle: Working on employees' homes and lawns.

    Idea: Offer employees the services of a handyman as a company benefit. Employees pay for materials; employer pays handyman to fix sinks, paint, hang wallpaper, and so on.

This idea is the result of unpredictable thinking that started with the absurd idea. It is not possible to think unpredictably by looking harder and longer in the same direction. When your attention is focused on a subject, only a few patterns are highly activated in your brain and these few dominate your thinking. These patterns produce only predictable ideas no matter how hard you try.

Peggy DuPre is the sales manager for a large automobile dealer. She and her staff brainstormed for crazy ways to sell cars. One absurd idea was to offer sex to anyone who bought a new car. They worked with that and determined that the principle of the idea was *romance*. They thought of many different ways you could use romance in selling. The idea they implemented was to have the salesperson personally deliver the car to the customer. When the customer checks out the car and opens the trunk, they discover it's filled with flowers. Customers become so overwhelmed with the gesture that they tell everyone they know.

An electrical distributor's human resource director was concerned about employee turnover. He and his team brainstormed crazy ideas on how to fix the problem. One of the ideas was to offer a secret hair tonic that would grow and beautify hair. You get the secret tonic after five years with the company.

The group then imagined the steps they would go through if they were actually going to buy a hair retention product. Among the steps were:

1. Checking out the reputation of the manufacturer.

2. Getting research documentation.

3. Finding out where to buy it.

4. Traveling to store.

5. Applying it regularly.

6. Checking in the mirror to evaluate the results.

7. Send complaints, if any, to the manufacturer.

Each of these steps inspired ideas on how to improve morale:

1. *Checking out the manufacturer* inspired the idea of enhancing the reputation of their own company so that employees feel proud to work there.

2. *Researching* inspired the idea of having exit interviews.

3. *Buying* inspired the idea of allowing employees to purchase stock or services at reduced rates from the company.

4. *Traveling* inspired the idea of awarding additional vacation time to employees who remain at the company for a certain number of years.

5. *Applying regularly* inspired the idea of making sure supervisors meet with workers on a regular basis.

6. *Checking in the mirror* inspired the idea of conducting employee attitude surveys to highlight major concerns and anticipate future problems.

7. *Send complaints* inspired the idea of implementing an employee suggestion system.

You need to will yourself to look at crazy and absurd ideas from different angles. Once you have the will, your intelligence is challenged to find as many positive, negative, and interesting points in the absurd idea as it can. Instead of using intelligence to support your prejudices, you are now using it to explore the subject matter.

When discussing absurd ideas with a group, elicit information on:

- What is useful about the idea?

- What is interesting about the idea?

- What is missing in the idea?

- How can the idea be implemented?

The studies of the Gestalt psychologists concluded that prolonged study of any subject will bring about spontaneous structural changes in the subject. The mind, through prolonged inspection of a subject, becomes bored with it and will explore alternative ways of perceiving it by deconstructing the whole into parts and looking for the interesting parts. In the early steps of this process, the effects of these changes remain below the level of awareness. After a while, they penetrate consciousness as new ideas and insights.

Years back, 3M invented a new adhesive for industrial use. No industries were interested, however, and 3M management ordered the project scrapped and had all the samples destroyed. One engineer thought the adhesive had interesting aspects, saved some samples, and took them home. He was intrigued by the simplicity of the adhesive, and he thought about the tape over the next few weeks. He observed his teenage daughters setting their hair, taping cloth and paper together, and using the adhesive in various other ways. He went to management and convinced them that what they had was a consumer product, not an industrial one. 3M manufactured and marketed it as Scotch Tape.

THE DREAMER, THE REALIST, AND THE CRITIC

Walt Disney allowed his vivid imagination to produce fantastical ideas, uncritically and unrestrained. Later, he engineered these fantasies into feasible ideas and then evaluated them. To evaluate them, he would shift his perspective three times by playing three separate and distinct roles: the dreamer, the realist, and the critic.

On the first day, he would play the dreamer and dream up fantasies and wishful visions. He would let his imagination soar without worrying about how to implement his conceptions. His fantasy analogies permitted him to connect words, concepts, and ideas with apparently irrelevant objects and events. The result was a rich treasure of associations; an imagination avalanche with whole mountains of ideas crashing down. The next day, he would try to bring his fantasies back to earth by playing the realist. As a realist, he would look for ways to engineer his ideas into something workable and practical.

Finally, on the last day, he would play the part of the critic and poke holes into his ideas. Is it feasible? Can you translate the idea's features into customer benefits, and, if so, can you make money with it?

BLUEPRINT

Dreamer. Ask the group to generate as many fantasies as they can to address the problem. Tell them to imagine that any idea they can come up with will be implemented. Encourage the group to imagine things that normally wouldn't be possible. Try to make each idea more improbable than the last.

Example: A city council wants to raise more money by more efficient policing of parking meters. Some fantasies were:

- Honor code; everyone keeps track of their own parking time and sends the money owed to the city treasurer.

- Cars vaporize when time expires.

- Incorporate sensor meters that record license numbers and how much time expired while parked. A bill is sent to the owner.

- Hire the homeless. In lieu of meters, a homeless person records the time expired. The motorist pays the person and is encouraged to tip the person as well.

- Repeat offenders are sent to prison for life without a trial.

Now ask the group to select the ideas they like best.

Example: The city council liked "hire the homeless" as one of their favorites.

Realist. Ask the group to play the realist by working the fantasy into a practical idea. Ask participants to extract a principle, feature, or some aspect of the fantasy that appeals to them.

Example: Some of the appealing features about the "hire the homeless" idea were:

- The principle of actually seeing whether a space is occupied.

- Parkers won't be able to pirate "unexpired time" from parkers who leave early.

- Provides new jobs. We have to hire somebody to watch the meters.

- Would modify behavior. Motorists would no longer spend time looking for unexpired meters or ways to beat the system.

Now, have the group imagine how that feature could be turned into a practical idea. The city council worked the concept of seeing the parking spaces into an idea of manufacturing parking meters with infrared sensors and lithium-powered computer chips to "see" parking spaces. The meter erases unexpired time when a car leaves to prevent another car from pirating the time.

Critic. Now, have the participants poke holes into the idea. In our example, the "seeing meter" is technologically possible. The major drawback is cost, as such a meter will cost at least four times the cost of a normal meter. The cost, however, will ideally be offset by a more efficient collection of revenues.

You can now go back and engineer other features of the same fantasy into workable ideas, or you can go back and work with one of the other fantasies. In our example, the city council approached a manufacturer with their idea and made a deal. The manufacturer agreed to install and monitor prototypes of meters with sensors for free. The city agreed to be a showcase of the meters for the manufacturer and keep the revenue that's generated.

Gino De-Gol, a robotic engineer, fantasized about a rollercoaster that would have the rider zooming through space without rails, blasting asteroids while executing a number of barrel rolls to avoid being pelted by debris. Then, without warning the rider sucked into a wormhole upside down. After that, the ride starts to get really interesting.

Gino became the realist and constructed the first part of his fantasy ride. His key discovery was the world's first industrial robot, the KR500, most commonly used to lift automobile engines for spot-welding. The arms six joints allow it to move any which way imaginable. His ultimate rollercoaster will propel a rider on a twisting, undulating trip while shaking him like a cat would a rat. His ride will combine the high G-forces of today's coasters, the computer generated trickery of virtual-reality simulators, and the interactivity of video games. Propelled through a snaking series of domed theaters, riders will swing far out into a computer-generated universe to come face-to-face with aliens. The beauty of the ride is that the violence of the ride and the virtual reality simulations can be reprogrammed constantly.

Finally, as the critic, he realized his biggest hurdle was the human upchuck factor. If an alien lands on your ship, but the rides jerks a tenth of a second later—the illusion is shattered and the body could revolt. The question was, how much can the human body tolerate?

MAGIC WAND

This is a similar technique to the one described above. The facilitator posts the topic on a wall or chalkboard. Participants imagine they have a magic wand. The wand will grant them any wish they desire. Participants silently write three to five wishes on index cards or sticky notes.

The wish cards are collected and posted around the topic card. The group leader organizes the cards and places related ones together. The group then tries to work the wishes into ideas.

The more interesting and unique the wish, the greater the possibilities are for an original idea or twist. Automobile windshields must be constantly cleared when there is inclement weather or road conditions, such as rain, sleet, snow, ice, frost, or dust. Wipers and washer fluid help, but grime is rarely eliminated completely. A group of engineers brainstormed for ways to improve the windshield. The wish they decided to work with was, "What if a windshield could clean itself?"

The group listed all objects and things that self-clean. One of the listed objects was camera lenses, which seem to be self-cleaning. One of the engineers investigated and discovered that the lenses are coated with titanium dioxide. When the sun's rays hit the coating, they set off a chemical reaction that strips the lens of organic matter. The engineers decided to see if they could adopt this process to the automobile windshield by modifying the way glass is coated. This process keeps the windshields clean of everything but large bird droppings.

THE EXQUISITE CORPSE

The harder and longer you focus on a subject, the more difficult it becomes to break out of habitual patterns of thinking. In fact, the harder you try, the stronger the same patterns become. If, however, you change your focus and combine your subject with something that is not related, then different, unusual patterns are activated.

Try an experiment. Pick eight random words and give the list to someone or to a small group (e.g., flowerpot, baby, glass, grasshopper, coffeepot, box, toast, and garage). Ask them to divide the words into two groups without giving them any rationale for the division. You'll discover that people will come up with some very creative classifications. They'll group them according to *words with the letter* o, *things that touch water, objects made in factories,* and so on. There are no connections between these objects except for those that the human mind invents. Though we seldom think about it, making random connections in such a manner is a conceptual creative act. Making random connections was a popular technique used by the Surrealists to create conceptual combinations in art. Artists in a group would take turns creating a sentence, each contributing any word that occurred to them without seeing what the others had written. The resulting sentence became a combination of concepts that the group would study and interpret, hoping to get a novel insight or a glimpse of some deeper meaning. The technique was named *the exquisite corpse,* after a sentence that happened to contain those words.

BLUEPRINT

1. *Have the group bounce ideas and thoughts about the subject off each other for five to ten minutes.*

2. *Then, ask the participants to think about what was discussed and silently write one word that occurs to them on a card.*

3. *Collect the cards and have the group combine the words into a sentence* (words can be added by the group to help the sentence make sense).

4. *Invite the group to study the final sentence and build an idea or ideas from it.*

An Alzheimer's organization planned to have an auction to raise money for their cause. They planned an elaborate, sophisticated evening and looked for unusual items they could auction. They tried the exquisite corpse technique. Some of the words they came up with were "people," "cruises," "creative," "furniture, "charity," "designer," "custom," "art," "thin air," and "celebrities." One of the connections that occurred to them was between "create," "art," and "thin air." This triggered an idea that became the sensation of the auction: They sold an idea for a work of art that doesn't exist. They talked a local conceptual artist into describing an idea for a work of art. The idea was placed in an envelope and auctioned off for $28,000. Legal ownership was indicated by a typed certificate, which specified that the artwork (10,000 lines, each ten inches long, covering a wall) be drawn with a black pencil. The owner has the right to reproduce this piece as many times as he likes.

SAND TRAY

The sand tray technique is an interesting way to get a group thinking metaphorically by substituting physical objects for mental images. You need a large sand tray. At first, the surface of the sand tray is raked smooth and clean. Surrounding it are hundreds of bright objects: tiny dolls, colored marbles, shells, feathers, bits of wood, plastic toy soldiers, a miniature bride and groom, fake dinosaurs, rubber snakes, toy sharks, toy pistols, and so on.

The group starts by discussing the subject and then one participant builds a scene that represents the subject in the sand tray using the objects. The group studies the scene and generates as many interpretations as possible. When interpreting the scene, everyone should be on the lookout for parts that are puzzling, seem to be missing, or that show up when focus is changed. Ask the group questions such as:

- "What is this?"

- "What could this mean?"

- "What does the frequency of this object mean?"

- "Who does this represent?"

- "What object comes closest to the essence of the subject?"

- "What does this remind us of?"

Among these questions, one may stand out as the key to solving the problem. Write out the interpretations. Search for clues, new ideas, insights, and new lines of speculation. Combine the interpretations into one all-inclusive narrative. Try writing a story explaining how the sand tray scene relates to the subject.

CREATIVE COLLAGES

Similar to the sand tray, the metaphorical collage is an assemblage of pictures, both whole images or fragments. Each element in the collage loses its separate identity as it becomes part of the whole. The collage is greater than, and often different from, the sum of it parts.

When two or more dissimilar images collide in a collage, the imagination transforms them into an altogether new reality that transcends the separate elements. For example, a picture of seals performing in a marine show next to a picture of a building may become a metaphor for salespeople performing for customers; a user-friendly computer program; how to perform for a job interview; and so on. The imagination transforms the picture into a symbol for many different things.

To create such a collage, cut out several pictures or parts of pictures from magazines, newspapers, catalogs, flyers, and so on. Mix and match the pictures by moving them around into different patterns and associations. Play with the pictures until you get a feeling for possible ways to use these patterns. Form patterns and associations without forcing them. Continue until your collage feels complete. Make one large metaphorical picture by assigning a word or phrase to each picture and then completing the sentence, "My subject is a lot like [insert a word or phrase from the collage] because it . . . " Think metaphorically and analogically.

The research and development staff for a furniture company looked for ways to develop a paint that does not fade, chip, or scratch. They made a collage that included pictures of various trees and plants. The collage triggered a discussion of how trees and plants get their color. Their subsequent research inspired the idea of "everlasting color." They came up with the idea of injecting trees with dye additives that impregnate color into the plant cells, spreading the color throughout the tree. The tree is painted before it is cut down.

People enjoy creating collages because it accesses the more visual, feeling part of their brain and gives them an entirely different way of looking at a problem. The guidelines for a small group are:

1. Pass out old magazines and scissors.

2. Ask each participant to cut out images and pictures from various magazines that metaphorically represent the subject or some aspect of it.

3. Have each person make a collage. Paste the images and pictures in an arrangement that's aesthetically pleasing.

4. Assign a word or phrase to each picture on the montage.

5. Each person then transforms the subject into one large metaphorical word-picture by completing the sentence, "Our subject is a lot like [insert a word or phrase from the collage] because it . . ."

6. Hang the collages on a wall and direct the group to compare them, looking for common points and trying to identify any gaps.

Another way to collage your subject is to create two separate collages to represent two separate aspects of your subject. Suppose you want to improve corporate communications. You could create one collage to represent upper management and another one to represent employees. With the two sets of visuals, compare the common points and identify the gaps between upper management and the employees.

THOUGHT WALK

Tell your group to take a walk around the building and the surrounding grounds. Ask them to look for objects, situations, or events that you can compare to your subject metaphorically. For example, suppose your problem is how to improve communications in your company. Take a walk and notice potholes in the road. How are potholes like your corporate communication problem? For one thing, if potholes are not repaired, they get bigger and more dangerous. Usually road crews are assigned to repair the potholes. Similarly, unless something is done to improve corporate communications, it's likely to deteriorate even further. An idea with a similar relation to "road crews" is to assign someone in the organization to fill the role of "communications coach." The role would entail educating, encouraging, and supporting communication skills in all employees. And just as road crews are rotated, you can rotate the assignment every six months.

The guidelines for leading a thought walk are:

1. Have the participants take a walk around the grounds and look for objects, events, or situations (e.g., children skipping rope, a pebble, a bag of jelly beans, a drinking fountain, and so on) that might make interesting metaphors with the subject at hand. Ask them to keep a list.

2. Upon their return, have the participants make as many metaphors as they can between their list and the subject. Look for similarities and similar circumstances.

3. Look for ways to transfer principles and similar circumstances from what the participants observed and the subject. Try to build at least one idea or solution from each metaphor. Ask what new insights, relating to how to solve the problem, the metaphors provide.

A few months back, engineers looked for ways to safely and efficiently remove ice from power lines during ice storms and were stumped. They decided to take a thought walk around the hotel. One of the engineers came back with a jar of honey he purchased in the gift shop. He suggested putting honey pots on top of each power pole. He said this would attract bears and the bears would climb the poles to get the honey. Their climbing would cause the poles to sway and the ice would vibrate off the wires. Working with the principle of vibration, they got the idea to bring in helicopters to hover over the lines. The hovering of the helicopters vibrated the ice off the power lines.

ASK YOUR KID

The great landscape artist J. M. W. Turner used an unusual technique to stimulate his imagination. Whenever he visited friends who had young children, he would give them watercolors and paper to make drawings. Sometimes he would suggest a general theme, and other times he would let them draw anything they wanted. The results were original and spontaneous expressions of primary consciousness. Turner would then take the drawings, observe them with an open mind, and create his own visual impressions from the children's work, in much the same way that Leonardo da Vinci imagined faces and scenes among stains on the wall. Turner would use these visual impressions to inspire his imagination to create new perspectives for the familiar landscape.

The chemist Karl Kreckman worked on various ways to protect seeds from the elements. One day, he leafed through a stack of his son's drawings. One intrigued him. It was a picture of a tree wearing a fur coat and hat. This got him thinking about synthetics, including polymers that make clothing. In turn, this triggered his idea for intelligent polymer seed coatings, which shift properties as conditions change. The seeds can be planted in any weather or season. They lie protected and dormant when it's cold outside and sprout as soon as the soil reaches the right growing temperature.

If members of your group have young children, try this technique. Ask the group to provide their children with drawing materials and ask them to make drawings. You could suggest a general theme. For example, if your problem is how to organize your company more effectively, you might suggest that they make drawings of people at work; or if you're worried about job security, ask them to make drawings of people in danger. Or, let them draw anything they want. Take the drawings and observe the images, patterns, and colors with an open mind. Then force connections between the images and your subject.

ASK A CRAB

Applying your senses to your subject can get you thinking about a problem in different dimensions. Consider the sense of sight. Pictures, photographs, and illustrations are excellent sources of unrelated stimuli.

The CEO of a Japanese perfume company asked his executives for ideas that would enable the company to survive poor economic times. Disappointed with their suggestions, he gave each of them a picture of a king crab and instructed them to study it and to look for ideas from the crab they could apply to their business. Some of their connections and ideas were:

- A crab can rejuvenate lost claws. We must develop backup product lines in case our primary line falters.

- A crab can see 360 degrees. We must improve our market intelligence.

- A crab moves slowly. We're moving too slowly. We cannot afford this. We must downsize so we can react more speedily to the market.

- A crab has distinct features. We need to develop a distinctive package that differentiates our perfume more clearly.

- A crab is a scavenger. We need to allocate resources to see what other uses and markets we can find for our products.

BLUEPRINT

1. *Read aloud a problem statement and ask the group to verbally brainstorm solutions.*

2. *Give each group member a folder containing two or three pictures that are not related to the problem area.*

3. *Instruct the group members to examine each picture and write their ideas.* After a designated period, ask the group members to read their ideas aloud.

4. *As each idea is read, ask the group members to discuss it and try to develop new ideas or modifications.* Record all new ideas as they are suggested.

5. *Collect and evaluate.*

An interesting twist is to provide participants with instant film cameras and ask them to take a stroll and photograph interesting objects and scenes. Use them as prompts. A group of managers from various departments met to seek better ways to mesh functions. One of their photographs showed birds looking at a pond of goldfish. To some, it seemed that the birds were trying to communicate with the fish, who of course could not hear them. As they discussed the photo, they realized they saw themselves as the unheard birds.

Marketers felt that the researchers were preoccupied with scientific rather than commercial matters; while researchers felt that marketers were deaf to new technical insights. The solution was to have teams of marketers and researchers meet quarterly to learn how to talk to each other.

SUMMARY

Think about a swimming pool with a lot of people jumping in and out forming a great choppiness of waves over the surface. Now, imagine that it's possible that in those waves there are clues to what's happening all over the pool. Imagine that an insect of sufficient cleverness could sit in the corner of the pool and, just by being disturbed by the waves and the nature of the irregularities, figure out who jumped in where, when, and how. It seems incredible, but that's what we're doing when we try to use learned logic to come up with original and unconventional ideas. You were born creative. Jump in the pool!

Try to represent the key elements of your challenge in mental images that symbolically represent your subject as you see it. Disassociate yourself of labels and words and just make mental pictures of the problem. Close your eyes and picture your challenge or problem in your mind. Block out verbal thoughts. (This can be done by repeating a simple word such as *om* over and over until it becomes meaningless.) Try to imagine images that symbolically represent your subject or some aspect of it. Write down or draw the images and associations that you conjure up. Draw analogies between these thoughts and your subject. Look for relationships and connections.

In the following illustration, the challenge is to rearrange the matches to make nothing. No matchsticks may be bent, broken, or placed over each other. First, try to solve it using your usual way of thinking. Most people cannot solve this problem. Next, close your eyes and imagine the concept of nothing. What symbolically represents it? Write down the images and associations that you conjure up. See if you can make the connection between your images and the challenge to solve it.

Some 60 percent of people who use this technique solve the problem. Some symbolically represent nothing as a zero, and others represent it as *nil*. Once they make a mental picture of the concept, they work back to the problem and rearrange the matches to correspond to their mental picture.

If you are adept at imaging, the ideas will emerge spontaneously and effortlessly. If a chain of images emerges, often the first ones are the most significant. If you have trouble conjuring up symbolic images, imagine you meet a Martian who does not understand any earthly language and who communicates with abstract symbols. You want to communicate your problem to the Martian, because you feel it will be able to help you. Write out your problem and then translate it into abstract symbols.

RAW CREATIVITY

PART FOUR

ENDTOYS

After you create ideas, you need to put them in some sort of order and evaluate them. The logic is similar to that which governs dynamics in music: Without accent, music has no life. The beat becomes monotonous, the melody lacks coherence, and the piece sounds aimless. Conversely, if every note, word, or movement is stressed, the result has even less meaning.

After you create ideas, you need to put them in some sort of order and evaluate them. The logic is similar to that governing dynamics in music: Without accent, music has no life. The beat becomes monotonous, the melody lacks coherence, and the piece sounds aimless. Conversely, if every note, word, or movement is stressed, the result has even less meaning. I find the most satisfying music is that which ends not in a clash of symbols, but with the brushes laid gently against the drums for a beat or so after the finale.

Thus, I prefer to end this book with a Thinkertoy to help you evaluate your ideas, and one last chapter on beliefs and perceptions.

—

CHAPTER THIRTY-EIGHT

MURDER BOARD

"What is called foreknowledge cannot be
elicited from spirits, nor from gods, nor by
analogy with past events, nor from
calculations. It must be obtained from men
who know the enemy situation."

SUN TZU

Look at the surf pounding on any beach. It is never exactly the same twice, nor will it ever be. The waves typify the infinitude of individualism in our universe.

For instance, no two people will give you the same opinion, in the same words, with the same emotions and beliefs about an idea. In the figure in the margin, one person may see a fish as large as a man, something to be cautious of. Another may see one as small as a dinner plate, something to eat.

Some people make the false assumption that anyone can dissect an idea and determine its true worth. If you believed the person who sees a fish only as a small thing, you would be misled; if you believed the person who sees a fish only as a large thing, you would also be misled. If you listened to both, you would consider the possibility that fish can be both large and small. This is why it is so important to get feedback about your ideas from many people.

Different people can help you modify and improve the initial idea. It's like sculpting: You start with a big block of marble and an idea. Others can suggest what parts of the block can be removed or discover cracks that you must take into account before you start sculpting. They might also offer suggestions as to how your idea for a sculpture might be improved or modified, suggestions that you may or may not take. Then you carve the remaining marble into a final shape.

Feedback is essential to the nurturing and critical development of ideas. It helps you look more closely and critically at your ideas.

Feedback is used to:

- Compare many different ideas to narrow down the field to one (or a few) of the most promising possibilities.

- Identify the strengths and weaknesses of an idea.

- Suggest modifications and improvements that will sharpen the idea.

- Determine business opportunities, or lack of them, for the idea.

- Identify marketing opportunities as well as marketing concerns.

- Determine the level of interest in the idea.

One of the CIA's favorite techniques for the critical analysis of ideas is the Murder Board. A Murder Board is a special group of selected individuals that evaluates and criticizes ideas before they are presented for final approval and implementation. The goals of the Murder Board are to:

- Terminate worthless ideas and proposals.

- Expose all the negative aspects of a viable idea so that corrective actions can be taken before final evaluation and implementation.

- Provide feedback.

The group critiques the idea as harshly as possible, attacking every weakness. If the idea has too many weaknesses, it goes no further. When the Board considers an idea viable, they suggest ways to modify or improve the idea to overcome each weakness.

The Board has saved the agency from considerable embarrassment over the years. For instance, many of the highly publicized anti-Castro plots such as poison cigars, powdered poison on his uniforms, drugs to render him impotent or make his hair fall out, and so on were terminated by the agency's Murder Boards.

The CIA adopted this technique from its predecessor, the Office of Strategic services. The OSS was awash with ideas during World War II, including one idea from behaviorist B. F. Skinner. He suggested using pigeons to control guided missiles, as pigeons could be conditioned to peck continuously for four or five minutes at the image of a target on a screen. The birds would then be placed in a nose of a missile, harnessed in front of a similar screen. The idea was that the pigeons would peck the moving image on the screen producing corrective signals to keep the missile on course. Skinner's idea was never used in actual warfare. The problem, according to the OSS, was that the members of the Murder Board couldn't stop laughing long enough to take the idea seriously.

Creating your own personal Murder Board is an excellent way to get feedback about ideas.

BLUEPRINT

1. *Verbalize the idea to your significant other or a trusted friend.* Sounding out the idea in detail with someone close to you will help clarify the idea, brighten its virtues, and expose its flaws. You need someone who is not afraid to tell the emperor he has no clothes. You need someone who is close to you so that he or she is not afraid to be honest.

2. *Detail your idea in writing.* Type up a detailed proposal, using graphics and illustrations if necessary. State your goals, your assumptions, your concerns, areas where you need information, your beliefs, what inspired the idea, and why you want others to evaluate it.

   State why you want feedback: Is it to decide the worth of the idea, determine its strengths and weaknesses, compare it to other products, plan funding, business opportunities, and marketing, or what?

   Your proposal should also list the questions you need answered. Remember that the questions themselves can stimulate creativity in others as they read your proposal. Emphasize that you are asking for feedback about your idea so that you can make decisions about implementing, terminating, modifying, or improving it. Some common categories for questions are: need, cost, marketing, and feasibility.

   SAMPLE QUESTIONS

   Need

   - Does the idea meet a real need?
   - Should a need be created through promotional and advertising efforts?
   - Who will resist?

- Does it sound like a good idea to you?
- Are there real benefits?
- Do you feel it is new and original?
- Do you think it is better than others on the market?
- Can you think of different variations of the idea?
- Can you offer alternative ideas?

Cost

- Is it worth producing or implementing?
- Will it provide enough benefit to outweigh the cost?
- How should it be financed?
- What immediate or short-range gains or results should be anticipated?
- What should the projected returns be?
- Do you feel the risk factors are acceptable?
- What are the economic factors—what necessary talent, time for development, investment, marketing costs—do you foresee?

Marketing

- How should it be marketed?
- What are some possible obstacles, objections, and concerns?
- Does it have natural sales appeal? How ready is the market for it? Can customers afford it? Will customers buy it?
- Is timing a factor?
- Are there possible user resistances or difficulties?
- What might go right?
- What might go wrong?
- Who should be involved?
- What special marketing programs can you imagine?
- What is the competition?

Feasibility

- Is the idea sound?
- What is the best thing that could happen?

- What is the worst thing that could happen?

- What are the faults and limitations?

- Do you feel the idea is original?

- Will it work in actual practice?

- What problems or difficulties do you think the idea might solve?

- Do you think I have the resources?

- How simple or complex will its execution or implementation be?

- What is most likely to help me implement the idea?

- What is most likely to hinder successful implementation?

- Is it possible to make it happen? How soon?

3. *Appoint a Murder Board.* Seek out people in your network of friends, relatives, and coworkers who have a creative mindset or are knowledgeable about your idea's environment.

 The perfect feedback person has good imagination, perception, vision, and is as cold-eyed and objective as a pawnbroker pricing a broken watch.

 Select as many people as you wish and ask each for their help in providing you with feedback (it is probably best to approach them one at a time). How you involve people in your idea can make or break the Board's effectiveness. Give each person your written proposal and listen carefully to what they say, without judging. Encourage each person to articulate his or her thoughts as they ponder your proposal and to brainstorm with you for ways to improve your idea or its implementation. Play devil's advocate. If you get objections, make them tell you why they feel it won't work. Get specifics.

 Make value judgments at a later date. The decision is ultimately yours no matter how positive or negative the feedback you receive. I worked with one fellow whose entire Board told him his idea wouldn't work. "It was incredible how everyone told me the idea sounded great, but it wasn't going to work," he said. "But they all had different reasons, so I ignored their advice." If they had all cited the same reason, he probably would have taken them more seriously. As it was, he sold the rights to his invention for a huge sum of money.

There are any number of methods for obtaining feedback about your idea. You may choose a quantitative or qualitative approach, depending upon the idea, the purpose of the evaluation, and the style of analysis you prefer. For instance, if you prefer to mix the two approaches, you could assign a numerical value to each question. In the eight-factor approach that follows, you would ask people to assign a point value to the questions that reflects their opinion (the point spreads are completely subjective). This would quantify your idea's perceived strengths and weaknesses; you could then interview people on selected questions for more information or opinions.

Eight Factors

1. Did I communicate the idea completely and clearly?
   (0–20 points)

2. Do you have interest in this idea?
   (0–20 points)

3. Are there good market opportunities?
   (0–20 points)

4. How good is the timing?
   (0–5 points)

5. Do you feel I have the competence to implement this idea?
   (0–10 points)

6. Is this a good application of my personal strengths?
   (0–10 points)

7. Does my idea have good competitive advantages?
   (0–5 points)

8. How unique is my idea?
   (0–10 points)

Now you can look at total points for all eight factors, or focus on specific questions. For example, if your point total for marketing opportunities is 0, you would probably ask a lot more questions about the market or marketing opportunities.

One inventor developed a commercial hair dryer that could dry hair in five minutes. He used the eight-factor method and got a 0 for marketing opportunities from hairdressers. The reason there was no market, he found out, was that stylists wanted slower dryers to keep patrons occupied for thirty minutes or so while they worked on other customers.

PMI

Edward de Bono, international authority on thinking, recommends using "PMI" to get people away from simply reacting to ideas and situations.

Subjects are asked to observe and list the pluses, minuses, and most interesting aspects of an idea or situation. The "most interesting" category is for all those things that are worth noting but do not fit under either "plus" or "minus."

PMI forces people into action, thinking, and focusing their attention in a specific direction rather than just reacting to an idea or situation.

A PMI list can help you:

- *Compare many different ideas and narrow them down to one or a few.* I know a sales manager who sends his staff several different sales strategies and asks them to do a PMI on each before he decides on a final strategy.

- *Focus objectively on the pluses and minuses of a proposition.* An inventor proposed a new hinged bottle top to make drug bottles "elder accessible." His friends did PMIs on this idea, and their feedback led him to a better idea. He decided to create a cap that works like a combination lock: turn right, turn left, lift off.

- *Make a decision about the worth of an idea.* An executive who had been arguing for weeks with his management team about an idea finally gathered everyone involved and asked them all to do a PMI. Once the problem had been laid out, a route could be chosen, and the matter was resolved in minutes.

OPUS

Opus is modeled after the market research technique used by TerraFirma AB, a Swedish research company that gets an amazing 92 percent response to its surveys.

Although you can certainly improvise, Opus seems to work best when you use a sleek, elegant-looking box, about 16 inches by 4 inches by 1 inch. The interior of the box should be divided into four compartments and contain a description of your idea, instructions for performing Opus, and about one hundred cards. On each card, type a statement of concern (not a question) about your idea.

Examples:

- I believe my product is superior to Brand X because . . .

- The major benefit is . . .

- I can produce this for a cost of . . .

- People will buy it because . . .

- The best way to market it is . . .

- I plan to finance it by . . .

- The problems it will solve are . . .

- I expect the following results . . .

You ask the respondent to put each card into one of the four compartments, labeled "agree," "partly agree," "disagree," or "no opinion." The cumulative results will give you a feel for how your idea will be received. You can reuse the box with several different people. It works because it's fast and easy to do, and most people enjoy doing this kind of physical survey.

An obscure artist had the idea to sell advertising space on his canvases. He had absolutely no idea whether this could work, so he used an Opus box to survey nightclubs, clothing boutiques, hair salons, art galleries, and trendy restaurants. He found that advertisers seemed happy to put up to $1,000 for space on a painting.

He had been successful in selling these paintings, which are heavy on stylized images of celebrity idols, with as many as a dozen ads, presented in foot-square boxes, adorning both sides and the bottom of each canvas. One art collector calls them "the cutting edge." The demand for his work became so large that he hired a full-time salesperson to sell advertising space and is planning a solo exhibition.

DEVIL'S FOOD

Most people love to help others with their business ventures or challenges, and their cooperation and compassion can be invaluable to you in your quest for feedback. An ancient story illustrates the radical difference cooperation and compassion can make. A man who led a basically good life died and was assigned to Hell for a short time. He discovered that the main torture in Hell was that everyone was forced to eat with spoons that were longer than their arms. The condemned spent eternity in the midst of excellent food they couldn't eat. When he was finally transferred up to Heaven, he found that the blessed were given the same spoons. In Heaven, however, no one went hungry because they fed each other.

An effective feedback system is one that works for you. A Murder Board is one way to get honest information and create an ongoing creative climate for modifying and improving ideas. Of course, advice and feedback mean nothing unless you listen to and evaluate them properly.

SUMMARY

When your idea feels final, implement it. Do not spend days, weeks, or months refining it. If you delay, you may find yourself in a situation like that of the Victorian portrait painter who chose not to seek immediate benefits from his talents. Instead, he spent years refining his craft and art until he finally reached a pitch of dazzling brilliance—just in time to be rendered obsolete by photography.

CHAPTER THIRTY-NINE

YOU ARE NOT A
FIELD OF GRASS

"Change the way you look at things
and the things you look at change."

SUN TZU

A field of grass is given its character, essentially, by those experiences that happen over and over again, millions of times: the germination of the grass seed, the blowing wind, the flowering of the grass, the hatching of insects, the beating of thunderstorms, the paths made by animals and hikers, and so on. It is a whole system of interdependent events that determines the nature of the field of grass.

It is also roughly true that the nature of our beliefs and perceptions is interpreted from our experiences. The field of grass cannot change its character. Grass cannot interpret and shape its experiences to create a different nature. We are not a field of grass. We can choose to interpret our experiences anyway we wish. You know as well as I do that few of us are even aware of what this means.

(*-*) AAA

(00) | 000000 |

^–^ | - - _ - - _ |

Look at the designs above. Assign names to these designs by selecting one of the following words: "Indians," "piggynose," "shy kitty," "woman," "sleeper," and "bathroom."

Now that you've assigned names, ask yourself: "Why is this so easy to do?" For example, if you labeled "AAA" as "Indians," how does an Indian village fit—with its ponies, tents, and campfires—so comfortably into three letters? These symbols have no meaning. We give them meaning by how we choose to interpret them. You have the freedom to select any meaning for any experience instead of passively assigning one, and only one, meaning to each experience.

We automatically interpret all of our experiences without realizing it. Are they good experiences or bad ones? What do they mean? We ask these questions without giving much thought, if any, to what the interpretations mean. For instance, if someone bumps into you, you wonder why. The event of her bumping into you is neutral in itself. It has no meaning. It's your interpretation of the bumping that gives it meaning, and this meaning shapes your perception of the experience.

You might interpret the "bump" as rude behavior. You might interpret the bump as deliberately aggressive. You might feel that you are of such little consequence that you're deliberately unnoticed and bumped around by others. Or, you might interpret the bump as flirting. Your interpretation of the experience determines your perception.

Think of roses and thorns. You can complain because roses have thorns, or you can rejoice because thorns have roses. You can choose to interpret experiences any way you wish. It is not the experience that determines who you are; it is your interpretation of the experience. You do not see things as they are; you see them as *you* are.

We are each given a set of experiences in life. The experiences are neutral. They have no meaning. It is how we interpret the experiences that gives them meaning. The interpretations of experiences shape our beliefs and theories about the world. Our beliefs and theories, in turn, determine what we observe in the world to confirm our beliefs, which, in turn, reinforce our interpretations.

In the diagram below, experiences both real and imagined are represented in the bottom box. Beliefs and perceptions are in the box above but are not directly linked. The dotted lines represent interpretations of experiences.

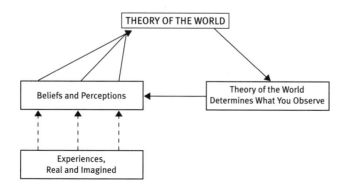

Psychologically, interpretations rest upon the experiences. There exists, however, no logical path from our experiences to our interpretations, only a subjective connection that is always subject to revocation. The interpretations shape our beliefs and perceptions.

It is the interpretation of these experiences that creates your beliefs and perceptions of the world.

Once upon a time, two explorers came upon a spectacular, perfectly tended garden of vegetables in the middle of a jungle. One explorer said, "What a beautiful garden. It looks so perfect. Surely, a gardener must tend this garden." The other disagreed, "There is no way a gardener can tend this garden. It is in the middle of the jungle, hundreds of miles from civilization. There is no sign of human life anywhere. Surely, it is some kind of natural phenomenon." After much argument, they agreed to set up camp and watch the garden to see if someone showed up to tend it.

They stayed for months and no one showed up. "See," said the Doubter. "There is no gardener, for surely he would have appeared by now to tend the garden, which is still perfect. It must be a random creation of nature." The Believer argued, "No, there must be a gardener. He may be invisible, intangible, and eternally elusive to our understanding. But it is not possible for such a beautiful, well-tended garden to exist in the middle of the jungle without being tended. The garden itself is proof of the existence of the gardener, and I have faith that the gardener will return to his garden."

Both the Believer and Doubter interpreted the garden differently, and these two different interpretations led to two different beliefs. When you believe something, you have the feeling that you chose to believe or not believe based on reason and rational thinking. But this is not so. Your beliefs are shaped by the way you interpret your experiences.

How you interpret experiences also helps determine how you feel. While researching happiness and well-being, professor Daniel Kahneman of Princeton University discovered that when he asked college students if they were happy, most said yes. However, when he first asked them how many dates they'd had in the last month and then asked if they were happy, most said no. Their interpretation of the questions determined how they felt.

Try this little exercise. Select something you "need" and then tell yourself it is something you "should have." Can you feel the shift in your psychology? Next, select something you "should have," then tell yourself it is something you "need." Try the following:

- Change something you have to do to something you choose to do: "I have to go to work" becomes "I choose to go to work."

- Change something you have to do to something you want to do: "I have to clean the house" becomes "I want to clean the house."

- Change something you ought to do to something you would love to do: "I ought to write her a thank-you note" becomes "I would love to write her a thank-you note."

Your theory about the world is deduced from your interpretations and beliefs. That theory then determines what you observe in the world. At one time, ancient astronomers believed that the heavens were eternal and made of ether. This theory made it impossible for them to observe meteors as burning stones from outer space. Although the ancients witnessed meteor showers and found some on the ground, they couldn't recognize them as meteors from outer space. They only sought out and observed things that confirmed their theory about the heavens.

We are like the ancient astronomers in that we actively seek out information that confirms our beliefs and theories about ourselves and the world. Religious people see evidence of God's handiwork everywhere; whereas, atheists see evidence that there is no God everywhere. Conservatives see the evils of liberalism everywhere, while liberals see the evils of conservatism everywhere. People who believe they are creative see evidence of their creativity everywhere, and people who do not believe they are creative see evidence that confirms this everywhere. Whatever does not conform to our theories makes us feel uncomfortable and confused.

Think, for a moment about words and sentences. Part of what a sentence means depends upon its separate words, and part depends on how they are arranged. Consider the following sentences:

"Round squares steal honestly."

"Honestly steal squares round."

What makes these sentences seem so different, when both use the same words? Immediately upon reading the first word string, you know exactly what to do with it, because it fits our learned beliefs about parts of speech (nouns, adjectives, verbs, adverbs, and so on) and how they should be positioned.

Because the first conforms to what we believe to be grammatically logical (adjective, noun, verb, adverb), it is easier to read it and then dismiss the content as nonsense. Our beliefs about grammar, however, are not confirmed by the second word string because the words are out of order and hard to parse out. This makes us confused and hesitant about what to do with it. It disturbs us and makes us uncomfortable because it does not conform to our learned beliefs.

Much of what causes us unhappiness in life are learned beliefs. Many of us have been taught that we aren't creative because we are left-brained. Therefore, when asked to generate ideas at work, we tend to be linear and analytical. We know what ideas to create to conform to our learned beliefs. When confronted with outlandish, absurd ideas, we become confused and uncomfortable.

Psychologists call this phenomenon "confirmation basis." This is a phenomenon whereby people, once they believe a theory is true, will force everything else to add fresh support and confirmation for it. Think of the last new car you bought. Remember how you continued to read ads and reviews about your new car but avoided all ads and reviews of other makes and models?

SUMMARY

Experiences and events are neither good nor bad. They are simply neutral. Good, bad, right, wrong, sad, angry, lazy, cruel, kind, and so on are all interpretations that people make. It's a matter of what perspective you choose to take. Blackcloud, my good friend who is Lakota Sioux, told me the following story, which his grandfather had told him.

An old Sioux warrior had eight magnificent horses. One night, during a great storm, they all escaped. The other warriors came to comfort him. They said, "How unlucky you are. You must be very angry to have lost your horses."

"Why?" replied the warrior.

"Because you have lost all your wealth. Now you have nothing," they responded.

"How do you know?" he asked.

The next day the eight horses returned bringing with them twelve new stallions. The warriors returned and joyously announced that now the old warrior must be very happy.

"Why?" was his response.

"Because now you are even richer than before." They responded.

"How do you know?" he again responded.

The following morning, the warrior's young son got up early to break in the new horses. He was thrown and broke both his legs. The warriors came, once more, and talked about how angry the old warrior must be at his misfortune and how terrible it was for the boy to break both his legs.

"How do you know?" the warrior said once more.

Two weeks passed. Then the chief announced that all able-bodied men and boys must join a war party to fight against a neighboring tribe. The

Lakotas won but at great cost, as many men and young boys were killed. When the remaining warriors returned, they told the old warrior that it was lucky his son had two broken legs, otherwise he could have been killed or injured in the great battle.

"How do you know?" the old warrior replied.

INDEX

About the Author

Michael Michalko is one of the most highly acclaimed creativity experts in the world. As an officer in the U.S. Army, he organized a team of NATO intelligence specialists and international academics in Frankfurt, Germany, to research, collect, and categorize all known inventive-thinking methods. His team applied these methods to various NATO military, political, and economic problems and produced a variety of breakthrough ideas and creative solutions to new and old problems. After leaving military service, he was contracted by the CIA to facilitate think tanks using his creative-thinking techniques. He specializes in providing creativity workshops, seminars, and think tanks for clients who range from individuals to Fortune 500 companies.

If you would like to share your thoughts or ideas about *Thinkertoys,* send them to:

Michael Michalko
165 Percy Road
Churchville, NY 14428
www.creativethinking.net